HARVARD ECONOMIC STUDIES

VOLUME CIX

Awarded the David A. Wells Prize for the year 1952–53 and published from the income of the David A. Wells Fund.

The studies in this series are published by the Department of Economics of Harvard University. The department does not assume responsibility for the views expressed.

Germany's Economic Preparations for War

BURTON H. KLEIN

HARVARD UNIVERSITY PRESS
Cambridge, Massachusetts
1959

© Copyright, 1959, by the President and Fellows of Harvard College

Distributed in Great Britain by Oxford University Press, London

Library of Congress Catalog Number 59-7655

Printed in the United States of America

Preface

The idea for this book came as a result of my experience with the United States Strategic Bombing Survey. It occurred to me that there were some interesting aspects of Germany's economic war preparations, only incidentally covered in the Bombing Survey reports, which might be of interest to economists and others. Accordingly the book deals mainly with the German prewar economy, and with the wartime economy up to the period of massive aerial attacks.

The research for this study was substantially completed during the years 1946 through 1948, and was made possible by a research grant from the Carnegie Corporation. I am also indebted to the RAND Corporation, where I am now employed, for permitting me time to complete the manuscript, and for editorial assistance. However, neither the Carnegie Corporation nor RAND has any responsibility for the ideas advanced in this book.

With the same qualification I wish to express my gratitude for many helpful suggestions to Professor William Capron of Stanford University, Russell Nichols of RAND, Professor M. A. Adelman of M.I.T., and Professors Carl Kaysen and J. K. Galbraith of Harvard. Most of all, I wish to thank Edward Mason, until recently Dean of the Littauer School of Public Administration.

Burton H. Klein

Santa Monica, California
October 1958

Contents

PART I

GERMAN REARMAMENT

1933–1938

I. *Germany's Economic Preparations for War: A Re-examination* 3

The role of the "fear of inflation" in general economic policy 4
The nature of the economic recovery 9
The magnitude of war preparations 16
The factors which limited economic mobilization 20

II. *Raw Material Preparations for War* 28

The raw material potential in 1933 28
The raw material production program 34
Raw material distribution controls 54
The stockpiling program 56
The raw material position as it affected foreign trade policy 59
The effect of Germany's raw material position on her war strategy 63

III. *Mobilization of Manpower* 65

Mobilization from the legal point of view 65
A statistical appraisal of Nazi labor mobilization 67

Conclusions on the economic rearmament of Germany 76

PART II

THE GERMAN WAR ECONOMY

1939–1944

IV. *The Magnitude of Germany's War Effort, 1939–1942* 85

Germany's total output and its major uses, 1938–1942 85
War expenditures further examined 90
Munitions production in the United Kingdom and Germany 96

A comparison of German munitions production with intelligence
  estimates   101
Possible explanations for the low level of military output   103

V. A Resources Limitation?   104

Industrial capacity   104
Raw materials   110
  Materials with which Germany was well supplied   110
  Materials with which Germany was not well supplied   112

VI. A Resources Limitation? (continued)   136

Labor   136

VII. The German Economic Administration, 1939–1941   147

The economic agencies   148
The system of economic controls in operation   152

VIII. "A Peacelike War Economy"   173

Hitler's war plans   173
Economic objectives, 1939–1942   185
A crisis needed   200

IX. A Summary of Germany's Economic War Effort, 1942–1944   206

Military supplies, late 1942 to mid-1944   206
Major factors accounting for the increase in military output   213
The collapse of military production   225
Some observations on strategic bombing   229

Summary and conclusions of Part II   235

Statistical Appendix   241

Bibliography   259

Index   265

List of tables

1. Total public expenditures and revenues for fiscal years beginning
   1 April   8
2. German economic indices 1928–1938   10
3. German gross national product — 1928 prices   11
4. Indices of private per capita consumption and investment expenditures   11
5. Total investment classified by purpose   13
6. Government expenditures — for goods and services   16
7. Crude steel production 1929   29
8. German crude steel output   30
9. Gross investment in plant and equipment in selected raw material industries   34
10. Production of major oil products   40
11. Production of iron and steel, 1929 and 1936   41
12. Copper, lead, and zinc metal and ore production   47
13. Domestic agricultural and industrial production of textile raw materials   48
14. Volume index of agricultural production   49
15. Stocks of ferroalloys, August 1939   57
16. Oil requirements, production and stocks   58
17. Composition of Germany's foreign trade, 1929–1939   60
18. Germany's major sources of imports   61
19. Wage and salary earners   67
20. Comparison of gainfully employed with population of working age   68
21. Ratio of gainfully employed to population of working age   69
22. Average weekly hours worked in German industry   70
23. Occupational distribution of the German labor force   72
24. Gainfully employed in the manufacturing industries   74
25. Gross national product in 1939 prices, 1938–1942   86
26. Germany's total available output and war output, 1939–1942   91
27. Munitions production in Germany and the United Kingdom   97
28. Output of particular types of armaments in Germany and the United Kingdom, 1940–1942   99
29. Comparison of the estimates of the ministry of economic warfare with actual German production of various types of war goods   102
30. German munitions expenditures   102
31. Net value of output and employment in the construction and machinery industries   105
32. Employees per machine tool in the industries using tools   108

33. *Copper supplies, consumption and stocks, 1938–1943*   113
34. *Domestic output and imports of iron ore, iron content*   116
35. *Crude steel output in greater Germany and the occupied areas, 1941 and 1942*   118
36. *Number of months' alloy consumption requirements covered by existing stocks and domestic output*   120
37. *Coal production in Germany and occupied territories, 1938–1943*   121
38. *Quarterly allocation of steel rights to major claimants*   131
39. *Indices of total steel supplies and armaments output*   133
40. *Total labor force, 1939–1942*   137
41. *Average weekly hours worked by wage earners in production and consumption goods industries, by sex and skill, selected periods 1929–1942*   138
42. *Number of gainfully occupied men and women in Germany and Great Britain, 1939 and 1942*   139
43. *Distribution of the civilian labor force, 1939–1942*   143
44. *Mobilization of manpower in Great Britain and Germany, 1939–1943*   144
45. *Reich expenditures, tax receipts, and annual deficit, fiscal year beginning April 1*   153
46. *Cost of living and wholesale price indices, 1936–1943*   154
47. *Production of selected classes of armaments, 4th quarter 1939 — 1st quarter 1941*   187
48. *Production of total and selected classes of armaments, 1941*   190
49. *Indices of aircraft, army weapons, and army ammunition production, 1941*   192
50. *Indices of aircraft, army weapons, and army ammunition production, 1942 and peak month of 1941*   196
51. *Increases in armaments production from April until October–November, 1942*   197
52. *Index of German munitions output 1942–1944*   207
53. *German and Russian production of military equipment, annual average 1942–1944*   211
54. *Indices of resource availability*   215
55. *Indices of consumption, selected years, 1928–1938*   246
56. *Indices of consumption, 1939–1944*   250
57. *Gross national product, 1928–1938*   251
58. *Gross national product by major components, 1928–1938*   252
59. *Gross national product by major component, measured in 1928 prices, 1928–1938*   253
60. *Budget expenditures of the Reich, states and municipalities, 1933–1938*   254
61. *Government expenditures for goods and services, 1928–1938*   254
62. *Public and private investment, 1928–1938*   255
63. *Public investment, 1928–1938*   255
64. *Private investment, 1928–1938*   256

65. Gross national product, 1938–1944   256
66. Gross national product, 1938–1944   257
67. National income, 1938–1944   257
68. Government expenditures, 1938–1943   258

PART ONE

GERMAN REARMAMENT

1933–1938

I *Germany's Economic Preparations for War: A Re-examination*

When Germany marched against Poland in September, 1939, her military might was not questioned. The Nazi government, it was commonly believed, had for six years concentrated the country's resources on preparation for war. This was a tacit assumption of the diplomacy of the period, and a point of major emphasis in the voluminous writings on Germany.

Nearly all the economic and political studies of prewar Germany agreed on three major propositions:[1] (1) that in the period before 1939 Germany had succeeded in building up a military machine whose comparative strength was enormous; (2) that a substantial part of the increase in production from the low level of the depression was channeled into the construction of a huge war potential; (3) that all economic considerations were subordinated to the central task of preparing for war.

Even a cursory examination of the official German data recently made available shows that the validity of these propositions is questionable. In regard to manpower, for example, mobilization fell nearly a million short of the number in the armed forces at the outbreak of World War I. Military production was on a much smaller scale than had been assumed: for example, German aircraft production at the beginning of the war, 675 per month, was about the same

1. See, for example: Gustav Stolper, *German Economy 1870–1940* (New York, 1940); Henri Lichtenberger, *The Third Reich* (New York, 1937); Jergen Kuczynski, *Germany: Economic and Labor Conditions under Fascism* (New York, 1945); Maxine Sweezy, *The Structure of the Nazi Economy* (Cambridge, 1941); "Germanicus," *Germany, the Last Four Years* (Boston, 1937).

as Britain's. Tanks, the main weapon of blitzkrieg warfare, were produced at the rate of 50 per month, a rate of output which was exceeded by the British. Another indication of Germany's preparedness was the state of her stockpiling program. In July 1939, the Wehrmacht estimated that such critical items as gasoline, fuel oil, iron ore, magnesium, and rubber were in sufficient supply for only a few months' fighting.[2]

Economic writers were, as subsequent events proved, correct in their belief that Germany was preparing for war. However, their interpretation of the character of the Nazi economic mobilization was wrong. In this volume it will be shown that the central proposition of these writers — that Germany was making massive war preparations — was very much exaggerated. Since a number of important economic conclusions were based on this assumption, the conclusions will have to be revised. In particular, it will be demonstrated that the proportion of output directed to war purposes was not nearly so great as has been usually supposed, and not sufficient to prevent a very substantial recovery of private consumption and investment. It also will be shown that monetary policy, far from having been made subservient to Hitler's political and economic aims, conditioned both the recovery strategy and economic mobilization for war.

I. THE ROLE OF THE "FEAR OF INFLATION" IN GENERAL ECONOMIC POLICY

When the Nazis came into power in the spring of 1933, economic activity had recovered only slightly from the lowest point of the depression. The index of industrial production in the second quarter of 1933 stood at 63 (1928–100), only 3 per cent above the depression bottom. Unemployment, which had reached 6 million in the early part of 1932, had declined by only 500,000. Other economic indices, such as gross national product, farm income, retail sales, and private capital investments, also show that in the spring of 1933 recovery had only begun.[3]

2. This paragraph is based on data from *The Effects of Strategic Bombing on the German War Economy*, U. S. Strategic Bombing Survey (Washington, 1945).

3. See Table 2 for annual data on the index of industrial production, gross national product, private investment, and employment and unemployment. Data for farm income and retail sales appear in the 1938 *Statistisches Jahrbuch*.

To solve Germany's economic problem, Hitler did not introduce a "New Deal." Germany's basic economic policy for the prewar period had been initiated before the Nazi accession to power.[4] The Brüning government (1930–1932) decided against devaluing the mark. Evidently the memory of the inflation was still too fresh, and the fear that devaluation would lead to a flight from the currency was a compelling argument in this decision. This meant, of course, that Germany's power to compete in international markets would depend on the decline of her internal prices at a faster rate than those of rival countries. To this end, the Brüning government sought to accelerate the deflationary process by raising taxes and reducing those prices and wages which had not been sensitive to the general decline. The unpopularity of these measures with both the industrialists and the laborers led to the overthrow of the government.

The von Papen and von Schleicher governments which succeeded the Brüning administration (July 1932 and January 1933) initiated a number of positive recovery measures. These included the remittance of business taxes, the reduction of interest rates, the allocation of more than a billion marks for various types of public works, and the adoption of a direct relief program.

The recovery program did not extend to the stimulus of exports by currency devaluation. This measure was not taken because these governments, like the Brüning government, feared that such a decision would lead to a currency crisis. Since it was impossible to force internal prices down further, the deterioration of Germany's competitive position — with respect to other countries which had devalued — was inevitable. As a final outcome it later became necessary to introduce exchange rationing and selective devaluation in order to obtain necessary imports. Aside from restrictions on the withdrawal of foreign currency, however, it was not at this time necessary to institute an elaborate system of exchange control because Germany still had a favorable balance of trade.

While it was not politically possible to continue a policy of forced deflation, the von Papen and von Schleicher governments had no in-

4. A detailed account of German recovery policy in the years 1930–1938 may be found in C. W. Guillebaud, *The Economic Recovery of Germany, 1933–1938* (London, 1939); Kenyon Poole, *German Financial Policies, 1932–39* (Cambridge, 1939); or the reports of the German Institute for Business Cycle Research.

tention of allowing prices to rise. Two circumstances dictated the retention of price and wage controls. In the first place, these governments were concerned with the possibility that government spending would lead to an internal price rise — something which was in itself to be feared. Secondly, given the decision not to devalue, an internal price rise would have made export difficulties even greater.

Thus, pre-Hitler German economic policy consisted of government spending and other fiscal measures designed to increase employment and income, coupled with strict control of wages and prices to insure that the impact of public expenditures would be on employment and output rather than on wage rates or prices. The Nazis did not change this basic strategy; they only attempted to make it more effective. Recovery expenditures were increased; controls over prices, wages, and foreign exchange were tightened. The measures they undertook could hardly be described as basic innovations in economic policy.[5]

In reaffirming the decision of previous governments not to devalue the mark, the Nazis were compelled to go much further in the direction of elaborate exchange controls. Early in 1934 the trade balance deteriorated to such an extent that Germany's gold and foreign exchange were almost depleted. In order to guarantee necessary imports, Economics Minister Schacht introduced his famous "New Plan." Under this plan, exchange was rationed in order to assure its use for only those types of imports deemed essential. The conclusion of a number of skillful barter agreements with other nations permitted their volume to expand.

As the inflationary pressure of government expenditures increased, controls over prices and wages were tightened. In 1936, selective price controls were superseded by a general price ceiling. All wage disputes were referred to state-approved Labor Trustees who were directed to grant wage increases only in exceptional cases.

Arguing that after 1934 or 1935 there was no longer any economic basis for the retention of these policies, a number of writers have made the point that the price policies and the foreign exchange policies of Nazi Germany can only be explained in terms of her preparations for war.[6] It is my hypothesis that Schacht was interested in con-

---

5. Many of the economic studies of prewar Germany have taken a contrary view. See, for example, Stolper, *German Economy 1870–1940*, p. 240ff.

6. ". . . exchange control from the monetary and financial angles were superfluous as early as 1933 in all probability, but by 1935 for a certainty." Howard

tinuing and strengthening these policies mainly because of his fear — however unfounded — of inflation. Any significant decline in the exchange rate or increases in prices were in themselves regarded as alarming. For an explanation of his policies it is not necessary to look further.

We now turn to the positive recovery measures. In the "First Four-Year Plan" the Nazis expanded expenditures on the various public works programs initiated by the von Papen and von Schleicher governments and added some new programs. The new programs were designed to further Nazi political and social aims.

For example, shortly after he came into power, Hitler became greatly interested in equipping Germany with superhighways and in providing for the mass use of automobiles. Excise taxes on new vehicles which, as in other European countries, had been extremely high, were discontinued. Expenditures on new vehicles were allowed as deductions for income-tax purposes, providing the purchaser scrapped his old car. The goal of self-sufficiency caused agriculture to be another favored sector of economy. Here, in contrast to the general economy, minimum rather than maximum prices were set in order to raise agricultural incomes. The granting of marriage loans was another measure which reflected National Socialist ideology. These monetary incentives, coupled with a propaganda campaign, were very successful in inculcating the idea that women should remain in the home. The measures were, in fact, too successful, for their effects persisted into the period when labor became scarce.

The most widely discussed aspect of Nazi recovery policy was deficit spending. Germany's experience provided a number of economists and publicists with an opportunity for expressing their views on this much-discussed subject.[7] The main issue in this case was whether or not large-scale deficits would lead to inflation and financial ruin. One side argued that the stringent controls over prices, wages, and the capital market ruled out the possibility of inflation. Others thought that the financial strains attendant on such a program were

---

Ellis, "Exchange Control in Germany," *Quarterly Journal of Economics,* Supplement, 53:126–127 (1940).

7. See Otto Nathan, *Nazi War Finance and Banking* (New York, 1944); Guillebaud, *The Economic Recovery of Germany, 1933–38;* Poole, *German Financial Policies, 1932–1930.*

more than Germany could bear and predicted a collapse of her economy.[8]

The fact of the matter is that in prewar years large-scale public borrowing was not undertaken. Until 1938, the total budget of the Reich, states and municipalities, was substantially in balance. As Table 1 shows, although total government expenditures increased from 15 billion RM in 1933 to 39 billion RM in 1938, more than 80 per cent of the funds expended during this period was raised by taxation. (In contrast, from 1932–1936, one half of the United States' government expenditures were deficit financed.) The 25 billion RM increase in the deficit from 1933 to 1938 presented no problem since national income had increased by 75 per cent, and tax receipts had doubled.

Since quick recovery was the primary aim, it may well be asked why the Nazi government chose not to reduce the high tax rates in-

Table 1. Total public expenditures and revenues for fiscal years beginning 1 April

	National income	Total government expenditures	Tax and nontax receipts	Annual deficit
1933	46.5	15.3	14.1	1.2
1934	52.8	17.4	15.5	1.9
1935	59.1	18.9	17.2	1.7
1936	65.8	23.0	19.5	3.5
1937	73.8	27.3	23.4	3.9
1938	82.1	39.4	26.5	12.9
Total		141.3	116.2	25.1

Source: See Appendix, Table 60.

stituted by the Brüning administration and to rely instead on public deficits to finance expenditures. Such a policy, in fact, was advocated by a number of German economists.[9] Their arguments, however, had no influence on the ultra-conservative Minister of Economics and President of the Reichsbank, Hjalmer Schacht. He was actually much disturbed that the propaganda machine allowed such unorthodox

8. See especially *The Banker Magazine* (London), 1937, 1938.
9. See, for example, Robert Noll von der Nahmer, "Die Deckung des oeffentlichten Bedarfsdurch nichtinflatorische Papierausgabe." *Finanzarchiv* (1934), p. 549.

theories of government finance to be published, "Thus causing anxiety for the economy. . . ." [10] This "anxiety" was not caused by a feeling that government deficit spending might lead to a general rise in prices. Such a possibility was precluded by the elaborate system of price and wage controls. The danger attendant on government deficits seemed to Schacht to be the destruction of confidence in the basis of the currency. And this danger could not be measured by a cost-of-living index. Just how far the government could go in increasing the debt was "something imponderable, to recognize the time of which must be left up to fine sensitivity." [11] Thus the fiscal policy pursued during the recovery is another piece of evidence regarding the Nazis' fear of inflation.

If it is denied that the "fear of inflation" was an important factor in Nazi economic policy, it may be possible to explain various decisions, but hardly the entire policy. For example, it is true that having made the decision not to devalue the mark it was to Germany's interest to prevent a further deterioration of her competitive position in international markets by keeping internal prices from rising. Given a policy of price controls, wage controls also became necessary. Controlling wages is facilitated, one may argue, by high taxes on profits. But it is nevertheless difficult to find a rational explanation for a program of high taxes, wage controls, price controls, and stabilization of the mark at a high value, in a time of depression. Under the circumstances, no one could have really feared a serious rise of prices.

However, it was not this type of inflation about which the Germans were concerned. What they feared, as Schacht's statements show, was a loss of confidence in the value of the mark, a frantic effort to convert money assets into real assets. In short, they feared a return to inflation à la 1922, and, as we pointed out, this factor was of considerable importance in explaining the Nazi attitude toward rearmament expenditures.

2. THE NATURE OF THE ECONOMIC RECOVERY

Though the Germans did not rely heavily on deficit financing, public expenditures were increased rapidly enough to result in sub-

10. Record of the Council of Ministers on 12 May 1936, International Military Trials, *Nazi Conspiracy and Aggression* (Washington, 1946), III, 879.
11. International Military Trials, *Nazi Conspiracy and Aggression*, III, 879.

stantial gains in total output and employment. As Table 2 shows, the current value of the gross national product rose from 59 billion RM in 1933 to 105 billion RM in 1938. Only a small portion of this increase was due to price rises. Measured in 1928 prices, the gross na-

Table 2. German economic indices 1928–1938

	Gross national[a] product, current RM	Gross national[a] product, 1928 RM	Index of[b] industrial production	Employment[b] of laborers	Unemployment[b]
	(billions)		(1928=100)	(millions)	
1928	90	91	100	18.4	1.4
1929	90	89	101	18.4	1.9
1932	58	72	59	12.9	5.6
1933	59	75	66	13.4	4.8
1934	67	84	83	15.5	2.7
1935	74	92	96	16.4	2.2
1936	83	101	107	17.6	1.6
1937	93	114	117	18.9	0.9
1938	105	126	122	20.1	0.4

a. See Appendix, Tables 57 and 59.
b. *Statistisches Jahrbuch* 1941/42, pp. 55, 410, and 426.

Table 3. German gross national product — 1928 prices
(billions RM)

	1928	1929	1932	1933	1934	1935	1936	1937	1938
Gross national product	91	89	72	75	84	92	101	114	126
Consumption	68	71	58	59	63	65	68	74	74
Private gross capital formation[a]	10	5	2	4	6	10	12	14	16
Net foreign investment[b]	−1	1	−1	−1	−3	−1	0	0	−3
Government goods and services	13	13	12	12	15	17	21	27	36

Note: Details will not necessarily add to totals because of rounding.
Source: Table 59.
a. Includes plant and equipment, inventory changes, and residential construction
b. Net exports of goods and silver and monetary uses of gold and silver.

tional product rose from 75 to 126 billion RM, some 70 per cent. In the same period the index of production nearly doubled, reaching a level which was 20 per cent above the 1929 peak. From 1933 to 1936 unemployment declined from 4.8 million to 1.6 million (approximately the predepression level) and by 1938 was less than 0.5 million.

As a result of these large gains in total output, private as well as public expenditures increased considerably.[12] As Table 3 shows, despite the fact that government expenditures measured in real terms almost tripled from 1929 to 1938, the 37 billion RM increase in total output over this period was sufficient to permit a higher level of private consumption and investment than had prevailed in the previous prosperity.[13] Consumer expenditures, which were more stable than other segments of the national product, fell by nearly 20 per cent in real terms during the downswing, but by 1937 they had surpassed the 1929 peak level. Private investment fell more rapidly but

Table 4. Indices of private per capita consumption
and investment expenditures
(measured in 1928 prices)

	Total consumption and investment expenditures	Consumption expenditures
1928–29 average	100	100
1933	81	84
1938	108	100

also recovered at a much faster rate than did consumer expenditures. Recovery in investment activity which already had begun in 1933 reached the 1928 peak level during 1935 and exceeded it by 60 per cent in 1938.

In per capita terms, the picture is substantially the same. From the 1933 depression level to 1938, total per capita expenditures in-

12. Figures used in the following discussion have been corrected for price changes.

13. National income, the index of industrial production, and employment reached their highest levels in the years 1928 and 1929. In these two years national income (measured in 1928 prices) was about 10 per cent higher than in the previous peak year — 1913.

creased 35 per cent, and in 1938 exceeded the 1928–1929 amount. Per capita consumption expenditures declined less than total private expenditures during the depression, and by 1938 were up to the predepression figure.

By contrast, in the United States it was not until 1939 that the 1929 level of total output was surpassed.[14] As in Germany, public expenditures increased greatly but the recovery in private expenditures was much slower. Although consumer expenditures (measured in 1939 dollars) surpassed the 1929 total as early as 1936, the highest level of private investment reached before 1940 was only 70 per cent of the 1929 figure.[15]

These comparisons indicate that a diversion of resources from the civilian economy occurred only to the extent that private output was prevented from increasing beyond the 1928–1929 peak level. But this is quite a different order of diversion than that which many economic writers have ascribed to the German rearmament period. Quotations from a few of the economic studies of prewar Germany show a very different picture from the one presented here:

> The Nazis have thus had remarkable success in achieving military goals, but the results of their policies from the point of view of civilian needs are less happy . . . per capita income, including both civilian consumption and investment, has increased only eight per cent since the depths of the depression.[16]

> We conclude that, because of the philosophy of the regime, German recovery was artificial almost from the first, controlled by the government and prevented from spreading throughout all industry in the manner familiar to most upswings.[17]

> During 1934, when it (the standard of living) was about 10 per cent below the 1928 standard, the production of consumptive goods (excluding the production of goods for their army, air force, and navy) had about reached its peak: 1935, 1936, 1937, 1938 and the first nine months of 1939 brought no increase in Germany proper.[18]

14. *Annual Economic Review,* Council of Economic Advisors, January 1952, p. 168.

15. *Annual Economic Review* (January 1952), p. 168.

16. Sweezy, *The Structure of the Nazi Economy,* p. 205.

17. Poole, *German Financial Policies, 1932–1939,* p. 218.

18. Kuczynski, *Germany: Economic and Labor Conditions under Fascism,* p. 60.

Our estimates of real consumption agree fairly well with other indices. For example, they are roughly consistent with the German data on food consumption.[19] They are in agreement with the data on retail sales, and on the output of industrially produced consumer goods. Several German statisticians have estimated consumer expenditures for two portions of the period being examined.[20] My estimates come out reasonably close to these.

That the level of civilian production in the last peacetime years was high can also be inferred from the level of output of civilian items which competed directly with war production for raw material use and which, therefore, should have been the first to show the impact of a large war program. Private residential construction and consumer durables are examples of such marginal items. Actually, we find that 336,000 dwelling units were erected in 1937, only 1 per cent below the high construction year, 1929.[21] The decline in residential construction in 1938 was less than 10 per cent. The 1938 production of automobiles for the civilian economy was at a record level, double the 1929 output.[22] The 1937 and 1938 production of such other consumer durables as furniture and radios was also appreciably above the 1928–1929 level.

How about capital formation? Were the Germans concentrating investment in those sectors of the economy especially important to her war production potential? To answer these questions we have classified the various types of investment activity under three main headings,[23] estimates for which are shown in Table 5.

19. Total per capita calorie consumption declined about 6 per cent from 1929 to 1933, and by 1937 was again at the prewar standard. A more detailed comparison of 1938 with 1928 shows that consumption of beer, eggs, cheese, wheat flour and margarine had decreased somewhat during this period. On the other hand, consumption of meat, lard, butter, fish, potatoes, rice, and coffee increased. *Wirtschaft und Statistik,* 1939, p. 463; *Statistisches Jahrbuch* 1937, pp. 362–363; 1941/42, p. 437.

20. See Appendix, Section 1.

21. *The Effects of Strategic Bombing,* p. 231.

22. *The Effects of Strategic Bombing,* p. 281.

23. There is no unequivocal method of classifying investments into war and nonwar categories. Almost every investment in plant, equipment, roads, etc., has some relevance for military output. In the case of Germany, the difficulty is further enhanced by the fact that the statistics do not permit as fine a breakdown of capital formation as is necessary to make the desired classification. In spite of these difficulties, however, much can be learned by classifying and studying the available data of these subgroups.

I. Armament Factories and Military Facilities
II. The Basic Industries
III. Civilian and Government Nonwar.

It will be observed that in the years 1933–1938 more than 50 per cent of total public and private investment fell into Group III. Even

Table 5. Total investment classified by purpose
(billions of RM)

	1928	1933	1934	1935	1936	1937	1938
Group I	0.8	0.2	0.4	1.9	3.3	4.0	5.3
Armament plants[a]	0.8	0.2	0.4	0.6	0.9	1.2	1.6
Military facilities[b]				1.3	2.4	2.8	3.7
Group II	4.2	1.5	2.1	2.6	3.0	3.7	4.5
Heavy industry[c]	0.9	0.1	0.3	0.6	0.8	1.0	1.3
Railroads and other transportation equipment	1.3	0.6	0.8	0.8	19	1.1	1.5
Agriculture	0.9	0.6	0.7	0.8	0.9	1.0	1.1
Public utilities	1.0	0.2	0.3	0.4	0.5	0.6	0.7
Group III	8.6	3.3	5.4	6.6	8.0	7.8	8.6
Other industry[d]	0.9	0.3	0.3	0.4	0.5	0.6	0.8
Residential construction	2.8	0.9	1.4	1.6	2.2	2.0	2.5
Commercial, handicraft, miscellaneous	1.7	0.7	0.7	0.8	0.9	1.0	1.0
Roads	0.5	0.3	0.6	0.9	1.2	1.2	1.8
Other government[e]	2.7	1.1	2.4	2.5	3.3	2.9	2.9
Total	13.7	5.1	8.3	11.2	14.3	15.5	18.8

Source: For total public and private investment by major category, see the Appendix. Details on industrial investment, *Statistisches Jahrbuch*, 1941/1942, p. 604; *Statistisches Jahrbuch*, 1937, p. 540. Investment in military fortifications, etc., estimated on the basis of an official report *Bericht vom Westwall*, and the total public investment estimates shown in Appendix, Table 63.

a. Electrical machinery, vehicle, locomotive, naval, metal-working, optical, and chemical industries.

b. Barracks, airfields, fortifications, etc. (more than 2 billion RM were spent on fortifications in 1938 and 1939).

c. Steel, coal, construction materials, and rubber industries.

d. Clothing, food, printing and publishing, linoleum, paper, and musical instrument industries.

e. Postal system, trams and subways, waterways, government and party buildings, municipal improvements, etc.

in 1938, the last peacetime year, the current value of these nonwar types of investment was as large as in 1928. Measured in constant prices, their real volume was 20 per cent higher in 1938 than it had been in 1928. Public expenditures on roads and buildings formed the largest component of Group III. In the years 1936–1938, such undertakings averaged about 4.5 billion marks annually — nearly 5 per cent of Germany's gross national product.

Inspection of the figures in Table 5 shows investment in armament plants and Germany's basic industries to be a surprisingly small part of total investment. Investment in Group II industries, which included the iron and steel plants, the coal mines, the transportation system and public utilities, was exceeded every year by expenditures on road construction and government buildings. Comparing the Group II totals of the rearmament period with the 1928 figure, we find that it was not until 1937 that the 1928 level was surpassed, even after allowance is made for the difference in the price level. Investment expenditures on that part of Group I which we have called armament plants were, relatively speaking, exceedingly small. Annual expenditures on these facilities for the years 1933 through 1938 averaged only half as much as those on residential construction. Thus, inspection of Germany's prewar pattern of investment shows that there was no pronounced concentration of investment in those activities associated with economic preparations for war.

Germany's actual war effort of course benefited from the large volume of prewar investment, though it was not specifically directed to war preparations. For example, expansion of the basic industries turned out to be very important. A significant proportion of the investment represented types of facilities which could be converted to war production purposes. More important, perhaps, capacity in the machinery and construction industries was vastly expanded. Between 1933 and 1938 the production of construction materials was more than tripled.[24] From 1936 to 1939 machinery production increased by 60 per cent.[25]

24. *Statistisches Jahrbuch,* 1941/1942, p. 218.
25. Des Reichsamts fur wehrwirtschaftliche Planung, *Die deutsche Industrie,* 1936, p. 101; *Industrial Sales, Output and Productivity, Prewar Area of Germany, 1939–1944,* United States Strategic Bombing Survey, p. 37.

Summing up concerning the composition of Germany's prewar gross national product, it is apparent that an enormous diversion of resources from the civilian to the war sector of the economy did not occur. Both consumption and nonwar types of investment reached the prosperity levels of 1928 and 1929. This is also true in regard to government nonwar expenditures.[26] Thus, it is only possible to speak of a diversion of resources in the sense that private expenditures did not rise more than they actually did.

3. THE MAGNITUDE OF WAR PREPARATIONS

Most discussions of Germany's war preparations begin with Hitler's boast that the Nazis had spent 90 billion RM on rearmament. It is paradoxical that this statistic was accepted quite uncritically at a time when nearly all other German data were suspect.[27] Actually,

Table 6. Government expenditures — for goods and services[a]
(billions RM)

Fiscal year beginning April	Total government expenditures for goods and services	Armament expenditures	Other public expenditures
1933–1934	21	4	17
1935	14	4	10
1936	17	6	11
1937	21	8	13
1938	33	18	15
Total	106	40[b]	66

a. See Appendix, Tables 60 and 61.
b. In answer to an American interrogation, Schacht stated that he and von Krosigk (Minister of Finance) placed total armament expenditures at 45 billion RM.

26. See Table 6.
27. In calculating a residual of private investment and consumption, Sweezy uses a figure of 90 billion RM (*Structure of Nazi War Economy,* p. 205). In *Nazi War Finance and Banking,* p. 88, Nathan uses his own figure of 75 billion RM, but thinks that it is understated. Neither of these authors defines armament expenditures. According to Churchill, two independent estimates made in Britain in 1936 placed German rearmament expenditures at an annual rate of one thousand million pounds sterling, or about 12 billion RM (*The Second World War.* Vol. I, *The Gathering Storm* [Boston, 1948], p. 226). Actual expenditures at that time were at an annual rate of about 5 billion RM; see Table 6.

according to the German budget data, total government expenditures — war and nonwar — amounted to not much more than 90 billion RM during the period 1933–1938.[28] Rearmament expenditures themselves totalled 40 billion in the six fiscal years ending March 31, 1939, and about 50 billions up to the outbreak of war. The figures include, besides Wehrmacht expenditures, public expenditures for fortifications, for armaments plants, and for stockpiling.

Public rearmament expenditures corresponded to less than 40 per cent of total public expenditures, excluding transfer payment, and about 10 per cent of the gross national product produced during this six-year period.

A German economist has pointed out that the proportion of total output devoted to rearmament, which was implied by Hitler's 90 billion figure, was reached only in the latter part of the war. Regarding the fact that foreigners were deceived, he remarks, "Public views of the scale of armament were very much exaggerated. The German government of the time did nothing to contradict the exaggerated ideas; on the contrary they were desirable propaganda, producing the illusion of a warlike strength which in reality was not available on that scale." [29] Up to the time of the German reoccupation of the Rhineland in the Spring of 1936, rearmament was largely a myth. In the three years ending March 31, 1936, some 8 billion RM were spent; more than one half of this in the fiscal year 1935–1936. In other words, about 5 per cent of the total national output went for war purposes.

It is perhaps easier to assess the state of preparedness by looking at the size of the army. At this time the German army was no larger than the French; it numbered less than 500,000 men and was composed of the equivalent of some 25 full-strength divisions.[30] Before 1936 plans for the speedy creation of a large offensive army did not exist. At the time conscription legislation was passed in March 1935,

28. See Appendix, Table 60.
29. Rolf Wagenfuehr, *Aufstieg und Niedergang der deutschen Rüstung*, Berlin, March 1945, p. 8.
30. *German Army Mobilization*, Intelligence Division, War Dept. (1946). This study is based on captured German documents. The estimate of French military strength comes from Paul Reynaud, *Le Problème Militaire Française*, 1937, p. 27. Reynaud's estimate of German strength at this time was 800,000; nearly twice the actual size.

it was planned to bring the army up to a strength of 700,000, and that only by 1939.[31]

The second phase of German rearmament began in the summer of 1936 when Hitler decided to start rearming on an intensive scale. Undoubtedly this decision was influenced by German intelligence reports which placed the strength of the Russian army at nearly one million. Such "Bolshevist" superiority was greatly feared, and preparations were begun under the Second Four-Year Plan to assure German dominance of Europe.

The language of the memorandum delivered to Goering on his appointment as Plenipotentiary of the Second Four-Year Plan in October 1936 leaves no doubt as to Hitler's desire to begin full-scale preparation for war.[32] This document begins with Hitler's declaration that war is inevitable. In the first place, Hitler asserts, "it will be Germany's task to defend Europe against Bolshevism" [33] and secondly, "a final solution of the food problem only can come through an expansion of living space [Lebensraum]." Following these pronouncements, Hitler denounced Schacht's Economics Ministry for sabotaging rearmament, accusing Schacht of having no comprehension of economic mobilization. Finally, Goering was given two commands:

I. The German Army must be ready for commitment in four years.

II. The German economy must be ready for war in four years.

Hitler did not indicate the strength of military forces or the size of the economic effort which would be required to prepare Germany for its "historic task." Nor, to my knowledge, has such a plan been found in the German archives. It is difficult, therefore, to gauge just how high the Nazis had set their sights. But at any rate it does not appear that the extent of mobilization before the actual outbreak of

31. *German Army Mobilization.*

32. A photostat of this document is in the files of the United States Strategic Bombing Survey.

33. ". . . the world is drifting with ever increasing speed into a new conflict, whose most extreme solution is called Bolshevism. One has to compare the Red Army as it really is today with the assumptions of the military ten or fifteen years ago to gauge the dangerous extent of this development. Germany will have to be considered as the focal point of the Occidental world against Bolshevist attack."

war measured up to the Fuehrer's edict of "unconditional subordination of all other desires to preserve Germany's national existence."

In the three fiscal years ending March 31, 1939, Germany spent 32 billion RM for rearmament. In 1938–1939, the last peacetime year, military expenditures amounted to 18 billion RM, a sum equivalent to 15 per cent of Germany's gross national product. Actually, the share of the German national output going for armaments was not much higher than that of the Allies, prior to their entry into the war. Total British war expenditures in 1939 constituted nearly 15 per cent of her gross national product, and were only slightly less than Germany's.[34] In 1941, the year before the United States went to war, the war expenditure ratio was about 10 per cent — and this would imply a higher absolute volume of armament expenditures than Germany's.

Comprehensive statistics on munitions production in the immediate prewar years are lacking. Such data on output or stocks as are available indicate that the production of war goods, like total military strength, has been considerably exaggerated.

The Nazis placed heavy emphasis on the importance of air power, allocating nearly one half of prewar military expenditures to the *Luftwaffe*. A large aircraft output was therefore to be expected. Total monthly aircraft production[35] rose from 30 in 1933 to 425 in 1936 and remained at this level through 1938. In 1939, total output rose by 60 per cent. At the outbreak of war output of combat types was 500 a month, 60 per cent of the production rate credited to Germany by British Intelligence.[36] Germany entered the war with an air force of 1000 bombers and 1050 fighters, which was still not an inconsiderable number compared to the air strength of her enemies.[37]

Before 1938 Germany produced only the very light Mark I and Mark II tanks — types which were outmoded soon after the beginning of the war. Production of the Mark III began in 1938, and the

---

34. *World Munitions Production 1938–1944.* War Production Board. The definitions of War Production and Gross National Product are roughly comparable to those which have been used for Germany.

35. *Effects of Strategic Bombing,* p. 149.

36. *An Appraisal of Pre- and Post-Raid Intelligence,* U. S. Strategic Bombing Survey.

37. *An Appraisal of Pre- and Post-Raid Intelligence.*

Mark IV in 1939. In the last three months of 1939, Germany produced 247 tanks,[38] 45 per cent of the Intelligence estimate of German
production.[39]

A more dramatic indication of Germany's state of preparedness is
to be found in the 1939 plot against Hitler. In the summer of 1938,
Hitler informed his confidants of his plans to invade Czechoslovakia
if it became impossible to strike a bargain with England. This plan
was opposed by a group of high army and civilian officials. Included
in the group were General Beck, Chief of Staff, General von Witzleben, Commander of the Third Army, General Thomas, production
chief of the High Command, former Economics Minister Schacht,
and Goerderler, former Lord Mayor of Leipzig. Some of these names
figured in the 1944 Plot. The opposition of this clique was based on
the assumption that the English would not back down, and that the
Wehrmacht was totally unprepared to withstand a coalition of European powers. (In the fall of 1938 Germany had 35 infantry and 4
motorized divisions, and, according to testimony of German generals,
these were neither fully equipped nor fully manned.) Foreseeing
another Versailles, these generals formed a conspiracy to seize Hitler
and remove the Nazis from power by a military *coup d'état*. According to the documentary evidence, Theodore Kordt, the German
chargé in London, informed Halifax of the plot and urged Britain to
stand firm. As it was planned, Beck resigned early in September when
he was informed of Hitler's certain decision to take action. Before
the date planned for the conspiracy, however, it was learned that
Chamberlain would go to Godesberg on September 13. This knowledge seemed to indicate that their original premise was wrong, that
Hitler's bluff would be successful. The plot was called off and von
Halder, one of the conspirators, accepted Beck's vacated post.[40]

4. THE FACTORS WHICH LIMITED ECONOMIC MOBILIZATION

A nation's real war potential is limited by two factors: the total
amount of production which can be obtained from its resources, and

38. An Appraisal of Pre- and Post-Raid Intelligence.
39. An Appraisal of Pre- and Post-Raid Intelligence.
40. An account of this plot is to be found in the "Twentieth of July,"
Franklin Ford, American Historical Review, July 1946. Also consulted were
interrogations of Thomas, Schacht, von Halder, documentary evidence presented at the War Crimes Trials, and Churchill, The Gathering Storm, p. 312:

the share of this output which can be converted to war purposes. In the prewar years, at least, there is no evidence that armaments output was circumscribed by either of these factors.

In the first place, it is clear that a much larger share of the 1938 national product could have been used for war purposes. Civilian consumption and investment, as we have seen, were at the 1928–1929 levels; while at the same time the government was undertaking a huge nonwar program. Thus it would appear that it might have been possible for the Germans to have doubled war output by cutting the over-all level of civilian production by 10 or 15 per cent.

Nor does it appear that it was at this time impossible for the Germans to have secured a larger war output through an expansion of their national product. Although full employment had been reached before 1938, and the 1929 level of production was exceeded by 25 per cent of this year, she had not exhausted her expansionary possibilities. Further evidence will be supplied when we examine the manpower and raw material situation (Chapters II and III), but the plausibility of this argument can be gauged by reference to the wartime records of Britain and the United States. In these countries it has been quite clearly demonstrated that full employment did not signify a capacity level of production. Subject to outside pressure, production showed an elasticity which was astonishing. This also was shown at a later date in Germany.

We may sum up this argument by saying that although it may not have been possible to increase war output while maintaining all types of civilian output (automobiles and refrigerators, for example), opportunity still existed as late as 1938 for increasing military preparations without causing an appreciable decline in the general level of civilian output. It is seen, therefore, that "real" factors cannot explain why Germany did not produce more war material.

The explanation of Germany's failure to prepare on a much larger scale is essentially a financial one. The German leaders simply did not at this time understand the elementary economic lesson that "a nation can finance everything which can be produced." [41] As will be shown, financing a higher level of war expenditures by raising already high tax rates was not regarded as expedient. Procuring additional

---

41. Nathan's conclusion that Germany had learned this before the democracies is hardly valid (*Nazi War Finance*, p. 90).

funds by borrowing, it was thought, would destroy confidence in the currency and lead to an inflation. This fear of inflation weighed heavily in the policy decisions of the whole decade. It was an important consideration in the decision of the Brüning government against devaluation and coincidentally in the adoption of the policy of forced deflation; it led to the retention of this policy after the inflationary argument was, from an economic standpoint, no longer valid; it prevented the Nazis from reducing taxes when their primary aim was a speedy recovery. And financial considerations also played a major role in impeding the rearmament.

One of the strongest exponents of this school of financial conservatism was Schacht. Although he was already in disfavor with Hitler by 1936, Schacht remained Minister of Economics until August 1937 and President of the Reichsbank until January 1939. And until his dismissal from the Reichsbank, his financial views to some extent dominated Nazi economic policy. Schacht's testimony indicates that he was dismissed, not because he opposed rearmament on social or political grounds, but because large rearmament expenditures were inconsistent with his views on sound finance.[42]

By 1937, he stated, the financial position of the Reichsbank had become so precarious that he advised Hitler that additional credits for rearmament could not be raised. Hitler finally persuaded him to provide the government with another three billions, but only on the condition that this was to be the last. After March 1938, Schacht stated that he refused to give another penny for rearmament, and in January 1939 his one-year appointment was not renewed. There is nothing in the documentary evidence which would deny the veracity of Schacht's story.

At the meeting of the Council of Ministers on May 12, 1936, the possibility of increasing armament expenditures was discussed.[43] The Minister of Finance, Graf Schwerin von Krosigk, did not think that an additional 6 or 7 billions could be raised by taxes. In conformity with universal standards of political behavior, this was denied by

42. This account of Schacht's dismissal is taken from his testimony to Clifford Hynning of the United States Group Control Council; from interrogation reports of the United States Strategic Bombing Survey made by Paul Baran and the author, and from the record of his testimony at the International Military Trial.

43. *Nazi Conspiracy and Aggression*, III, 878–884.

none of the Ministers. This passed the responsibility for obtaining more funds to the Reichsbank; Schacht summed up the past accomplishments of the Reichsbank, declaring that with unswerving loyalty to the Fuehrer he had raised 11 billions for rearmament and re-employment. The Reichsbank could go on, he said, and raise some 2 billions annually, but, he asserted, the money market would not support the 8 or 9 billion requested. If the Reichsbank were to be pushed further, Schacht left no doubts as to his own position:

> Dr. Schacht will never be part to an inflation; the Fuehrer also has decided in this sense. The danger of such a development is imminent. If a road is to be taken, which contains this danger, Dr. Schacht would like to drop out on time, so that he does not disturb the new course.[44]

Goering voiced his skepticism by commenting that "Measures which in a state with a parliamentary government would probably bring about inflation, do not have the same results in a totalitarian state." [45] But he did not press his argument further.

It might be pointed out that Schacht quite successfully withstood the pressure for higher armament expenditures. In the fiscal year 1936–1937, they were only 4 billions more than in the previous year. Whenever the question came up, Schacht took the same firm position of the danger of public deficits. At a meeting of the Council of Ministers in May 1936,[46] Goering began by asking what objections there might be to producing substitute materials in the Reich. Schacht replied that there were no theoretical objections, that self-sufficiency was absolutely necessary, but that on the practical side there would be serious difficulties — the question of finance. "Providing money by taxing capital is impossible. Circulation of money cannot be increased beyond a certain amount. Previous measures were executed correctly and without danger to monetary value. Further increase seems precarious; a matter of confidence." [47]

By 1938, when Hitler was completely out of patience with Schacht's economic ideas, it might have been expected that the Nazis

---

44. *Nazi Conspiracy and Aggression,* III, 879.
45. *Nazi Conspiracy and Aggression,* III, 883.
46. *Nazi Conspiracy and Aggression,* III, 886.
47. *Nazi Conspiracy and Aggression,* III, 886–887. It may be noted that the debt increased by more than 250 billion RM during the war, with neither a substantial rise in prices nor a financial collapse.

would have at last freed themselves from their financial yoke. But the evidence does not confirm this suspicion.

During the fall of 1938 when the Sudetenland issue was pending, military expenditures were increased sharply. On the 7th of December, an order signed by Keitel went to the commanders of the three services stating that:

> The strained financial situation of the Reich makes it necessary that for the rest of the current fiscal year 1938–39 the expenses of the Armed Forces, which in the last months under the strain of extraordinary circumstances have undergone a very considerable increase, should be lowered again to a level, which would be tolerable for some time.[48]

It was ordered that total military expenditures for the last five months of the fiscal year were not to exceed 6.9 billion. The provisional budget for 1938–1939 was set at 11.5 billion RM, 30 per cent below expenditures of the previous fiscal year.[49]

For the purpose of explaining why Germany's war preparations were not larger, the financial bottleneck provides us with the necessary but not the sufficient conditions. For, if additional funds could not be obtained through borrowing or taxation, it still would have been possible to obtain these by cutting nonwar expenditures. There were some 15 billion RM, in the fiscal year 1938–1939, nearly 75 per cent greater than when the Nazis came into power. Especially prominent in the civil budget were public investments in highways, party buildings, municipal improvements, and the like.[50]

If nonwar expenditures were not reduced, it was not the fault of Schacht; in every discussion of public finance, he preached economy in government expenditures. In proposing specific cuts, however, he was invariably opposed by some faction of the party, and succeeded only in getting himself thoroughly in disfavor with the Nazi politicians. It was, in fact, even difficult for Schacht to compel the semiautonomous political organizations to submit their budgets to the Ministry of Finance.[51]

When rearmament was speeded up during the time of the Czech

---

48. *Nazi Conspiracy and Aggression*, III, 907.
49. *Nazi Conspiracy and Aggression*, III, 908.
50. See Table 4.
51. *Nazi Conspiracy and Aggression*, III, 845–846, 878.

crisis, Goering began to take a firmer stand on the reduction of nonwar expenditures. However, not much was done in this respect before the beginning of the war. Goering's speech before the Air Ministry in October 1938 was a forecast of action which was to come only at a later date:

> He [Goering] is going to make barbaric use of his plenipotentiary power which was given to him by the Fuehrer.

> All the wishes and plans of the state, party and other agencies which are not entirely in this line have to be rejected without pity. . . .

> He warns all agencies, particularly the labor front, price controller, etc., from interfering with these proposals in any way. He is going to proceed ruthlessly against every interference on the part of the labor front. The labor front would not receive raw materials and workers for its tasks any more. Similarly all other party requirements have to be set aside without consideration. Foreign workers can continue being employed except in the particularly secret sections of the enterprise. At the present time the plants should not be burdened with unnecessary demands, such as athletic fields, casinos or similar desires of the labor front.[52]

This discussion of financial impediments to rearmament provides some insight into Nazi politics. The fear of increasing the debt because it would destroy confidence, the unwillingness to raise taxes, the difficulties of reducing particular types of government expenditures — all indicate that Hitler was less able to subordinate the various private interests to his central task of preparing for war than has been commonly assumed.

These fiscal considerations do not explain, however, why Germany did not undertake really large-scale preparations for war. The various minutes of meetings pertaining to the discussion of the rearmament question indicate that the Nazi leaders were thinking only in terms of increasing military expenditures by a few billion reichmarks, or of adding several divisions to the army. It is unlikely, therefore, even if finances had not stood in the way, that the rearmament program would have been more than, say, some 20 or 30 per cent larger.

The fundamental reason why large war preparations were not undertaken is simply that Hitler's concept of warfare did not require them. Documentary evidence and interrogation of his confidants in-

52. *Nazi Conspiracy and Aggression,* III, 902–903.

dicate that for the fulfillment of his territorial desires, Hitler did not expect to fight a protracted war against a coalition of major powers. Rather he planned to solve Germany's living-space problem in piecemeal fashion — by a series of small wars. His strategy, as it developed, was to undermine an enemy's internal and external political unity, to intimidate with threats of military destruction, and, if this were not successful, to force a speedy capitulation by blitz warfare. All this was to occur in so short a time that the democracies could be presented with a *fait accompli* while they were still debating whether or not to intervene.[53] Italy's experience against Abyssinia, the occupation of the Rhineland, the conquest of Czechoslovakia, all indicated that the process could be repeated against Poland, the Balkans, and, after a period of consolidation, against the coveted Ukraine.

The only nations which could be considered as threats to German expansion were the United States, Russia, France, and England. Before the outbreak of war, the possibility of American intervention was considered remote. Although Hitler frequently spoke of Germany's future task of defending Europe against Bolshevism, Russia was not considered an immediate threat. Russia could be dealt with in the future, after Germany was able to draw on the war potential of Western Europe. For this conflict Hitler counted on the neutrality, if not the active participation, of the democracies. Hitler always took England and France into account in his war plans, but he did not think that they would intervene.[54] England, he thought, would not be able to fight without the support of the Commonwealth. And he doubted if the Commonwealth would support the mother country in a European conflict.[55] Also, he thought it unlikely that England would wish to destroy Europe's "bulwark against Communism." As early as 1937 Hitler saw the possibility of a social and political decay

53. The directive for the operation "Gruen" (conquest of Czechoslovakia) stated: ". . . it is essential to create — already in the first 4 days — a military situation which plainly proves to hostile nations eager to intervene, the hopelessness of the Czechoslovakian military situation. . . ." *Nazi Conspiracy and Aggression,* III, 311.

54. Hitler was confident that the invasion of Poland would not bring England and France into the war, and later, after Poland was conquered, he expected that they would agree to his peace terms.

55. *Nazi Conspiracy and Aggression,* III, 297–304.

in France which would leave her incapable of offering active resistance.[56]

Hitler's strategy, then, did not involve large war preparations, but only immediate military superiority over France and England. For this 50 or 60 well-trained divisions and an air force of 2000 planes were regarded as adequate. This hypothesis was confirmed by the first two years of fighting.

The faulty appraisal of the prewar Nazi economy was due primarily to the inability of political and economic writers to appreciate the economic significance of this blitzkrieg strategy. They failed to see that such a strategy did not involve a large use of resources and that it permitted, together with minimal war preparations, a prosperous civilian economy. Their economic picture was distorted also because of the implicit belief that Nazis would make their financial policy subservient to the economic rearmament program rather than adapting the scale of war preparations to the principles of financial conservatism.

56. Conference of the Reichskanzlei, November 1937. "Should the social tensions in France lead to an internal political crisis of such dimensions that it absorbs the French Army and thus renders it incapable for employment in war against Germany, then the time for action against Czechoslovakia has come." *Nazi Conspiracy and Aggression,* III, 301.

II *Raw Material Preparations for War*

A principal factor in Germany's defeat in World War I was her inability to obtain adequate supplies of foodstuffs and industrial raw materials. The Nazis were well aware of this lesson, and from the beginning of their regime they placed great importance on becoming self-sufficient in raw materials. The German General Staff, especially, was impressed with the necessity of making adequate economic preparations. Had Hitler deferred to their judgment, Germany's second attempt to conquer Europe would have been delayed for five or ten years.[1]

I. THE RAW MATERIAL POTENTIAL IN 1933

A precise description of Germany's 1933 raw material potential would require data on the productive capacity of her various raw material industries and data on the volume of raw material imports required for this level of production. Since such data are not available, we shall use as an approximation the actual production and import figures for years of record levels of output.

A. *Steel*

One of the most frequently used measures of a nation's war potential is its steel capacity, and there is ample indication that this was the standard which the Nazis accepted for judging their own

1. A thorough investigation of the Nazi program for raw material self-sufficiency would involve a major study. We shall concentrate our discussion on industrial materials and only mention the agricultural self-sufficiency program. The raw materials to be included in the discussion are steel, iron ore, ferro-alloys, nonferrous metals, coal, chemicals, oil, rubber, and textile raw materials.

strength and that of their enemies. In terms of this standard, Germany had a marked advantage over her potential European enemies. German steel production in the peak years of the 1920's was greater than 16 million tons and, as Table 7 shows, exceeded the output of any of the other European powers. Germany's lead appears even more impressive when it is remembered that 35 per cent of her crude steel capacity had been lost at the peace settlement following World War I (see Table 8). In 1922 her steel production was around 11 million tons, or only slightly larger than that of Britain or France; by 1929 it was more than 60 per cent above the production of either country.

Several factors contributed to Germany's rapid expansion of

Table 7. Crude steel production 1929
(millions of metric tons)

Germany	16.2
Great Britain	10.0
France	9.7
Russia	4.7
United States	57.3

Source: *Statistisches Jahrbuch*,
1931, p. 62.

steel capacity in this eight-year period. The government subsidized expansion by indemnifying owners of lost steel properties on the condition that the funds be reinvested in German steel plants. The inflation provided a stimulus by placing an enormous premium on the conversion of liquid assets into real property. The formation of a German steel cartel, in 1924, and the participation of German firms in an international cartel several years later, provided another impetus to expansion. It is somewhat paradoxical that this should be so, since the cartels were formed primarily because a large capacity threatened the price of steel and the profits of producers. Nevertheless, once a cartel was formed it was to the interest of the individual firm to enlarge its capacity and thereby secure a higher sales quota. Finally, expansion was facilitated by the ease of obtaining funds from foreign investors — among which American banking firms were not unimportant.

As a result of this expansion of capacity, production increased rapidly. As Table 8 shows, steel output in Germany proper reached a level in 1927 which was nearly 50 per cent above the 1913 near-capacity level for the corresponding area. Just how large 1929 capacity was is difficult to ascertain because reliable estimates do not exist. There is no doubt that steel plants were producing less than capacity levels. Discussions of the German steel cartel have stated that in the latter part of the 1920's they were operating at only 70 to 80 per cent of capacity.[2] On the basis of these estimates steel capacity can be conservatively estimated at about 21 million tons. Thus in steel capacity Germany had a large margin of superiority over any of her potential European enemies. Indeed, her capacity did not fall far short of that of France and Britain combined.[3]

Table 8. German crude steel output
(millions of metric tons)

	1913	1922	1925	1927	1929
Prewar area	16.8				
Area as of 1922	11.0	9.5	12.2	16.3	16.2

Source: *Konjunktur-Statistisches Handbuch*, 1936, p. 234.

But steel-making capacity does not give the whole picture. When Germany's resources of those raw materials used in steel production are considered, her position appears much less favorable. The principal steel input items are iron ore, coal, scrap, ferroalloys, and limestone. Of these Germany was self-sufficient in only three — scrap, coal, and limestone. For iron ore and ferroalloys she had to rely almost exclusively on imports.

In 1929, about 80 per cent of the ore supplies (by iron content) were imported. This heavy dependence on foreign ores was partly compensated for by Germany's ample scrap supplies, which are highly substitutable for iron ore. But this factor should not be overemphasized, because a large percentage of the scrap supplies are ob-

2. George W. Stocking and Myron W. Watkins, *Cartels in Action*, New York, 1946, p. 178.
3. It is assumed that the French and British steel plants were operating about as much below capacity as were the German plants.

tained in the process of producing steel, which in turn is dependent on ore supplies. Without foreign ore, therefore, the greater part of the steel industry would have had to close down. Germany's most important source of ore was Sweden, supplying in the 1920's about a half of the total imports. Another quarter came from Spain, Luxembourg, Norway, and Greece.

Ferroalloys imposed the severest limitation to self-sufficiency in steel input items. For practically all of her supplies, Germany was dependent on foreign sources, most of them non-European. Manganese was the only alloy produced in Germany.[4] In 1929 about one half the total supplies came from German mines.[5] For the other alloys — nickel, molybdenum, chrome, and tungsten — Germany relied exclusively on imports, the chief sources of which were not on the continent of Europe. Molybdenum came almost exclusively from the United States, chrome from the Union of South Africa and from Southern Rhodesia, and tungsten from India and China.

B. *Nonferrous Metals*

Other metals of considerable importance in the manufacture of war material are aluminum, copper, lead, and zinc. Aluminum is the most important of these because it is practically indispensable in aircraft production and has a variety of other important uses. The Nazis began their war preparations with the handicaps of having only a very small capacity for the reduction of ores, and practically no bauxite ore mining. Construction of new capacity had not been undertaken since the end of World War I because cheap electric power, one of the principal requisites for aluminum production, was not available. Most of the aluminum used in German manufacture had to be imported. Such ore as was reduced in Germany during the pre-Nazi period came from France, Yugoslavia, Hungary, and Italy.

Germany had a large copper smelting and refining capacity, but very little copper ore. In the decade of the 1920's her output of refined copper reached 125 thousand metric tons, which placed Germany second only to the United States.[6] But even with this produc-

4. During World War I, nickel was mined in Germany, but only to the extent of one tenth of her consumption.
5. *Konjunktur-Statistisches Handbuch*, 1936, p. 236.
6. *Konjunktur-Statistisches Handbuch*, 1936, p. 220.

tion she could satisfy only half of her peacetime consumption requirements for refined copper. Practically all the ore that was smelted in
Germany had to be imported. In 1928 and 1929, German ores provided for only a tenth of her total consumption.[7] About one half of
these imports came from overseas, mainly from the United States
and Chile.

Lead and zinc are of somewhat lesser importance for the production of war material. During the latter part of the 1920's about 60
per cent of the consumption of these metals was covered by German
resources.[8] But unlike copper, lead, and zinc, deposits existed in
Germany which at some additional cost could be mined much more
intensively.

Although, with the exception of aluminum, Germany was well
situated with respect to capacity for the conversion of ores into
semifinished products, her pre-1933 position in ore resources was
not as fortunate.

C. *Oil*

Germany's position in oil was especially weak. Both as an oil
producer and as an oil consumer, she lagged far behind other industrial countries. In the middle of the 1930's, when German consumption of petroleum products was higher than it had ever been,
she used only about one half as much oil as Great Britain, one fourth
as much as Russia and about 5 per cent of the amount consumed in
the United States.[9] Even for this modest consumption, domestic resources were inadequate. In 1934, Germany consumed about 3.0
million metric tons of gasoline, fuel oil, and various other petroleum
products.[10] Eighty-five per cent of this was imported (mainly from
North and South America)[11] and the other 15 per cent came from
domestic crude oil and from a synthetic oil industry which was still
in its infancy. The Fischer–Tropsch and Bergius processes for the
synthetic production of oil had been perfected only in the late 1920's,
and at the time the Nazis came into power only three small plants
were in operation. The reason that the industry had not developed

7. *Konjunktur-Statistisches Handbuch*, 1938, p. 220.
8. *Statistisches Jahrbuch*, 1930, pp. 197 and 209.
9. *Effects of Strategic Bombing*, p. 73.
10. *Statistisches Jahrbuch*, 1941/1942, p. 228.
11. *Statistisches Jahrbuch*, 1941/1942, p. 70*.

further is not difficult to find — synthetic oil costs four to five times as much as crude.[12]

D. *Rubber*

The process for the manufacture of synthetic rubber had also been developed before the Nazis came into power. By 1930 I. G. Farben had perfected "Buna S," a satisfactory tire rubber. However, this product too was very costly because its process demanded enormous quantities of electric power. At this time Germany still relied almost exclusively on natural rubber imports for her consumption requirements.

E. *Coal*

The only important raw materials of which Germany had abundant supplies were coal and chemicals. Second to Great Britain, Germany was the largest producer and exporter of coal in Europe. In the high production years of the 1920's, bituminous output averaged about 155 million tons.[13] (In addition, Germany also produced nearly 200 million tons annually of *Branukohle* — a form of lignite having a low heat value.) A high degree of mechanization in German mines was an important factor in her relatively high output. In 1938 output per man shift in the Ruhr was about a third greater than British mines, and double that of the French and Belgian mines.[14]

The supply of coal was ample not only for very extensive internal use but also for exports. In the decade of the 1920's, Germany supplied about a quarter of total European coal imports.[15] This abundance of coal formed the basis for a large sector of German industry. Electric power was derived almost exclusively from coal; it was the key material in the synthetic rubber and oil industries developed later; and it made possible the development of a gigantic chemical industry.

F. *Chemicals*

The most important wartime chemical was nitrogen, the basic material for the manufacture of explosives. Germany's synthetic

12. *Final Report,* Oil Division, p. 15.
13. *Konjunktur-Statistisches Handbuch,* 1936, p. 200.
14. *Effects of Strategic Bombing,* p. 91.
15. *Statistisches Jahrbuch,* 1931, p. 100.

nitrogen industry dates back to World War I. Methanol and calcium chloride were also produced synthetically. Methanol is an important ingredient in explosives; calcium chloride is used in the manufacture of synthetic rubber and other basic chemicals. Since coal was the principal input item for all three of these chemicals, there was no supply problem. Sulfur and phosphorus, of somewhat lesser importance in war production, could not be manufactured synthetically, and for their supplies Germany had to depend mainly on imports.

2. THE RAW MATERIAL PRODUCTION PROGRAM

It is apparent that the Nazi war leaders could not have been satisfied with Germany's raw material potential as it appeared in the initial phase of their regime. However, before 1936, little was done to make Germany more self-sufficient in industrial raw materials. Indeed, at this time the raw material industries were still in the process of recovering from the depression.

Table 9 shows how expenditures on plant and equipment in the major raw material industries during the 1930's compared with the figures for the prosperous years of the previous decade. Thus, in 1935 the current value of investment in these industries was 40 per cent below the 1928 level. Measured in 1928 prices, it was 20 per cent

Table 9. Gross investment in plant and equipment
in selected raw material industries
(millions of RM)

	1924–28 (annual average)	1928	1932–36 (annual average)	1935	1936	1937
Heavy industry[a]	403	570	181	276	381	540
Other metal mining and smelting	40	47	42	75	87	143
Chemical industry[b]	212	333	170	178	423	563
Total	655	950	393	529	891	1246

Source: *Statistisches Jahrbuch*, 1941/1942, p. 604; *Statistisches Jahrbuch*, 1937, p. 540.
a. Includes coal, iron, and steel.
b. Includes synthetic rubber and oil as well as chemical plants.

below. By 1936, capital outlays in the chemical industries surpassed the 1928 amount but investment in the heavy industries was much less than in 1928, measured in current or in 1928 prices.

A large volume of investment was needed in the years following 1936 if only to bring total capacity up to the predepression level. As Table 9 shows, from 1932 to 1936, average annual gross investment in these major raw material industries was 395 million marks. According to the estimates of the German Business Cycle Research Institute, annual depreciation over this period averaged 580 million marks, or 185 millions more than gross investment.[16] For the six-year period this would mean a total *net disinvestment* of nearly one billion marks. While the accuracy of the depreciation estimates is questionable, it is not unlikely that capacity in 1936 was smaller than it had been in the predepression years.

Until 1936, when the responsibility was transferred to Goering, Schacht, in his capacity as Minister of Economics and Plenipotentiary of the War Economy, was in charge of the raw material production program. His approach in raw materials planning, as in other matters, was cautious. In a series of letters beginning in 1935, Hitler accused Schacht of being more interested in foreign trade questions than in raw material production, of being unduly concerned about the higher cost of producing materials synthetically, of being unwilling to raise adequate funds for increasing the capacity of these industries, and of representing the interests of the industrialists rather than those of the State.[17]

Finally, in 1936, Schacht's direction of the raw materials economy was transferred to Goering upon the latter's appointment as Plenipotentiary of the Second Four-Year Plan. Hitler's directive to Goering sharply criticized Schacht's policies, stressed the urgency of increasing the output of strategic materials, and set production targets for some of the important materials.[18]

Hitler summed up Germany's raw material situation as it appeared in 1936 in the following manner: Raw material requirements, he said, could not be satisfied to a very large extent by imports be-

16. *Statistisches Jahrbuch,* 1941/1942, p. 604.
17. *Nazi Conspiracy and Aggression.* VII, 564.
18. Hitler's 1936 Directive to Goering. A copy of this directive is in the files of the United States Strategic Bombing Survey.

cause of the shortage of foreign exchange. The limited supply of exchange had to be used mainly for food and could not be increased appreciably because export markets were limited. The only alternative was to increase the domestic production of raw materials. Complete self-sufficiency in raw materials, he recognized, was out of the question; a permanent solution to the raw material problem could come only through conquest.

In contradiction to Schacht's often enunciated views, Hitler declared that in this expansion of the raw material base "the question of costs of raw materials is absolutely irrelevant, for it is still preferable if we produce more expensive tires which are available, rather than if we buy theoretically cheap tires for which the Ministry of Economics cannot allot the foreign exchange." [19] After reciting a number of such examples Hitler placed the blame for cost considerations on the "capitalistic system" and more specifically on the industrialists. He ordered that their interests no longer play a part in production decisions and announced that if the industrialists refused to cooperate "the National Socialist State itself will know how to perform this task."

After pages of such pronouncements Hitler finally took up the more specific issue of what was to be done to prepare the raw materials economy for war. "One hundred per cent self-sufficiency achieved with iron determination in all fields where it is possible," [20] was the general directive. Expanded output was regarded as most urgent in oil, steel, iron ore, synthetic rubber, and aluminum. Hitler ordered that the oil, rubber, and steel industries were to be ready for war in eighteen months. How large an expansion was required to make these industries ready for war? This subject is mentioned only in the last paragraph of the directive:

"Almost four precious years have now elapsed. There is no doubt that we could have been completely independent of foreign countries today in the supply of fuel, rubber and partly also iron ore. Just as easily as we produce 7–800,000 tons of gasoline at present, we could produce 3 million tons. Just as we manufacture a few thousand tons of rubber today, we could produce already 70–80,000 tons per annum. Just as we raised iron ore output from 2½ to 7 million tons, we could process 20 to 25 million tons from German iron ore, and if necessary even 30. One

19. Hitler's 1936 Directive to Goering.
20. Hitler's 1936 Directive to Goering.

has had enough time to find out in four years what we cannot do. It is now necessary to accomplish what we can do." [21]

In view of all that has been written about economic planning in dictatorships, it is of some interest to see what principles were used in determining the various production goals. If it is assumed, as many writers have assumed, that Nazi economic planning was highly rational, then it might be expected that the plans would have been developed approximately as follows: First, the high command would have planned its war strategy. Next, this strategy would have been translated into weapons requirements of the armed forces. The production of these weapons would, in turn, require a certain amount of raw materials. This amount plus that which was needed for the supporting economy would constitute total raw material requirements. From this a balanced raw material production plan could be formulated.

There is no evidence, however, of such an order of rationality in Germany's prewar planning.[22] Testimony of German officials indicates that not until a few months before the march into Poland was the number of divisions which could be supported finally decided upon. Prior to 1939, war plans were being continuously revised and at no time was there a clear idea of the role to be played by the various branches of the armed forces. Each of the branches was making its own plans with little central coordination. In all phases of war planning — from over-all strength to material requirements — the Air Force was a completely autonomous organization. The armed forces did not even have a central economic agency which could review the various demands for materials and formulate some sort of a reasonable requirements picture. According to the writings of British and American experts this was the function of the War Economy and

21. Hitler's Directive to Goering, 1938.

22. The following summary of German raw material planning is based on interrogations of General Thomas, mentioned above, General von Halder, Chief of Staff, Goering, Speer, later head of the Armaments Ministry, Kehrl, later head of the raw materials section of the Armaments Ministry, Wagenfuehr, chief economist for the Ministry's Planning Board, and also on Minutes of Meetings of the Four-Year Planning Office and on a history of the War Economy Office referred to below. The interrogations were conducted by the United States Strategic Bombing Survey, by the technical intelligence agency FIAT, by the War Crimes Trial Commission, and by various war department intelligence agencies.

Armament Office of the High Command. However, in a history of this organization written during the war by its chief, General Thomas, it is stated that the Office was informed neither of strategic plans nor of total material requirements.[23] Its sole function was to expedite the procurement of certain scarce materials. Actually, the branches of the service independently presented their raw material requirements, drawn up on the principle that they were later going to be cut, to the Four-Year Planning Office or to the Economics Ministry. There, with little attempt to coordinate the demands for the various raw materials, Goering passed the individual requests on to the commodity experts. Many of them were prominent industrialists, others occupied key positions in German trade associations. These experts often retained not only their industrial positions but also their industrial interests. Their knowledge of the over-all war plans was slight; it was a cardinal policy of Hitler that war strategy was not a concern of economic planners. Since they were given only the inflated demands for raw materials of the various claimants, it was impossible to put together a very intelligent picture of requirements.

In such an atmosphere one could hardly expect to find rational, highly coordinated economic planning. Indeed, since the German officials did not think in terms of a raw material program as a whole, it is difficult to state what general principles were used in drawing up the various production plans. Hitler and Goering seem to have thought only in terms of securing the largest possible production of each material. In his history of the War Economy Office, General Thomas has stated that Hitler believed he could command industries, just as he could army divisions, to make a maximum achievement. Whether or not Germany had enough resources to make a number of these "maximum achievements" simultaneously did not concern him. Nor does it appear that he or Goering were concerned with planning the production of the various materials in accordance with their expected wartime requirements. The maxim was the largest possible production of each.

However the production goals were initially conceived, they were not, in most cases, the demands finally presented to industry. Plans were modified either because they were impossible to realize, or be-

23. "A History of the War Economy Office." This document is in the files of the Historical Division of the U. S. War Department.

cause they seemed to impose too great a financial burden, or because industrial interests were opposed.

Oil

In May 1936, a few months before the introduction of the Second Four-Year Plan, Goering instructed Schacht to draw up a comprehensive plan for increasing Germany's oil production. By 1940, oil supplies were to be sufficient for a wartime level of consumption. Total wartime requirements of these oil products were estimated at nearly 5.0 million tons annually. The 1936 level of production plus scheduled increases in capacity would have resulted in a total 1940 production of 4.3 million tons, 15 per cent less than estimated requirements. Approximately 3.1 million tons of this total was to come from Fischer–Tropsch and hydrogenation plants, the remainder from crude oil, alcohol, benzol, and tar distillation. The plan involved the construction of ten synthetic plants at a total cost of 1,150 million reichmarks.

Some notion of the adequacy of these plans may be had by comparing them with actual consumption of oil during the war. Approximately 2.3 million tons of aviation and motor vehicles gasoline were consumed in 1940, a year of relatively inactive warfare.[24] This consumption was about 15 per cent greater than that contemplated in the plan. Consumption of gasoline in 1941, the first year of war with Russia, was 3.8 million tons, 70 per cent greater than the 1936 requirement estimates.[25]

The Four-Year Plan was superseded in July 1938 by the Karin Hall Plan. Realizing the inadequacy of previous planning, the members of Goering's staff now proposed to bring total production up to 11 million tons — this by the beginning of 1944.[26] The immediate production goal, however, was set about 15 per cent below the earlier plan, because in 1938 it was recognized that the objectives of the Four-Year Plan could not be realized.

In order to provide monetary incentives for the expansion, an extremely high tariff was placed on imported oil, exploratory drilling for new wells was government subsidized, and loans were made for

24. *Effects of Strategic Bombing*, p. 77.
25. *Effects of Strategic Bombing*, p. 77.
26. *Effects of Strategic Bombing*, p. 74.

the construction of new plants. The tariff duty amounted to 270 reichmarks per ton of oil — 500 per cent ad valorem at the import level.[27]

From 1936 to 1939, synthetic oil capacity was more than doubled. When war broke out, fourteen hydrogenation and Fischer–Tropsch plants were in operation and, in addition, six plants were under construction. Capacity reached 1,470 thousand tons per year in 1939 and 1,850 thousand tons in May of 1940.[28] Although no new oil fields were discovered, crude oil output increased beyond anticipation. Between 1936 and 1940, output in Germany doubled, reaching in the latter year approximately one million tons.[29] The annexation of Austria added another 400,000 tons per year. By 1940 refining capacity had become more than ample for domestic production and imports.

In spite of the unforeseen gains in crude oil production, the output of oil products fell short of the modest goals set forth in the Four-Year Plan and even of the reduced target of the Karin Hall Plan. Production of the major oil products is shown in Table 10. In the

Table 10. Production of major oil products
(thousands of metric tons)

	1936	1939	1940
Gasoline	900	1135	1769
Diesel oil	280	510	781
Heating oil	270	385	728
Lubricants	20	275	462
Total	1470	2305	3740

Source: *Final Report*, Oil Division, p. 19.

Four-Year Plan, total output of these products was scheduled to have been 3.9 million tons in 1939 and 4.7 million tons in 1940. Actual production fell about 40 per cent short of the plan in 1939 and 20 per cent below it in 1940. In this year total production of these products was about 5 per cent below the amount scheduled in the 1938 Karin Hall Plan.

27. *Effects of Strategic Bombing*, p. 73.
28. *Final Report*, Oil Division, p. 17.
29. *Final Report*, Oil Division, p. 19.

These aggregate comparisons, moreover, conceal the failure of the synthetic program. Although capacity was more than doubled between 1936 and 1939 and nearly tripled by 1940, this was much less than had been contemplated in the Four-Year Plan. In both years, actual output was 45 per cent below planned output.

Thus, the oil expansion hardly measured up to Hitler's 1936 edict — "that the oil industry be prepared for war in eighteen months." On the one hand, the plans grossly underestimated actual wartime requirements; on the other, they were only partially executed.

Steel

In 1936, production of iron and steel in Germany proper reached 16 million tons, the 1929 level. This output plus that of the newly acquired Saar area gave Germany a total steel production of nearly 19 million tons. This level of production was not sufficient, however, to satisfy all demands. The synthetic oil program, construction of armament plants, expansion of the steel industry, fortifications in the West, construction of the *Autobahnen*, the large volume of nonwar construction, and growing export demands — all required still more steel.

The immediate limitation on a rise in output was not steel capacity. Total capacity of German plants (including those in the Saar) was at this time, according to a German report, 3 or 4 million tons higher than actual production.[30] More serious was the difficulty of obtaining the additional ore supplies. As Table 11 shows, in 1936, as in 1929,

Table 11. Production of iron and steel, 1929 and 1936[a]
(millions of metric tons)

	1929	1936
Crude steel	16.2	18.8
Pig iron	13.4	15.3
Iron ore production[a]	2.1	2.0
Scrap consumption[a]	8.5	9.6
Iron ore imports[a]	8.5	9.2

Source: *Statistisches Jahrbuch*, 1941/1942, p. 75.
a. In metal content.

30. "Germany's Raw Material Supply," *DAF Rohstoffe-Dienst*, II, 1937.

more than 80 per cent of the ore supplies were obtained from foreign countries. A shortage of foreign exchange limited the possibility of expanding ore imports. In fact, in the summer of 1936 ore imports had to be curtailed and this resulted in a decline in pig iron production. The only solution to the ore problem, therefore, was an expansion of ore mining in Germany itself. Moreover, such a solution was imperative if even a moderate degree of self-sufficiency was to be attained.

A survey conducted by the Prussian Geological Institute showed the existence of substantial deposits of ore in Germany. The Salzgitter area in Hanover was estimated to contain reserves of more than 500 million tons, the South German areas, 350 million tons.[31] These ores were, however, of a low iron content — about 30 per cent, compared to a 60 per cent iron content for the Spanish and Swedish ores and to a 40 per cent content for the French ores.[32]

In 1936 Goering, in his capacity as Plenipotentiary of the Four-Year Plan, asked private producers to undertake an expansion of ore production amounting to 10 or 11 million tons. Germany's total ore supply, if such an increase had occurred, would have provided for about a half of the 1936 level of ore consumption. The producers, however, resisted these demands. The cost of making pig iron from the low grade ore was about 10 per cent greater than from the Swedish ore;[33] and further, utilization of this ore required the installation of special types of equipment. Unless the price of steel was raised by more than Schacht's Economics Ministry was willing to allow, producers were unwilling to incur the greater expenses or to make the additional investments.

The only alternative was for the government itself to undertake the expansion. This too was resisted by the steel interests. In a report made to the government in 1936, the German iron and steel trade association (Wirtschaftsgruppe Eisenschaffende Industrie) said that Goering's requests for increased mining and steel output were preposterous, that if the contemplated plans were realized Germany would have more steel capacity than she could ever use, that the

31. "Germany's Raw Material Supply," *DAF Rohstoffe-Dienst,* II, 1937.
32. "Germany's Raw Material Supply," *DAF Rohstoffe-Dienst,* II, 1937.
33. U. S. Bombing Survey, *Special Report on the Hermann Goering Works,* p. 51.

price of steel would sink to an impossibly low level, and that the costs of mining the ore would be prohibitive.[34]

Nevertheless, and in spite of continued resistance to such a measure, the government made plans for entering the iron mining and steel producing business.[35] Paul Pleiger, a steel expert, and later manager of the Hermann Goering Works, was sent to inspect a plant using ores similar to those found in Germany located in Corby, England, and he also visited several plants in the United States. Following these visits a contract was entered into with an American construction firm to build a steel plant in the Salzgitter district designed to utilize the low grade ores.

To operate the Salzgitter mines and the plant at Watenstedt, a corporation known as the Hermann Goering Ore and Foundry Company (Reichswerke Aktiengeseelschaft fur Erzbergbau and Eisenhutten "Hermann Goering") was organized in 1937. The capital of the company was 400 million marks and most of it was provided by the government. Actual construction of the plant at Watenstedt was begun in 1938.

It was planned that in four years the plant would have an annual capacity of 4 million tons of pig iron, and a like amount of steel. The ore requirements, some 14 million tons annually, were to be satisfied by the Salzgitter mines. By 1944 annual output of these mines was to have been 24 million tons, and in addition it was planned to increase mining operations in South Germany to 6 million tons annually. If these plans had materialized, Germany's total ore output would have eventually been nearly 10 million tons annually (in iron content), enough to support a steel output of some 18 million tons. Total steel capacity would have been in the neighborhood of 30 mil-

34. A copy of this report was found in the documents of the Planning Board of the German Armaments Ministry.

35. Hitler in his directive to Goering stated: "It is further necessary to raise German iron production to a maximum. The objection is irrelevant, that we are not able to produce a similar cheap pig iron from German ore with 26 per cent yield as from 45 per cent Swedish ore, etc., as we are not faced with the question of what we would rather do, but merely what we can do. The Ministry of Economics merely has to formulate the national economic tasks, and the private economy has to execute them. But if the private economy does not believe itself capable of doing it, then the National Socialist State itself will know how to perform this task." Hitler's 1936 directive to Goering. (Files of United States Strategic Bombing Survey.)

lion tons. The purpose of constructing the steel plant in Central Germany was to save the cost of transporting pig iron to the Ruhr and the cost of transporting finished steel to fabricators in the area. It is interesting to note that the construction of facilities to produce high grade steel, which became short during the war, was an unimportant part of the steel plan.

These elaborate schemes to attain a high degree of self-sufficiency in ore supplies and concurrently to increase steel capacity were never realized. By 1942, when construction was to have been completed, the pig iron capacity of the Watenstedt plant was only 1.0 million tons, a fourth of the amount which had been planned.[36] Only about a half of the originally contemplated steel capacity was completed.[37] What is more important, moreover, is that plans for the expansion of ore mining, the *raison d'être* for the whole scheme, did not materialize. In 1941, output of the Salzgitter mines was only 3.4 million tons, and in 1942, 4.2 million tons — 30 per cent of the amount which was called for by the Four-Year Plan.

In 1938, with the annexation of Austria, the Goering Corporation acquired the Alpine Montangesellschaft, a subsidiary of the German firm Vereinigte Stahlwerke. This firm owned the Erzberg mines whose ores were superior to those in the Salzgitter area. On taking over this Austrian concern, the Goering Company made plans for expanding its mining operations to 6 million tons annually and for the construction of a steel plant at Linz with a capacity of 1 million tons. Concurrently, the ambitious plans for expansion of operations in Germany were sharply curtailed. However, there was no compensating expansion of output in Austria. The steel mill at Linz was never completed; and even by 1941 the Austrian mines produced only 2.9 million tons of ore.[38] The acquisition of the Austrian iron resources, therefore, cannot explain the halfhearted attempt to realize the objectives of the Second Four-Year Plan.

As a result of these limited preparations prior to 1939, Germany's 1939 steelmaking capacity was hardly greater than it had been in 1929; moreover, the great bulk of the ore supplies still had to be imported. The 1939 capacity of steel plants in Germany proper and in

36. *Special Report on the Hermann Goering Works*, p. 46.
37. *Special Report on the Hermann Goering Works*, p. 50.
38. *Special Report on the Hermann Goering Works*, Appendix, p. 2.

the Saar area was estimated at approximately 23 million tons, or about the same for the comparable area as in 1929.[39] The Austrian and Czechoslovakian plants added another 3 million tons, bringing total capacity up to 26 million tons. Although ore production had doubled since 1929, two thirds of the total ore consumed still came from foreign countries.[40]

Rubber

Rubber is one of the few materials for which both the program and the implementation were adequate. The process for the manufacture of synthetic rubber was perfected in about 1930. In 1936, the date of the Second Four-Year Plan, a small pilot plant was in operation at Leverkusen. The Four-Year Plan called for the construction of three additional plants, each with a 25,000 ton capacity.[41] This would bring total synthetic capacity up to about 80,000 tons, approximately the level of consumption in 1936.

To make the expansion profitable, a high tariff was placed on rubber, and plant construction was subsidized by the government. Construction of the first plant was begun in 1937 at Schkopau, and by September 1939 the annual rate of production was near the initially planned capacity level. But while the plant was still under construction its ultimate capacity was raised to 72,000 tons, which represented 70 per cent of the total rubber consumption in 1936.[42] Construction of the second plant at Huels was begun in 1938 and shortly afterwards its planned capacity was raised to 48,000 tons.[43] Building of the third plant envisioned in the Four-Year Plan was not begun until 1940.

Production of synthetic rubber was 22,000 tons in 1939, 69,000 tons in 1942.[44] The level of synthetic output in this year was more than total civilian and military consumption.[45] This output, plus the natural rubber obtained through blockade-running from Japan, permitted, in addition to domestic consumption, a sufficient supply

39. Übersichten über die eisenschaffende Industrie Deutschlands, 1937.
40. *Statistisches Jahrbuch*, 1941/1942, p. 301.
41. *Nazi Conspiracy and Aggression*, Vol. I, pp. 350–352.
42. *Final Report, Oil Division*, p. 49.
43. *Final Report*, Oil Division, p. 49.
44. *Effects of Strategic Bombing*, p. 83.
45. *Effects of Strategic Bombing*, p. 84.

of rubber for 32,000 tons of exports and a substantial accumulation of stocks.[46]

Aluminum

For aluminum, too, the production planning was adequate. A large expansion of capacity was already begun before the introduction of the Second Four-Year Plan. In 1936 aluminum production was 97,000 tons, three times the 1929 rate.[47] Between 1936 and 1939 existing facilities were expanded further and a large new plant was constructed. By 1939 output reached 199 thousand tons, a rate of production which was 40,000 tons greater than the goal set by the Four-Year Plan.[48] In this year German production amounted to 30 per cent of the total world aluminum output, and was about a third greater than United States' production.[49] Even this output, however, did not permit an accumulation of stocks of finished metal. Aluminum consumption in 1939 was about 20 per cent more than the current rate of supply.[50]

Despite the expansion of bauxite ore mining from 7 thousand tons in 1929 to 104 thousand tons in 1939, domestic ores in the latter year still provided only about 10 per cent of the total ore consumption.[51] Unable to do very much toward satisfying requirements from domestic ores, German firms had developed mines in other European countries which had greater ore resources. Through the Bauxit-Trust A.G., a Swiss holding company organized in 1923, German firms acquired mining properties in Hungary, Yugoslavia, Romania, and Italy. In 1939 more than 80 per cent of the bauxite imports came from the Hungarian and Yugoslavian mines.[52]

Other Metals

Copper, lead, and zinc refining capacity was greatly expanded in the prewar period. But the rise in the output of these metals was not equalled by an increase in domestic ore production, with the result

---

46. *Effects of Strategic Bombing*, p. 84.
47. *Statistisches Jahrbuch*, 1941/1942, p. 79.
48. *Statistisches Jahrbuch*, p. 79.
49. *Statistisches Jahrbuch*, p. 79.
50. *Effects of Strategic Bombing*, Appendix Table 83, p. 263.
51. *Statistisches Jahrbuch*, 1941/1942, p. 67.
52. *Statistisches Jahrbuch*, 1941/1942, p. 67.

that Germany's dependence on foreign sources of copper, lead, and zinc ores was greater in 1939 than it had been before the Nazis came to power.

As Table 12 shows, the output of refined copper increased steadily, even through the depression years, and in 1938 stood at twice the 1929 level. This period, however, saw no expansion of copper ore mining. From 1929 through 1938 lead and zinc output also rose rapidly; the production of the former by 60 per cent, the latter by 80 per cent. The output of lead ores increased by about as much as lead metal production, but zinc ore mining fell behind the rise in the

Table 12. Copper, lead, and zinc metal and ore production
(thousands of metric tons)

	Refined copper	Copper ore	Lead	Lead ore	Zinc	Zinc ore
1929	119	29	110	52	108	125
1933	162	32	119	49	51	104
1934	168	28	122	53	71	128
1935	189	30	129	54	124	131
1936	208	29	144	61	136	148
1937	224	30	166	64	164	158
1938[a]	243	30	176	87	193	192
1939	—	—	177	—	194	—

Sources: *Statistisches Jahrbuch,* 1941/1942, pp. 66, 67, 78, 79. *Statistische Schnellberichte zur Kriegsproduktion,* pp. 12, 13.
a. Includes Austrian output.

metal output. Inspection of minutes of meetings of the Four-Year Planning Office shows that Goering's staff was concerned about this heavy reliance on foreign copper and lead ores. But there appears to have been no plans for large increases in domestic mining.

Textile Raw Materials

Textile raw materials were a much less important item in the raw material program, but in view of the fact that the Nazi attempt to achieve textile self-sufficiency was so widely advertised, something should be said about them. Plans for a rapid increase in textile raw materials production were made in 1934. The original impetus of the program does not appear to have been preparations for war, but rather

a desire to economize on the use of foreign exchange which at [
time was very short.

In terms of predepression standards, the program succeeded ill
increasing the production of agricultural textile materials moderately
and of industrial materials enormously. Table 13 shows that from
1933 to 1938 the total output of textile materials increased more than
fivefold. In the latter year the production of agricultural textile
materials was three times the 1928 prosperity level, and the production of synthetic materials was ten times the amount produced in
1928.

Table 13. Domestic agricultural and industrial production
of textile raw materials
(thousands of metric tons)

Year	Agriculturally produced	Industrially produced	Total
1925	39	13	52
1928	19	23	42
1933	9	34	43
1936	42	92	134
1938	56	220	276

Source: *Weekly Report*, German Institute for Business
Research, March 9, 1938; *Statistisches Jahrbuch*,
1941/1942, p. 202.

Although this greatly increased production of textile materials
helped to reduce import requirements at the beginning of the war,
Germany still depended on foreign sources for a major share of her
textiles. In 1938 80 per cent of the total textile supplies were imported.[53]

Agricultural Raw Materials

Remembering the consequences of Germany's deficiency of foodstuffs during World War I, the Nazis placed a very high priority on
increasing the domestic production of food. In this they were emi-
nently successful. Table 14 shows that from 1932 to 1939 the volume
of agricultural output was increased nearly 20 per cent. This was

53. *Weekly Report,* German Institute for Business Research, March 9, 1939.

achieved without increasing the number of acres under cultivation and despite a reduced agricultural labor force (see Table 23). The gains in output were achieved by a much greater use of farm machinery and fertilizers.

Despite the fact that food consumption increased from 1933 to 1939, reaching in that year approximately the level of 1929, the increase in domestic food production was sufficient to permit a reduction of imports. A German index of self-sufficiency in foodstuffs (calculated on the basis of caloric value) shows that the degree of self-sufficiency was 89 per cent in 1939, as compared to 81 per cent in 1933 and 71 per cent in 1928.[54] At the outbreak of war, Ger-

Table 14. Volume index of agricultural production
(1927–1928 — 1928–1929 = 100)

Crop year	Including share due to foreign fodder	Excluding share due to foreign fodder
1928–1929	102	104
1932–1933	104	108
1933–1934	111	118
1934–1935	114	122
1935–1936	110	120
1936–1937	114	124
1937–1938	119	127
1938–1939	120	127

Source: *Weekly Report*, German Institute for Business Research, May 22, 1940.

many was virtually self-sufficient in bread, potatoes, sugar, meat, milk, and coarse vegetables. The main import items were fodder, fruit, eggs, fats, and oils. The shortage of fats and oils, 40 per cent of which came from imports, was the only serious food problem. Aside from this, Germany entered the war with a very adequate supply of foodstuffs.

Conclusions on the Raw Material Production Program

It is evident that the various raw material programs differed widely in their degree of success. For some important commodities, the

54. From an unpublished study by Dr. Woermann, "Die Ernaehrungslage der Welt" (The RAND Corporation library).

expansion of production was adequate to cover Germany's wartime requirements. For other important materials, the programs failed to provide even a moderate degree of self-sufficiency, and if an all-out war effort had been immediately necessary, Germany would have had to gamble on continued access to foreign sources.

As we have seen, the agricultural, rubber, and aluminum programs were relatively successful. The iron ore and oil programs, on the other hand, failed to make Germany independent of foreign countries for a major share of her requirements. In 1939 she still had to rely on imports for 65 per cent of her iron ore requirements. Only about 35 per cent of oil consumption was provided by domestic crude and synthetic production. If cut off from foreign sources of either oil or iron ore, Germany's industrial war potential would have been crippled.

How are we to explain the failure to undertake more adequate measures for the increased production of these key items? One possible explanation is that by 1937 or 1938 political events had indicated to Hitler that military conquest could be achieved without pressing for the completion of the costly iron ore and synthetic oil programs. This factor may have had some part in the decision to scale down the initial plans, but its importance should not be overrated. Although Hitler hoped to avoid a major war, he never completely dismissed the possibility that Britain and France might ally themselves against him. In fact, until the conquest of France, both Hitler and the General Staff were very concerned about Germany's being isolated from Northern Europe and the Balkans. That overseas sources would be lost was a foregone conclusion.

Moreover, even if Germany continued to get iron ore from Sweden, Norway, Luxembourg, and Spain, and oil from Romania, total supplies of these materials still would not satisfy the stated requirements. Imports of iron ore from these countries plus domestic production only accounted for about 75 per cent of domestic ore consumption in 1939. The remainder came from France and non-European countries. Even if Germany received the total 1939 exports of iron ore from these countries, this amount in addition to domestic output would not have been adequate for the current rate of consumption, not considering expanding steel output to the proposed goal of 30 million tons.

In oil, the situation was even less favorable. In 1939 only 35 per cent of the German oil supply was domestically produced and only 50 per cent came from the continent of Europe.[55] Even if the entire Romanian oil production could have been obtained, loss of overseas sources, chiefly in North and South America, would have left supplies 25 per cent short of 1939 consumption.[56] In these circumstances it would appear that an increased confidence in being able to retain European oil and iron ore sources of supply could not have been the principal factor in keeping the Germans from carrying out their programs for the domestic production of these materials.

Were these plans so expensive in labor and raw materials that they could not have been carried out? Let us look at the labor and materials requirements of the planned expansion of synthetic oil capacity. The Karin Hall plan, referred to above, called for 57,600 construction workers before July 1939 and 70,000 from October of that year onward. [57] Since employment in the construction industry totalled 2,485,000 in 1939, it hardly appears that labor could have been the bottleneck.[58] The most important material needed for the construction of the oil works was steel. To have brought actual capacity up to the plan would have required another 950,000 tons of steel.[59] This amount could not have been impossible to supply for such top priority projects. Germany's production of finished steel in 1937 and 1938 averaged 15 million tons.[60]

The original plan for developing Germany's iron ore deposits was less expensive than the oil program both in total cost and in labor and steel requirements. It hardly seems, therefore, that either program failed because Germany was unable to provide the necessary labor or materials.

It appears that the Germans were dissuaded from undertaking more energetic preparations in these fields because the planned expansions of capacity would have involved large public outlays, and

55. *Effects of Strategic Bombing,* p. 74.
56. *Statistisches Jahrbuch,* 1941/1942, p. 64*.
57. *Final Report,* Oil Division, United States Strategic Bombing Survey, p. 14.
58. *Statistisches Jahrbuch,* 1939/40, p. 148.
59. *Final Report,* Oil Division, p. 14.
60. *Statistisches Jahrbuch,* 1939/40, p. 148.

because, in the case of iron ore, the plan was firmly opposed by the industrialists. These assertions cannot be supported by direct evidence, such as the minutes of meetings where the scaling down of the programs was discussed, but there are other indications of their plausibility.

In Chapter I it was shown that the fear of larger deficits kept the Nazis from having a larger rearmament program. On these grounds Schacht opposed a large raw materials expansion program, and specifically the proposals for increasing iron ore and synthetic oil capacity.[61] Although Hitler dismissed Schacht from the Ministry of Economics for holding such views, this did not eliminate his restraining influence on raw materials expansion. For, until he was dismissed from the presidency of the Reichsbank in January 1939, Schacht, as controller of Germany's purse strings, was in a position to make his views effective. As we have seen, the principles of financial conservatism played an important role until the outbreak of war and there is good reason to believe that they continued to be an important factor in limiting the size of the iron ore and synthetic oil programs. This view has been expressed by several important German officials. When questioned about the small prewar oil and iron ore expansions, Albert Speer, Germany's wartime Minister of Armaments

61. Schacht's objections to a general program for the increased production of raw materials are summarized in a statement made to the Council Ministers in 1936.

Goering: "What objections are made to the production of war raw materials within the Reich?"

Schacht: "Principally there is nothing to object; a solution of the raw material problem by self-producing is absolutely necessary and agreed with, theoretically. Difficulties are encountered with regard to: (1) serious monetary strain because of investments. . . . (2) special scruples, regarding the cases where prices for substitute material are far beyond world-market prices" (*Nazi Conspiracy and Aggression*, III, 886–887).

Schacht's views on the establishment of "Hermann Goering Works" are contained in a letter written to Goering in August, 1937. "That brings me to the question of cost. Lacking more detailed information from you I must limit myself to the statement that your proposal would obviously entail the expenditure of many hundreds of millions of Reichsmarks, for which, according to information furnished me by the Reich Ministry of Finance, no financial provisions exist as yet. . . . I am not in a position to raise the financial means for projects, the effectiveness of which cannot be anticipated any more than their extent, or the length of their period of productivity" (*Nazi Conspiracy and Aggression*, VII, 574).

Production, Hans Kehrl, chief of the Ministry's raw material division, and Karl Hettlage, its financial advisor, all replied that it was impossible to raise sufficient funds to carry out the programs.[62]

There is also reason to believe that Goering's elaborate scheme for self-sufficiency in iron ore and expansion of steel capacity could not be carried through in the face of the opposition of the steel interests. We have pointed out that this group refused to undertake the expansion, because of the extra costs involved in mining low grade ore and because they believed that there would not be a profitable market for additional steel after the rearmament had been completed. Although Hitler stated in his directive on the Second Four-Year Plan that the state would undertake the task if the industrialists continued to refuse to cooperate, it is evident that his threats did not change their attitude; as we have seen, the state created the German Goering Works to carry out the expansion.

After construction of the project was begun, representatives of the steel cartel continued to voice their opposition. They were joined by Schacht, who, although an avowed enemy of the cartels, supported the position taken by the steel cartel.[63] The main reason for Schacht's action was no doubt the one mentioned above — the additional strain which the project would have put on the financial position of the Reichsbank.

In 1938, with the acquisition of the Austrian iron ore mines, the original plans for the Herman Goering Works were sharply curtailed — although its ore production was not nearly sufficient to warrant a drastic downward revision of the program. The available records of the Four-Year Planning Office show no reason for this decision. A plausible interpretation of the decision is that the acquisition of the Austrian mines gave Goering an excuse to avoid the embarrassment of not being able to raise sufficient funds to finance the project and an excuse to make peace with the steel interests (which also owned the major part of Germany's armaments industry). The latter interpretation has been emphasized by Paul Pleiger, manager of the

62. United States Bombing Survey and FIAT interrogations of Speer, Kehrl, and Hettlage.

63. Letters to Goering in 1937 and 1938. *Nazi Conspiracy and Aggression,* VII, 550 and 567.

Hermann Goering Works.[64] Although his opinion is admittedly not impartial, it is not contradicted by other evidence.

3. RAW MATERIAL DISTRIBUTION CONTROLS

In 1939 Germany was approximately in the same position vis-à-vis direct raw material controls as the United States in 1941 and probably behind Britain in this respect. In other words, until the outbreak of the war, Germany relied very largely on the ordinary market mechanisms to control the production and distribution of resources. This does not mean, of course, that this mechanism was not used to influence the distribution of resources into desired channels. Restrictions on wage increases, for example, served to restrict consumption and thus make a greater volume of resources available for public uses. Tariffs, subsidies, government loans, and import controls also played a part in encouraging production deemed essential. But these measures were far from the direct controls that Germany was compelled to introduce later and far from the controls involved in wartime Britain and the United States.

As for the more direct techniques of channelling resources into war output — as, for example, prohibitions against the manufacture of certain items using scarce resources, measures forcing producers to adapt their techniques to use more accessible materials, or the direct allocation of raw materials — these were seldom used prior to the outbreak of the war. Thus, direct rationing was introduced in August 1939, but at that time applied only to some types of food and to soap. Investment bans, designed to prevent the flow of steel and building materials into nonessential projects, were instituted as early as 1934 for a few types of manufacture and subsequently extended.[65] Even in 1939, however, the bans affected only a minor part of the consumers' goods industries.[66]

It was steel which gave the Germans most trouble.[67] By 1937, as

64. Interrogations of Paul Pleiger by representatives of the United States Strategic Bombing Survey.

65. See Samuel Laurie, *Private Investment in a Controlled Economy; Germany, 1933–1939*, New York, 1947.

66. That the bans were not very widely used can be readily seen by an examination of prewar private investment. See Chapter I.

67. This account is based on the United States Bombing Survey's interrogatory of a number of officials who administered the allocation system, on reports of the Four-Year Planning Office, on reports of its successor, the Central Plan-

a result of the heavy combined demands of the rearmament program, the synthetic programs, government nonwar building programs, and the civilian economy, the industry had orders on hand which greatly exceeded its production. An important factor reinforcing these high demands was the anxiety of manufacturers to put their funds into durable products as a hedge against inflation.

Because of the difficulty of satisfying high priority programs, Goering, in the spring of 1937 in his capacity as director of the Four-Year Plan, ordered the initiation of an allocation system. The scheme subsequently put into effect called for the cancellation of all orders as of a particular date and the renewal of orders under the inspection of his office. However, these measures proved to be quite ineffective. There was not a standard prcedure for deciding the urgency of orders and as a result the influence of the claimant played as large a role in the certification as did the importance of the order. In addition, there was no means of ascertaining whether or not the claimant actually used the steel for the specified purpose. The total number of orders which were granted each quarter greatly exceeded the capacity of the steel industry (in 1938 the excess of orders over production averaged 35 per cent) with the result that the total backlog became larger and larger.

Finally, in 1939 it again became necessary to cancel all the orders and start the system anew. This time, to facilitate a better classification of orders, a priority system with two classes of priorities was instituted. This system broke down because of a "priorities inflation." As claimants of steel for less urgent uses secured higher priority designations, new special designations were created and the process was repeated again and again. In 1941 a modification was made to correct some of the abuses of the system, and in 1942 a scheme for directly allocating steel was finally introduced. Although this will be dealt with later, it is sufficient to say here that the controls for the distribution of steel, said by the Germans to have been more elaborate than the several others which were used at the time, were extremely primitive and largely ineffective in the prewar period.

It is impossible to know how much steel was actually going into various types of uses because there are no data on the quantity of

ning Board, and on several reports written by the Iron and Steel Trade Association.

steel consumed by the various user industries. There are several pieces of evidence which show, however, that even as late as 1938 a large amount of steel was going into nonwar uses.

One of these is the composition of the 1938 national product. In this year, as we have seen in Chapter I, the production of consumer durables was at a record level, the government was undertaking a large nonwar construction program, and private investment in plant and equipment was larger than the 1928–1929 amount. All of these required large amounts of steel. Another indication of the pattern of steel consumption is the data on steel orders. These data show that 30 per cent of the 1938 volume of steel orders was placed by armaments producers, and 70 per cent by all other users.[68] Included in the armaments industry, moreover, were claimants not ordinarily regarded as belonging to this industry, as, for example, the railroads.

Thus, both the method employed for controlling the distribution of steel, and its actual uses, indicate that much more steel could have been directed into the war program.

4. THE STOCKPILING PROGRAM

For those materials which could be produced in insufficient quantity or not at all, there remained the possibility of providing for war requirements by building up stocks of raw materials. The scale of the stockpiling program, however, was much smaller than has been generally assumed. Supplies of important items like copper, iron ore, gasoline, and rubber were, in August 1939, in sufficient supply for only 3 to 6 months of contemplated war needs.

Several general reasons may be given why the stockpiling program was not larger. In the first place, the shortage of foreign exchange placed a general restriction on imports. It appears that, in the interest of obtaining more raw materials, food imports could have been cut even further, but this would have entailed a reduction of civilian consumption, a consequence which the Germans were unwilling to incur. Another obstacle to more stockpiling was the technical difficulty of storing some materials, and the lack of storage facilities for others. The latter, especially, limited the attempt to build up large reserves. Finally, a large stockpiling program was not advocated by

68. From a memorandum on steel allocation found in the files of the Ministry of Armaments Production.

Hitler. To him, accumulation of stocks meant that producers were not turning raw materials into finished armaments fast enough.[69] A war, he said, could not be fought with iron ore or stocks of unfinished aluminum; it was only important that these materials should be speedily transformed into planes and guns.

In August 1939, when last-minute preparations for the attack on Poland were being made, Goering ordered a comprehensive picture of Germany's raw material war requirements and supplies to be drawn' up. It is on the basis of the data presented to him that we are able to gauge the success of raw material stockpiling.[70]

It will be recalled that in 1939 Germany's steel economy was dependent on foreign sources for 65 per cent of the ore supplies and practically all of the ferroalloys. In August of 1939 current production and ore supplies were sufficient to cover only about six months of estimated needs. In a longer conflict the German economy would have collapsed without continued access to foreign ore supplies. The supply situation for ferroalloys was somewhat more favorable, ranging, as Table 15 shows, from a 6-month supply of nickel to a 36-month supply of vanadium.

Aluminum stocks in various stages of processing and current aluminum production were sufficient to cover an estimated 5.5

Table 15. Stocks of ferroalloys, August 1939

Material	Number of months coverage of requirements
Nickel	6
Chrome	8
Wolfram	11
Molybdenum	17
Manganese	20
Vanadium	36

Source: The document containing this information, *Raw Material Situation in Case of Mobilization*, August, 1939, is in the files of the War Department.

69. Hitler's directive to Goering; see above, footnote 18.

70. The document containing this information, *Raw Material Situation in Case of Mobilization*, August, 1939, is in the files of the War Department.

months of war needs. For copper, a period of 4.5 months was given. For both of these materials, as has been indicated, Germany's iron ore supplies could furnish only a modest proportion of her total needs; the bulk of them had to be imported. Moreover, in 1939 only a quarter of the copper supplies came from the continent of Europe. The lead and zinc situation was more favorable. Lead supplies were sufficient for 9 months, and zinc for 39 months of estimated war needs.

Synthetic rubber capacity, already in operation or in the process of construction at the beginning of the war, would have been ample for war needs, but not before 1942. Stocks of rubber were not nearly sufficient to cover requirements in the interim period. Synthetic and natural rubber stocks in August 1939 totaled only 19,000 tons, enough for two months of predicted wartime needs. Nor did Germany have large stocks of finished rubber products. Tire stocks in August 1939 were estimated at 500,000, 1.2 months of peacetime consumption.

The Germans assumed their greatest risk with regard to oil supplies. Stocks and current production of oil products, as Table 16

Table 16. Oil requirements, production and stocks[a]
(thousands of metric tons per month)

	Total requirements	Domestic output	Stocks	Number of months coverage of requirements
Aviation gasoline	152	46	480	4.8
Other motor gasoline	185	90	350	3.5
Diesel fuel	299	83	1068	4.9
Fuel oil	25	6	50	2.6

a. Several of the production figures and consequently the number of months coverage figures presented in "The Material Situation in Case of Mobilization" were revised on the basis of data later appearing in *Monatliche Rohstoffübersichten,* Statistisches Reichsamt.

shows, could guarantee consumption requirements for a period of only three to six months. After the exhaustion of these stocks Germany's own output would have been able to satisfy only a fraction of stated requirements.

There is no doubt that the supply situation for oil alone, not to mention iron ore, rubber, or copper, made the Nazi leaders well aware of the risks attendant on Germany's becoming involved in a major war.

5. THE RAW MATERIAL POSITION AS IT AFFECTED FOREIGN TRADE POLICY

The raw material situation itself played an important role in the development of foreign trade and a vital role in the formulation of the war strategy. Hitler's directives to Goering in 1936 regarding Germany's raw material preparations for war were concerned not only with increasing domestic production but also with foreign trade policy. The elements of this policy were an increase of raw material imports at the expense of other imports and the development of trade with countries which were less likely to be cut off from Germany in wartime.

The accomplishment of these objectives required no fundamental change in foreign trade policy. The Brüning and von Papen governments, as a result of their decision not to devalue the mark, were forced to contend with a sizable contraction of all types of imported goods. In order for Germany to absorb such a shrinkage with the least possible disorganization of the economy, imports of foodstuffs were more severely restricted than raw material imports and the growing of more food in Germany was encouraged. Thus, even agricultural autarky was a pre-Hitler policy.

The effort to increase trade with the Balkans, regarded as a source of supply not so likely to be lost in a war, was also begun before 1933. When, in 1931 and 1932, in the face of a world depression and an overvalued mark, exports fell very rapidly, it became imperative to take measures to prevent foreign markets and material sources from being eliminated altogether. Given the decision not to devalue, the only possibility of maintaining foreign trade was the development of bilateral trade with those countries with which Germany could come to terms. In 1932 trade agreements were concluded with Bulgaria, Greece, Yugoslavia, Romania, and Hungary. It was possible to make these agreements because these countries, importing manufactured goods and exporting raw materials, were complementary to the German economy, and because they also were short of foreign exchange. Foreign trade with these countries was transacted on essentially a barter basis and without need for official devaluation of the mark.

In 1934 Schacht, in his capacity as Minister of Economics, assumed the direction of Germany's foreign trade policies. Motivated by the same considerations as the previous governments, his "New Plan" for foreign trade tightened import controls, took stronger measures to limit agricultural imports and hence make more foreign exchange available for raw materials, and introduced a number of ingenious devices to promote bilateral trade.[71] Trade relations with the Balkans were strengthened and similar bilateral arrangements were made with a number of South American countries. These policies were well suited to Germany's rearmament needs and when Schacht's direction of foreign trade was taken over by the Four-Year Plan, Goering's only request was for a more energetic implementation of this policy.[72]

In their aim of changing the composition of foreign trade the Nazis were not very successful. As Table 17 shows, until 1936 there

Table 17. Composition of Germany's foreign trade, 1929–1939
(billions of marks at 1928 prices)

	Food		Industrial raw, semifinished, and finished materials		Raw materials		Total
	value	percentage	value	percentage	value	percentage	
1929	5.5	41	8.0	59	4.0	30	13.5
1933	3.6	39	5.7	61	3.4	37	9.3
1934	3.7	38	6.1	62	3.4	35	9.8
1935	3.2	36	5.8	64	3.4	38	9.0
1936	3.1	36	5.4	63	3.2	37	8.6
1937	4.1	41	5.9	59	3.5	35	10.0
1938	5.0	42	6.9	58	3.8	32	12.0
1939	4.4	42	6.0	57	3.3	31	10.5

Source: *Statistisches Jahrbuch*, 1941/1942, p. 284.

71. For a complete discussion of German prewar foreign trade policy see Howard Ellis, *Exchange Control in Central Europe*, Cambridge, 1941.

72. When Schacht's powers were being successively taken away from him, one of his grounds for protesting was that his "New Plan" had contributed greatly to preparing Germany for war. Letter to Goering, April 2, 1937. *Nazi Conspiracy and Aggression*, VII, 380–388.

was a comparatively larger reduction of food imports than of raw material imports. In the expansion of imports in 1937 and 1938, however, food imports increased faster than raw material imports with the result that the composition of imports was almost the same in 1938 as it had been in 1929.

They were more successful in developing new sources of imports, which were less likely to be lost in a war. The most important area for the expansion of trade was the Balkans. As Table 18 shows, the

Table 18. Germany's major sources of imports

	1929	1932 (per cent)	1937
Balkans	4.4	5.9	12.3
South and Central America	11.4	9.6	15.5
Northern and Western Europe	23.0	21.5	22.4
Great Britain	6.4	5.5	5.7
Russia	3.2	5.8	1.2
United States	13.3	12.7	5.2
Rest of the world	38.3	39.0	37.7
Total	100.0	100.0	100.0

Source: *Weekly Report*, German Institute for Business Research, July 29, 1939.

share of Germany's total imports supplied by the Balkans rose from 4 per cent in 1929 to 12 per cent in 1937. There was also some rise in the share of trade with South and Central America, but in absolute volume, imports from these countries in 1937 were still very much below the 1929 level. During this period the importance of the United States as a trading partner declined significantly. In 1929, 13 per cent of total German imports came from this country; in 1937, 5 per cent.

By 1937 Germany had succeeded in becoming the most important customer of the Balkans. In this year approximately 40 per cent of the total exports of these countries went to Germany and Austria.[73] In value terms, foodstuffs bulked largest in these exports, but more important to Germany's war preparations were several scarce materials which she was able to obtain from the Balkan countries. Most

73. *Weekly Report*, German Institute for Business Research, May 4, 1938.

important of these was bauxite. From 1934 to 1938 bauxite supplies received from the Balkans and Italy tripled, accounting in the latter year for 75 per cent of the total imports of this material.[74] The bulk of the bauxite imports came from Yugoslavia and Hungary. As has been mentioned above, German firms participated in the development of bauxite mines in these two countries. Another material for which the Balkans were a major source of supply was chrome, an important steel alloying material. From 1933 to 1938, chrome exports of the Balkan countries to Germany increased from 14 thousand tons to 79 thousand tons. Turkey was the most important source, accounting in 1938 for about 30 per cent of German supplies.[75] Germany had to rely on one of the Balkan countries, Romania, for practically all of her wartime oil imports. In 1939 about one fifth of the total imports of oil products came from Romania.[76] Although Romanian exports of oil to Germany had increased fourfold since 1929, 60 per cent of her 1939 oil exports were still going to non-Axis countries.[77] Discussions of the members of the Four-Year Planning Office indicate that the securing of a larger share of Romanian oil exports was, before the war, considered one of the most important tasks of Nazi diplomacy.[78]

To exploit the Balkans even more fully, the Germans, in 1939, were making pacts with these countries which went far beyond the scope of trade agreements. This is shown in the German–Romanian treaty of March 1939. Under the terms of this treaty the Germans were to assist in the drawing up of an economic plan for Romanian agricultural and industrial production and German–Romanian companies were to be set up to develop Romanian ore and oil deposits.[79] At the same time, similar arrangements were being worked out with Hungary and Bulgaria.

Hitler's final attempt on the eve of the war to make Germany's raw material position more secure was the reestablishment of commercial relations with Russia. The main purpose in making the pact with Russia in August 1939, undoubtedly, was the desire to prevent

74. *Statisches Jahrbuch*, 1941/1942, p. 67*.
75. *Statistisches Jahrbuch*, 1941/1942, p. 67.
76. *Statistisches Jahrbuch*, 1941/1942, p. 194*.
77. *Effects of Strategic Bombing*, p. 74.
78. Minutes of meetings of Four-Year Planning Office, 1939.
79. *Weekly Report*, German Institute for Business Research, July 27, 1939.

a war on two fronts. It cannot be assumed, however, that the opportunity to obtain much needed raw materials was an unimportant factor. In addition to substantial quantities of foodstuffs, textile raw materials, and timber, Germany was also able to get from Russia a substantial amount of several scarce raw materials. In 1940, 40 per cent of the German manganese supplies and 70 per cent of the chrome supplies came from Russia.[80] Oil imports from Russia in 1940 amounted to 620,000 tons, or nearly a third of the total amount of oil products imported in that year.[81] Before 1939, Germany had received only a negligible quantity of these materials from Russia.

6. THE EFFECT OF GERMANY'S RAW MATERIAL POSITION ON HER WAR STRATEGY

Although it is true that material supplies from the Balkans and Russia were important to Germany, nonetheless her raw material position was, at the outbreak of war, very weak. In the first chapter of this study, it was pointed out that Hitler's plans for the conquest of Europe did not involve a prolonged war against a coalition of major powers, but rather a series of minor wars in which Germany's territorial desires would have been satisfied in a piecemeal fashion. A survey of the raw material situation makes it evident that this was the only type of strategy which could have been seriously entertained. Germany's weakness in raw material supplies was admitted both by those who were opposed to the attack on Poland before additional preparations could have been undertaken and by Hitler and his followers who saw no gain in delaying the attack. Hitler believed that Germany's preparedness was sufficient to achieve a cheap victory and that a delay would only narrow Germany's advantage over England and France whose material strength, he believed, was increasing faster than Germany's.[82] Hitler's opponents, on the other hand, believed that his strategy would sooner or later involve Germany in a major war in which a lack of raw materials would place her at a decided disadvantage.

Mussolini was one of those who thought that Germany's material preparedness was insufficient to risk her involvement in a major war.

---

80. *Statistisches Jahrbuch,* 1941/1942, pp. 303–304.
81. *Statistisches Jahrbuch,* 1941/1942, pp. 303–304.
82. Hitler's speech to the Commanders in Chief, *Nazi Conspiracy and Aggression,* III, 581–585.

The autobiography of his foreign minister, Count Ciano, shows that for this reason Mussolini implored Hitler not to attack Poland, and proposed, instead, an international conference[83] (a strategy which already had paid large dividends).

Another group which was opposed to Hitler's strategy on similar grounds was the conservative faction of the German General Staff. The opinion of this group is indicated in the writings of General Thomas, chief of the War Economy Office of the High Command:

> During this time many conferences were held with the then Generaloberst Keitel discussing our readiness for war and conditions in regard to armaments as compared with that of the prospective enemy states. During all these discussions I maintained the point of view that a war with Poland would present no problem for us, but that for a great war of long duration, our economic structure would be too weak. . . .[84]

Hitler's position is summarized in his speech to the Commanders in Chief on August 22, 1939:

> Our economic situation is such, because of our restrictions, that we cannot hold out more than a few years. Goering can confirm this. We have no other choice, we must act. Our opponents risk much and can gain only a little. England's stake in a war is unimaginably great. Our enemies have men who are below average. No personalities. No masters, no men of action.[85]

The "Memorandum and Directives for the Conduct of the War" stated that Germany's only hope lay in a short war. Three reasons were given for the necessity of avoiding a long war. In the first place, a long war would eventually bring into the conflict against Germany countries which would not be able to take such action in a shorter period. Secondly, a long war would in itself indicate that Germany's defeat was inevitable, and would bring countries into the war otherwise not inclined to take such a step. Finally, in the words of this document, "The third danger, in a lengthier war, lies in the difficulty, owing to the limited food and raw material basis, of insuring the food supply of the people, and of finding the means for carrying on the war." [86]

83. *Ciano Diaries, 1939–1943* (New York, 1945), pp. 124–132.
84. *Basic Facts for a History of German War and Armaments Economy* (Nurnberg Trial Documents).
85. *Nazi Conspiracy and Aggression*, III, 582.
86. *Nazi Conspiracy and Aggression*, VII, p. 804.

I I I *Mobilization of Manpower*

Two things are meant by labor mobilization: First, expansion of the total supply of labor. This may occur through reducing unemployment, recruiting men and women previously not in the labor force, or through lengthening working hours. Second, labor mobilization means the concentration of manpower in those activities more or less directly concerned with war preparations. These would include military service, the production of war goods, and the production of basic materials. In short, labor mobilization is measured in terms of two attributes: the relative size of the labor force and its distribution.

That the German labor force was highly mobilized prior to the outbreak of the war scarcely was denied in any of the writings on the Nazi economic system.[1] There were several reasons for this widespread belief. In the first place, a high degree of labor mobilization was to be expected in an economy which was believed to be directing all of its energies into preparation for war. Secondly, the fact that unemployment had practically disappeared by 1938 was taken to mean that Germany had virtually exhausted her labor reserves. Finally, the various Nazi labor control measures strongly indicated that by 1939 actual mobilization must have gone very far.

I. MOBILIZATION FROM THE LEGAL POINT OF VIEW

Not long after they came into power, the Nazis abolished the traditional rights of organized labor. In May 1933 independent trade

1. See, for example: Nathan, *The Nazi Economic System,* pp. 170–214; Kuczynski, *Germany: Economic and Labor Conditions under Fascism,* chapters 3 and 4.

unions were dissolved and all laborers were compelled to join the German Labor Front. This organization was controlled by the Nazi party; its leader, Dr. Ley, was a prominent National Socialist. The primary function of the Labor Front, however, was not the control of labor but the inculcation of National Socialist ideology in its members and the improvement of their welfare. The supervision of the labor force became the direct responsibility of the state.

The Regulation of National Labor Law of January, 1934,[2] was the first of a series of decrees which finally succeeded in giving the government complete control over manpower. This decree prohibited strikes and lockouts, and provided for the settlement of labor disputes by state appointed labor trustees.

The government's control over labor was subsequently broadened by a number of specific decrees. In May 1934, to implement the program for agricultural self-sufficiency, it was decreed that agricultural laborers could not leave their occupation and that industrial workers who had been employed in agriculture during the previous three years were to be dismissed.[3] A number of similar decrees were designed to meet other labor shortages. In December 1934 skilled metal workers were forbidden to take employment outside of their district without the consent of their employment office;[4] in 1936 the regulation was extended to unskilled metal workers.[5] In October, 1937, carpenters and masons and, later, all building workers were restricted from leaving their occupations.[6] Finally, in March 1939, such measures were extended to include workers in the forestry, mining, and chemical industries.[7]

Another measure seemed to denote a change in Nazi policy regarding employment of women. In 1939 it was decreed that women receiving marriage loans were no longer forbidden to accept employment.[8] Earlier these loans were made only on the condition that the recipient withdraw from employment.

The various partial mobilization measures were finally succeeded

2. *Reichsgesetzblatt*, 1934, I, 45.
3. *Reichsgesetzblatt*, 1934, I, 381.
4. *Reichsgesetzblatt*, 1934, I, 202.
5. *Reichsgesetzblatt*, 1936, I, 311.
6. *Reichsgesetzblatt*, 1937, I, 248.
7. *Reichsgesetzblatt*, 1939, I, 444.
8. *Reichsgesetzblatt*, 1939, I, 400.

by a decree giving the government direct control over the whole labor force. In June 1938, more than a year before the outbreak of war, the Nazis ordered general conscription of labor. Power was given to the employment offices to conscript laborers for any work which was considered of national importance. The act[9] limited the term of service to six months, but in March 1939, a new measure[10] made it indefinite. Thus, before the war, Germany had a far more comprehensive system of labor controls than was introduced in this country during the whole war period.

To conclude from this evidence alone, however, that Germany had achieved a high degree of mobilization prior to the outbreak of war would be wrong. Indeed, as we shall see, the actual degree of mobilization was quite different from that implied in these decrees.

2. A STATISTICAL APPRAISAL OF NAZI LABOR MOBILIZATION

The most obvious method of increasing the size of the working force is the reduction of unemployment. As Table 19 shows, if this were the only way of increasing the labor force, Germany could be considered virtually fully mobilized in 1938; unemployment in this year averaged just above 400,000 workers, 2 per cent of the total number of wage and salary earners.

If we consider the total number of workers (employed as well as

Table 19. Wage and salary earners[a]
(millions)

| | Employed | | Unemployed | | Total | |
	Total	Men	Total	Men	Total	Men
1929	18.4	12.3	1.9	1.3	20.3	13.6
1933	13.4	8.7	4.8	3.9	18.2	12.6
1934	15.5	10.4	2.7	2.2	18.2	16.6
1935	16.4	11.2	2.2	1.8	18.6	13.0
1936	17.6	12.1	1.6	1.3	19.2	13.4
1937	18.9	13.0	0.9	0.8	19.8	13.8
1938	20.1	13.8	0.4	0.3	20.5	14.1
1939	20.8	14.0	0.1	0.1	20.9	14.1

Source: *Statistisches Jahrbuch*, 1941/1942, pp. 410, 426.
a. Old Reich.

9. *Reichsgesetzblatt*, 1938, I, 652.
10. *Reichsgesetzblatt*, 1939, I, 126.

unemployed), however, the picture is somewhat different. The total labor force as a percentage of the working population actually declined. Wage and salary earners in 1929 constituted 41 per cent of the population of working age (14 and over); in 1939, 38.5 per cent.[11] From an examination of these figures it would appear that the German labor force was more fully mobilized in 1929 than in 1939.

The data just cited do leave out of account the self-employed, a large share of the government workers, and the members of the armed forces. For this reason it is necessary to examine census data which include the entire occupied population.

The labor force figures taken from the three most recent census compilations are shown in Table 20. It is apparent that the inclusion

Table 20. Comparison of gainfully employed with population of working age[a]
(millions)

	1925	1933	1939
Total gainfully employed	32.0	32.3	36.2
men	20.5	20.8	23.3
women	11.5	11.5	12.8
Population of working age	47.6	50.2	54.3
men	22.7	24.1	26.3
women	24.9	26.1	28.0
Percentage employed	68	64	67
men	90	87	88
women	46	44	46

Sources: *Statistisches Jahrbuch*, 1941/1942, p. 33; *Statistisches Jahrbuch*, 1936, p. 15; *Statistisches Jahrbuch*, 1934, p. 13.
a. Age 14 years and over; includes the unemployed.

of the armed forces and the self-employed do not alter the observation that Nazi labor mobilization was reflected only in the decline of unemployment. Withdrawals from the labor force during depression years is a common phenomenon.[12] However, in 1939 the total labor force, including the armed forces, was not larger relative to the population of working age than it had been in 1925.

11. *Statistisches Jahrbuch*, 1941/1942, pp. 410, 426.
12. See, for example, *Weekly Report*, Institute for Business Cycle Research, May 5, 1937.

These results cannot be explained by statistical incomparability of the census figures for these three years. Corrections for statistical bias would alter the figures but slightly. They would increase the numbers of gainfully employed in 1925 and perhaps in 1933,[13] thus making the degree of mobilization in 1939 appear even less. There is one statistical factor, however, which could understate the relative mobilization in 1939 with respect to the earlier years. This is a peculiarity in the German method of counting the number of gainfully employed in agriculture. Here, the generous way of including "unpaid family helpers" in the labor force results in abnormally high proportion of the agricultural population counted as gainfully employed (in 1939, 70 per cent). A migration of farmers such as took place over this period would of itself, therefore, tend to lower the total percentage of gainfully employed. If we leave agriculture out of our calculations, however, and compute the ratios for the gainfully employed in nonagricultural occupations as shown in Table 21, the comparisons for three years are only slightly modified.

Table 21. Ratio of gainfully employed
to population of working age

	Total	Nonagricultural
	(per cent)	
1925	68	61
1933	64	58
1939	67	61

Source: See Table 20.

Another, though somewhat more questionable, method of gauging the degree of Germany's labor mobilization in 1939 is a comparison of the German with the British manpower figures. The ratio of gainfully employed in Germany, 67 per cent, was appreciably higher than Britain's. This is explained primarily by the German method of counting the occupied population in agriculture. Comparing the ratios of gainfully employed in nonagricultural occupations to the corresponding populations of working ages, we find that the German

13. The comparability of the census figures for 1925, 1933, and 1939 is discussed in a memorandum prepared by the Statistisches Reichsamt, "German Labor Force Estimates" (files, United States Strategic Bombing Survey).

ratio was only slightly higher than the British — 61 per cent as compared to 58 per cent. Nor can it be said that Britain's labor reserves were completely exhausted in 1939; during the war the number of gainfully employed increased by 14 per cent.[14] Furthermore, there was no increase in the total working population.

Another method of increasing the effective size of the labor force is the lengthening of working hours. Statistics on average weekly hours for the entire German industry, as well as various segments, are shown in Table 22. These figures show a substantial increase, 15

Table 22. Average weekly hours worked in German industry

	1929	1932	1933	1934	1935	1936	1937	1938	1939
Total industry	46.04	41.47	42.94	44.56	44.44	45.56	46.06	46.54	47.8
Production goods	46.34	41.16	42.96	45.15	45.87	46.61	47.25	47.84	48.8
Consumer goods	45.65	41.80	42.89	43.81	42.60	44.23	44.54	44.91	43.5
Selected industries									
Steel industry	48.24	39.38	41.94	45.67	46.83	47.53	47.43	47.96	
Transportation equipment	45.02	39.32	43.12	44.50	45.12	45.81	45.66	45.93	
Machinery	49.01	40.31	42.66	47.18	49.07	49.00	49.86	50.07	
Electrical	44.71	35.30	38.79	43.88	45.07	46.13	46.67	46.39	
Leather	45.34	43.57	44.13	45.19	44.73	44.31	44.18	45.04	
Textile	44.73	40.95	42.37	42.93	40.78	42.30	43.07	43.95	
Clothing	45.80	42.59	43.75	44.01	41.46	43.96	43.52	44.40	
Food and tobacco	47.00	43.11	43.26	44.99	44.76	45.03	45.47	45.46	

Sources: *Statistisches Jahrbuch*, 1939/40, p. 384, and *The Effects of Strategic Bombing*, p. 215. Individual industries not shown separately.

per cent, in working hours from 1932 to 1939. This comparison, though often used in discussions of Nazi labor mobilization, is misleading. The increase is due almost entirely to the fact that working hours were curtailed during the depression. For a more proper comparison, we must go back to a predepression year. The average increase in weekly hours from 1929 to 1939 was only about 3 per cent. Of course, in those segments of industry directly or indirectly associated with rearmament, or the nonwar investment program, the rise was slightly more pronounced. In the basic industries, the metalworking industries, the machinery industry, and the transportation

14. *Statistics Relating to the War Effort of the United Kingdom*, Cmd. 6564, His Majesty's Stationery Office, 1944.

equipment industry, the average rise was some 5 per cent, about 2½ hours per week. Figures have often been cited showing long hours worked in particular plants or by certain types of skilled labor. These are exceptional cases. For the overwhelming portion of industry, it must be concluded that in 1939 the possibilities of increasing working hours were by no means exhausted.

A more indirect method which the Nazis could have used to augment their labor supply would have been to increase its efficiency. About 1925, a general rationalization movement was begun in German industry, and it might be expected that the Nazis would have carried it further as a part of their economic preparation for war. The German estimates of labor productivity, however, do not show any evidence of this. Estimates of the German Institute for Business Cycle Research show that from 1925 to 1933 hourly productivity in German industry as a whole rose by nearly 30 per cent, or about 3½ per cent annually.[15] From 1933 to 1939, however, the figures indicate no general increase in productivity. While there were productivity increases in several branches of industry, notably iron and steel and the automobile industries, productivity in several others, textiles, for example, declined.

How are we to explain the fact that productivity in German industry did not generally increase after 1933? One possible explanation might be that the composition of industrial output shifted in favor of the low productivity industries. This, however, did not take place. Such changes in the composition of output as did take place between the prosperous years of the 1920's and the prosperous years of the 1930's favored the metal-working industries where productivity was comparatively high (see Table 24). Another possible explanation of the failure of productivity to increase from 1933 to 1939 is that German industry was, on the whole, subject to increasing average costs as output increased. But this is contradicted by the fact that productivity increased substantially from the years 1924 to 1929, which were also years of rising industrial output. The only possible explanation of the phenomena seems to be that so much repair and replacement of German plants was postponed during the depression years that the large investments of 1936 could only restore them to prewar efficiency (Table 5). Although German economists have

15. *Vierteljahrshefte zur Wirtschaftsforschung,* 1938/39, Heft 1.

called attention to the failure to continue the rationalization movement after 1933, they have made no serious attempt to explain it.[16]

Thus, with respect to the total supply of labor, it can be said that
German manpower was fully mobilized in 1939 only in the sense that
there was no unemployment. In terms of recruiting additional members into the labor force, lengthening working hours, or generally
increasing industrial labor efficiency, manpower in 1939 was hardly
more mobilized than it had been in the previous decade.

The second aspect of manpower mobilization concerns the distribution of the labor force. More specifically, we are here concerned
with the question of the extent to which the civilian labor force was
shifted to war-associated activities. We shall judge this by a comparison with the occupational distribution of the gainfully employed
in the census years 1933 and 1925.

The numbers of gainfully employed in the major occupational
groups and their percentages of the annual totals are shown in
Table 23. These data show that the distribution of the labor force
over this fourteen year period was surprisingly stable. Pronounced
shifts occurred in only two of the occupational groups — agriculture and public employment. The large rise in the number of govern-

Table 23. Occupational distribution of the German labor force[a]
(in millions)

	1939		1933		1925	
Total	36.14	100.0	32.30	100.0	32.0	100.0
Agriculture and forestry	8.94	24.8	9.34	28.9	9.76	30.5
Mining	1.33	3.7	1.31	4.0	1.53	4.8
Manufacturing	9.69	26.7	8.50	26.3	8.85	27.6
Construction	3.17	8.8	2.87	8.9	2.67	8.4
Transportation	1.87	5.2	1.55	4.7	1.52	4.8
Trade and finance	3.63	10.1	3.81	11.9	3.26	10.2
Services	3.07	8.5	3.13	9.7	3.05	9.5
Government	4.43	12.2	1.79	5.6	1.35	4.2
Civilian	2.43		1.64		1.21	
Army and para-military organizations	2.0		0.15		0.14	

Source: See Table 20.
a. Old Germany without the Saar.

16. *Vierteljahrshefte zur Wirtschaftsforschung*, 1938/39, Heft 1.

ment employees is not difficult to understand. The size of the armed forces increased from 100,000 in 1933 (the limitation imposed by the Treaty of Versailles) to nearly 1.5 million in 1939. In addition, there were in 1939 500,000 men in para-military organizations, and the civilian employees of the government were nearly 800,000 more than in 1933.

The migration of farm workers cannot be explained by Nazi policy; it was in fact contradictory to the objective of agricultural self-sufficiency. In spite of the decrees binding farm laborers to their occupations, more than 400,000 migrated during the period 1933 to 1939. The annual average decline in the agricultural population during this period was greater than that which occurred between 1925 and 1933.

Changes in the percentages of gainfully employed in the other occupational groups were not so pronounced as in the cases mentioned above, and there was no general tendency for manpower to shift into those occupational groups more or less closely associated with rearmament. In the transportation and construction industries relative employment increased slightly. The increase in construction represented for the most part, however, an expansion of building activity not associated with rearmament (see Table 5). In mining, where an expansion of production and employment was even more important for war preparations, the number of gainfully employed in relation to the total declined between 1933 and 1939 as it had in the period 1925 to 1933. In manufacturing where, on the basis of the wartime experience of Britain and the United States, we should expect to see a considerable increase in the proportion of gainfully employed, the ratio was nearly constant for all three of the census years. In the typically nonwar occupational groups there were likewise no pronounced changes. Relative employment in trade and finance remained about the same; in the various service occupations it declined slightly.

One of the service occupations, domestic service, provides a good example of the degree of labor diversion from an occupation not essential for war preparations. In 1933, there were 1,270,000 domestic servants. By 1939 the number had not been reduced. Indeed, it had increased about 75,000.[17] This increase in the number of domestic

17. *Statistisches Jahrbuch*, 1941/42, p. 33.

servants cannot be explained by the fact that it permitted more German women to seek employment. For, as we have seen, relative to the female population of working age, there was hardly any increase in the employment of women from 1933 to 1939 (Table 20).

Considering the composition of each of the major occupational groups, we find that there was only one in which there were important changes — manufacturing. The gainfully employed in the manufacturing industries both in absolute numbers and as percentages of the annual totals are shown in Table 24. These figures show that

Table 24. Gainfully employed in the manufacturing industries

	1939		1933		1925	
Total manufacturing	9691	100.0	8500	100.0	8851	100.0
Iron and other metals production	645	6.7	459	5.4	580	6.6
Metal fabrication	3892	40.0	2681	31.5	2997	33.8
Chemical	497	5.1	363	4.3	352	3.8
Textile and clothing	2460	25.5	2596	30.3	2796	31.6
Paper production	511	5.3	536	6.3	536	6.1
Rubber and leather	236	2.4	235	2.8	243	2.7
Food, drink and tobacco	1450	15.0	1630	19.2	1347	15.4

Source: See Table 20.

between 1939 and the earlier census years there was a significant increase in employment in the metal and chemical industries, both absolutely and relative to total manufacturing employment. Employment in the various consumer goods industries, on the other hand, declined. The relative decline in those industries which typically produced consumers goods (the last four entries in Table 24) was some 15 per cent, the absolute decline about 5 per cent.

It is undoubtedly true that rearmament was one of the factors explaining the larger number of gainfully employed in the metal industries. But it was not the only factor. For, in the manufacture of durable goods, production and employment are more sensitive to general business conditions than they are in other types of industry. The fact, then, that 1939 was a year of high economic activity compared either with 1933 or 1925 would in itself be of considerable importance explaining the larger employment in the metal industries.

Because the level of economic activity is itself an important deter-
minant of the distribution of the labor force, it would be better to
compare 1939 with another high production year, such as 1928 or
1929. Since census data for these years are unavailable, it is only
possible to make the comparisons on the basis of statistics for employed wage and salary earners. As we might expect, the differences
in the distribution of the industrial labor force are much less when
we compare 1939 with 1929 than when we compare 1939 with either
of the census years, 1925 or 1933. Employment in the consumer
goods industries in absolute numbers was about the same in both
years[18] (whereas it was slightly higher in 1925 and in 1933). Although the number of employed in the metal industries was higher
in 1939, the difference was much less than when the comparisons
are made with either 1933 or 1925.[19]

In summary, the statistics for the occupational distribution of labor
show only two discernible effects of preparations for war, a growth
in the size of the armed forces, and a redistribution of the industrial labor force in favor of the metal working industries (although,
as we have seen, part of this shift must be attributed merely to the
higher level of economic activity). More important is the fact that
there were large sectors of the economy in which manpower was un-
affected by war mobilization. The numbers of gainfully employed in
occupations not associated with war preparations such as retail and
wholesale trade, banking, consumer goods production, or personal
services were not on the whole reduced before 1939. As evidence of
the fact that in 1939 the civilian economy[20] still possessed large
reserves of labor by 1943 (when, as we shall see, the labor reserves
were by no means exhausted) some 3 million men and women had
been shifted to either the armed forces or to war industry.

If the Nazis had gone very far in mobilizing their labor force in the
prewar period, we would expect to see a growth of the labor force in
excess of the number which came from the reduction in unemployment and the growth in the working population. But these two

18. *Statistisches Jahrbuch,* 1939/40, p. 383.
19. *Statistisches Jahrbuch,* 1939/40, p. 383.
20. Includes retail and wholesale trade, banking, consumer goods production,
domestic services, amusements and other types of services, and nonwar construction. The estimate is for the area of old Germany and excludes foreign
laborers.

factors explain the entire growth of the number of workers and self employed during the Nazi prewar period. This total growth amounted to some nine millions. Of these, nearly five millions came from the unemployed and four millions from the increase in the population.

The growth in the total labor force (employed and unemployed) and the migration of farm laborers in the period 1933–1939 made 4.3 million additional workers available for employment in non-agricultural occupations. Of these, 3.9 millions were absorbed by the government, the army, the metal industries, construction, and transportation. Thus the modest requirements of war preparations were satisfied without an actual diversion of labor from the civilian economy.

It can be concluded that Germany's labor reserves were by no means exhausted in 1939. With respect to both the size of the labor force and to the number of workers still engaged in civilian type occupations, the country was still essentially on a peacetime footing.

CONCLUSIONS ON THE ECONOMIC
REARMAMENT OF GERMANY

In the prewar period, the German economy produced both "butter" and "guns" — much more of the former and much less of the latter than has been commonly assumed. By 1937, civilian consumption, investment in consumer goods industries, and government nonwar expenditures equalled or exceeded previous peak levels. There is no question, therefore, of a rearmament program so large that it prevented a substantial recovery of civilian production.

The volume of expenditures for rearmament was actually quite modest. In the period 1933 through 1938 rearmament expenditures absorbed less than 10 per cent of Germany's gross national product, and even as late as 1938, only 15 per cent. The volume of munitions production and the number of divisions which Germany mobilized was, by comparison with published appraisal, small. Investment in those industries comprising the war potential was not much larger than the volume reached in the prosperous years of the previous decade and was small in relation to total investment.

The review of Germany's raw material preparations for war shows that at the time the Nazis came into power Germany was not self-sufficient in such important materials as iron ore, ferroalloys, oil, copper, rubber, aluminum, bauxite, and foodstuffs. Of these, only in foodstuffs and rubber did the Germans attain a substantial degree of self-sufficiency prior to the war. They found it impossible to become independent of foreign sources for such important materials as copper ores, bauxite, and ferroalloys because Germany lacked the basic resources. For other important raw materials, notably iron ore and synthetic oil, the self-sufficiency programs were largely unsuccessful because they were begun too late and were inadequately implemented.

Raw material distribution controls were largely unsuccessful in increasing the flow of raw materials into the war sector of the economy. Priorities and allocation schemes were applied to only a few commodities and in those cases where they were used they were largely ineffective.

The stockpiling program also did little to improve Germany's raw material position. At the beginning of the war such important materials as gasoline, rubber, iron ore, copper ore, and bauxite were in sufficient supply for less than six months of estimated needs. After this period Germany's current output of these materials could cover only a fraction of stated requirements. The weakness of Germany's raw material position at the beginning of the war was recognized both by Hitler and by the German General Staff.

Concerning Germany's mobilization of manpower, the Nazis increased their total labor supply only insofar as they eliminated unemployment. A larger percentage of the population was not taken into the labor force, working hours were increased only slightly, and labor efficiency in industry was not, in general, improved. Second, it was shown that the Nazis did not shift a large proportion of the labor force into war activities. The only two major changes in the distribution of the labor force between 1925 and 1939 were a decline in agricultural employment and an increase in public employment. The shrinkage in the agricultural labor force was contradictory to Nazi policy. A large increase in the army from the 100,000 limit set by the Treaty of Versailles is hardly surprising. What is surprising, however, is the fact that the relative size of the industrial labor force was no greater in 1939 than in 1925, and that the relative numbers engaged in civilian production hardly declined.

On the basis of these observations it was concluded that there was no real mobilization of manpower prior to the outbreak of war.

Thus, whether we examine the general nature of the German economic recovery, or the raw material self-sufficiency program, or the mobilization of manpower, the same general conclusion is evident: The scale of Germany's economic mobilization for war was quite modest.

A number of reasons have been given why the rearmament was not, in general or in special aspects, on a larger scale.

A basic reason why the Germans did not have a rearmament on the scale popularly assumed is simply that their war plans did not require such a large effort. As we have emphasized, Hitler hoped to satisfy his territorial ambitions in a piecemeal fashion; he hoped to conquer each enemy so speedily that the democracies would not have time to intervene, and to have a breathing space after each conquest during which preparations could be made for the next. There is no doubt that this type of strategy called for less massive preparations than one involving a prolonged struggle against a coalition of major powers.

While this blitzkrieg strategy explains why Germany did not undertake preparations on an enormous scale, it cannot explain why they were not at least moderately larger. In the first place, while Hitler hoped not to get involved in a major war, he did not dismiss that possibility. Moreover, there is ample evidence that both he and the General Staff wanted a larger economic effort.

This was prevented by a variety of factors, consideration of which yields four principal reasons why the German rearmament was not, in fact, larger. The first and probably the most important reason is that the government was unwilling to increase public expenditures and incur larger deficits. A larger deficit, it was thought, would destroy confidence in the currency and lead to inflation. This fear of inflation was a major factor in explaining economic policy of the pre-Nazi governments. It played an important role in determining Nazi policy for economic recovery, and it was a restraining influence on both total military expenditures and the development of Germany's raw material industries. There is no doubt that without this concern about inflation, and without such an effective exponent of financial conservatism as Schacht, Germany would have had a larger rearmament.

The second reason was the unwillingness of the Germans to surrender a part of their prosperity level of consumption. The government's disinclination to ask for civilian sacrifices was demonstrated in a number of instances. One of these was its refusal to consider higher taxes as an alternative to deficit spending; another was its unwillingness in 1937 to cut food imports in favor of increased raw material imports; still another was its failure to transfer workers out of unessential occupations.

Until 1936, rearmament and increased civilian consumption could be achieved simultaneously by drawing on unemployed resources. Indeed, the rearmament deficits had a stimulating effect on consumption. There was no conflict, therefore, in having both more "butter" and more "guns." In the years 1937 and 1938, however, the German economy was operating at near full employment, and a sizable increase in armament expenditures could have been achieved only at the expense of some decline in civilian consumption. It would have required at least a sharp curtailment of some types of civilian goods production, notably consumer durables and residential construction. It appears, however, that the German government was unwilling to ask for such sacrifices.

It must be admitted that even if the above factors limited the amount of resources available for war preparations, the size of these preparations to some extent was dependent on the efficiency with which the program was directed. Nazi inefficiency in planning and carrying out their war production program is the third reason why war preparations were not larger. Note, for example, the manner in which the various branches of the armed forces procured their material. It is a first principle of war economy that competition between the branches of the armed forces for supplies is not the most efficient method of procurement; this was learned in World War I. Yet, as we have seen, before the outbreak of war there was no central agency which examined and coordinated the material demands of the German army, navy, and air force.

The review of Germany's raw material preparations for war showed a lack of efficiency in both the planning and execution of the program. In drawing up the plans the idea of attaining a balanced program seems to have been given little consideration. As a result the planned production of some commodities was ample, if not excessive, for wartime requirements, while for others it was not nearly sufficient. Once drawn up, the adequacy of the measures taken to implement the various plans was not solely a matter of their importance. The iron ore and synthetic oil programs were designated by Hitler as top priority projects; yet it was in these fields that Germany's preparations were most deficient. The Nazi prewar experience with raw material distribution controls is another example of inefficient economic administration. A steel priority system was instituted in 1937, yet by 1941 an effectve method still had not been found.

Something else which makes us suspicious of Nazi economic organizational ability is the composition of their governmental expenditures. Given the difficulty of increasing public outlays, and assuming that preparations for war had priority over other governmental activities, it follows that the latter should have been cut to an absolute minimum. But, as we have seen, public nonwar expenditures in 1937 and 1938 were much above any previous peak. Especially prominent in the German budget were expenditures on highway construction, municipal improvements, and party buildings.

In the light of such evidence, it would be difficult to deny that a more rational and better executed program would have given the Nazis larger rearmament.

The fourth reason why war preparations were not larger was that Hitler was unable to subordinate various vested and emerging interests to his central task of preparing for war. One of these interests was the Nazi party itself. The opposition of this group made it difficult to cut public nonwar expenditures. When Schacht attempted to cut expenditures for municipal improvements, he was invariably opposed by some prominent party members. When, on numerous occasions, he tried to reduce the budget of the German Labor Front, the issue was taken to Hitler, who invariably decided in favor of the latter. Because it was contradictory to its ideology, the party also opposed measures to force a larger number of women into the labor force.

The German industrialists were another group whose interests could not be disregarded. In our account of Germany's iron and steel expansion program, we showed that the interests of the steel cartel conflicted with those of the state; that the industrialists refused to carry out the program themselves; that they strongly voiced their opposition to the government's undertaking of the project; and that eventually the government had to drop its elaborate plans for expansion of iron ore and steel capacity.

Part of the government's reluctance for incurring large deficits may have been the concern that they would destroy the confidence of the industrialists in the regime and hence their cooperation in rearmament. Certainly there was little ground for fearing that moderately larger deficits would have led to a runaway price inflation. For by 1936 Germany had adequate machinery for controlling wages and prices; this was demonstrated during the war when, in spite of enormous government outlays and deficits by prewar standards, prices increased very little.

An adequate account of the importance of pressure groups in Nazi Germany will have to wait the studies of political scientists who were close to the situation. When such studies are made, it is likely that it will be found that the resistance of particular groups to Hitler's aims, for one reason or another, was as effective in circumscribing the German war potential as a lack of iron ore or oil.

The contrast between the conclusions reached in this summary of Germany's economic preparations for war and those of earlier studies should be reemphasized.

That the Nazis were undertaking massive preparations for war was the central assumption of practically all political and economic writings on Nazi Germany. In achieving this end, it was supposed that only money and not resources mattered to the Germans, that the civilian population as well as various private interests were compelled to make large sacrifices, and that the government was super-efficient in directing the program.

Actually, Germany's rearmament was on a much smaller scale than was generally assumed and it did not involve a large drain of resources from the civilian economy. The factors which prevented the Nazis from having a larger rearmament were, first, the fear of larger deficits; second, the government's unwillingness to ask for civilian sacrifices; third, Hitler's inability to subordinate various private interests to his aims; and, finally, a lack of efficiency in the direction of the program. Even without these restraining influences, however, it is unlikely that Germany would have made the tremendous preparations with which she was credited. Such an economic effort was not required by Hitler's strategy.

PART TWO

THE GERMAN WAR ECONOMY

1939–1944

I V *The Magnitude of Germany's War Effort, 1939–1942*

I. GERMANY'S TOTAL OUTPUT AND ITS MAJOR USES, 1938–1942

The economic developments of the early years of the war are broadly indicated by the changes in Germany's national output, by the additional output supplied by the occupied countries, and by the changes in the major uses of the total available output.[1]

After increasing substantially from 1938 to 1939, Germany's gross national product gradually rose in the following three years to a level of 136 billion RM, which was 15 per cent above the 1938 total. The considerable rise in total output was accomplished with no increase in the total civilian labor effort. Actually, the draft into the armed forces reduced the civilian labor force by some 4 million workers between 1939 and 1940.[2] From 1938 to 1942, after adjustment for difference in territorial coverage, there was a reduction in civilian employment of around 5 per cent.[3] This reduction was approximately offset by the lengthening of the workweek — in industry average weekly hours rose from about 46.5 in 1938 to nearly 49 in 1942.[4]

1. The construction of the national product estimates and their major weaknesses are described in the Appendix. The figures appearing in the text have been adjusted for price changes. The estimates refer to the prewar Greater Germany, which in addition to Germany proper includes Austria and the Sudeten. Total available output includes, in addition to Germany's gross national product, the net economic contributions from all other areas.

2. *Effects of Strategic Bombing,* appendix table 1.

3. *Effects of Strategic Bombing,* appendix table 1.

4. *Effects of Strategic Bombing,* appendix table 14.

The pronounced expansion in total output was mainly attributable to the shift in the structure of production in favor of the manufacturing industries. The extent of this shift is indicated by the fact that whereas total national output increased only about 6 per cent between 1939 and 1942, industrial output is estimated to have increased about 20 per cent.[5] Moreover, in industry itself, there was a substantial increase in productivity (about 15 per cent from 1939 through 1942);[6] which in turn was mainly associated with the shift in industrial output towards munitions production.

The output which Germany could draw upon for war and nonwar

Table 25. Gross national product in 1939 prices, 1938–1942
(billions of RM)

	1938	1939	1940	1941	1942
Government expenditures for goods and services	33	45	62	77	93
Consumer expenditures	70	71	66	62	57
Gross capital formation	14	13	1	−8	−14
Home	13	14	10	7	6
Net acquisitions from foreign countries	1	−1	−9	−15	−20
Gross national product	117	129	129	131	136
Gross national available product	116	126	138	146	156

Source: See Appendix, Table 66.

uses was increasingly augmented by the exploitation of other European countries. This surplus was entirely supplied by the occupied countries, through such devices as the imposition of occupation levies and forced loans and the printing of invasion currency. Neutral and allied countries were not as a group net suppliers.

From the records of the German War Economy Office and other sources, estimates have been prepared of the value of goods and services received from the occupied and other European nations, net of

5. *Die Industriewirtschaft: Entwicklungstendenzen der deutschen und internationalen Industrieproduktion (1860–1932) Sonderheft 31, I.K.*; and *Industrial Sales, Output and Productivity Prewar Area of Germany*, U. S. Strategic Bombing Survey.
6. *Industrial Sales, Output and Productivity.* . . .

German exports to them.[7] The estimates attempt to measure the contribution in terms of prices paid in Germany for the same types of output. They are understated inasmuch as they do not include stores of military equipment, materials, and foodstuffs taken directly by the Wehrmacht, and they make insufficient allowance for the contribution of foreign laborers (a rough notion of the contribution of foreign workers is indicated by the fact that in the years 1940–1942, about 8 per cent of the total labor force was made up of foreign workers).

On the other hand, in another sense they overstate the real net contribution of the occupied areas since they do not make any allowance for the use of German manpower and resources required for economic exploitation of the occupied areas. A notion of the real value of the occupation to the Germans is given in the next section.

As Table 25 indicates, the net acquisition of goods and services from areas outside of Germany's prewar boundaries increased from 1 billion marks in 1939 to about 20 billion in 1942 (measured in 1939 prices). In the latter year, foreign acquisitions augmented Germany's own total output by about 15 per cent.

Relative to the total output of the exploited countries, these were very substantial amounts. According to Colin Clark's recent estimates, the prewar national incomes of all the occupied countries amounted to about 85 per cent of Germany's prewar national income, which suggests that their total gross national product was in the neighborhood of 100 billion RM.[8] In the period 1939–1942 as a whole, their estimated contribution was 8 per cent of this amount; in 1942 it reached 20 per cent.[9] (After 1942 there was very little increase in Germany's net acquisitions from outside areas.)[10]

The industrial nations supplied a much higher percentage of their total output for German use. During the same four-year period, the contributions of France and Belgium averaged nearly one fifth of their prewar output.[11] In 1943, the net contribution of France

7. See Appendix, Section B, for a description of sources and methods.
8. *The Conditions of Economic Progress,* London, 1951, chapter III.
9. See Tables 26, 65, and 66.
10. *The Conditions of Economic Progress,* chapter III.
11. *The Conditions of Economic Progress,* pp. 80, 84; and *Nazi Conspiracy and Aggression,* VII, 264ff.

amounted to nearly one quarter of her estimated 1938 national product.[12]

Moreover, the available evidence indicates that there probably was a substantial decline in the total output of the occupied nations during the war; i.e., that the proportion of output taken by the Germans was actually much larger than the above figures indicate. Two French statisticians, Mm. Froment and Gauanier, estimated that France's real output declined by nearly 40 per cent between 1938 and 1942, and that in 1942, over 30 per cent was "transferred" to Germany.[13] On the assumption that total real output actually declined by 40 per cent, their estimate of the transfer is consistent with the estimates presented above. However, as will be suggested in section 2, a substantial part of the "transfer" remained in France, e.g., was used to finance the cost of the occupation.

The estimates presented above — admittedly very crude — indicate that the total output available for Germany's use increased more than one third between 1938 and 1942. During the same period, there was a substantial curtailment of private activities. Consumer expenditures and domestic investment together (measured in real terms) fell by 20 billion dollars, or by nearly one quarter. Government expenditures, on the other hand, nearly tripled, increasing as a proportion of total available output from about 30 per cent in 1938 to 60 per cent in 1942. Indeed, total public expenditures in 1942 were equal to about 80 per cent of Germany's entire output in 1938 (measured in constant prices).

By comparison with Britain's wartime experience, and certainly by comparison with the United States' experience, the German decline in real consumption was considerable. The 20 per cent decline in aggregate real consumption (about 15 per cent on a per capita basis) that occurred between 1938 and 1942 brought consumption down to almost the depression level. Per capita consumption in 1942 was not more than 5 per cent above the 1934 amount.[14] In Britain, the decline in total real consumption was about 15 per cent from 1938 to

12. *Nazi Conspiracy and Aggression,* VII, 264ff.

13. *The Conditions of Economic Progress,* p. 82.

14. For estimates of total consumption in constant prices, see Statistical Appendix. Population data: *Effects of Strategic Bombing,* appendix table 1, p. 202.

1942.[15] In the United States, aggregate real consumption rose throughout the whole war, and in 1942 the level of real consumption was estimated at nearly 50 per cent above the depression level.[16]

Civilian per capita food consumption (measured in 1939 prices) fell nearly one fifth between 1938 and 1942.[17] This decline was not, to an appreciable extent, caused by a reduction in the quantity of food consumed by the average German, but rather by a deterioration in the quality of his diet. According to estimates of the German Food Ministry, average caloric consumption was 2800 in 1942; only 50 calories below the average for 1938.[18] The principal cuts in food consumption came in the meat and fat rations. This was compensated for by increased consumption of potatoes, cereals, and legumes. Although the average German became increasingly a vegetarian in World War II, his position was much better than in World War I. At that time, the shortage of meat and fats was much more severe and was not nearly compensated for by an increased consumption of vegetable foods.[19]

Private gross capital formation, that is, investment in machinery, buildings, and inventories, fell much more precipitously than private consumption. As Table 25 shows, by 1942 the real volume of private capital formation had fallen to 40 per cent of the 1938 level. However, investment in manufacturing plant and equipment was maintained at nearly the 1938 level throughout the first four years of the war. But in 1938 such investment amounted to less than a quarter of total private capital formation.[20] Other types of private investment were nearly eliminated. Residential construction, a very important part of total prewar investment, fell nearly 80 per cent between 1939 and 1942.[21]

15. *National Income and Expenditures of the United Kingdom, 1938–1946*, p. 15.
16. *January 1952 Annual Economic Review*, Council of Economic Advisors, Appendix Table B-2.
17. Monograph on Consumer Expenditure, 1936–1944, Alfred Jacobs (see Statistical Appendix, Section B).
18. *Die Entwicklung der Rationssätze in den Kriegen 1914/1918 und 1939–1943*. A study prepared by the German Food Ministry.
19. *Die Entwicklung der Rationssätze. . . .*
20. See Chapter I.
21. *Effects of Strategic Bombing*, appendix table 39, p. 231.

2. WAR EXPENDITURES FURTHER EXAMINED

As a result of the increase in total output in Gemany itself, the economic exploitation of other nations, and the compression of domestic investment and consumption, it was possible for total war expenditures (measured in 1939 prices) to increase from 30 billion RM in 1939 to about 90 billions in 1942. In 1942, as Table 26 shows, war expenditures accounted for more than half of Germany's total available output. While such aggregate measurements exaggerate the increase in real resources made available for the war effort, there is no doubt that the increase was very considerable.

Such an over-all shift in the broad pattern of resource use is not, however, very surprising. By 1942, the level of war expenditures in Britain accounted for somewhat over half of her total available output.[22] The 1943 level of war expenditures in the United States represented more than 40 per cent of the total gross national product.[23] What is surprising is the very small level of direct military production that accompanied this apparently huge economic war effort. Indeed, one of the most surprising facts of the whole history of the war is Germany's very modest level of military output during the period of her great military successes.

While total war expenditures (measured in real terms) increased about 60 billion RM between 1939 and 1942, total armed forces expenditures, including military pay, increased by only about 30 billions, or about half as much. In 1942, armed forces expenditures accounted for only 55 per cent of total war expenditures, and about 30 per cent of the total output available to Germany. Excluding military pay, they took less than one quarter of the total output available to Germany. Munitions output itself increased from 8 billion RM in 1939 to only 16 billions in 1942, and as a proportion of total output showed no significant increase from 1940 to 1942.

An obvious question at this point is the use which was made of the substantial volume of expenditures not directly associated with the armed forces budget. During the period under review, as Table 26

22. *National Income and Expenditure of the United Kingdom,* April 1946 and April 1947. War expenditures adjusted to include lend-lease and Canadian contribution.

23. *January 1952 Annual Economic Review,* appendix table B-2.

Table 26. Germany's total available output and war output, 1939–1942
(billions of RM, 1939 prices)

	1939	1940	1941	1942
Total output available to Germany[a]	126	138	146	156
War expenditures[b]	30	53	71	91
Internal Wehrmacht expenditures	19	31	39	45
Industrial sales to armed forces[c]	14	19	24	28
Munitions[d]	8	12	12	16
Military pay[e]	5	12	15	17
Other war expenditures including war expenditures in occupied nations[f]	11	22	32	46
Total Wehrmacht purchases in the occupied countries[g]	—[a]	—[a]	3	4
War expenditures as a percentage of total output	24	38	49	58
Total Wehrmacht expenditures (internal and external) as a percentage of total output	16	23	29	31
Munitions output as a percentage of total output	6	9	8	10

a. See Appendix, Table 66.

b. See Appendix, Tables 66 and 68.

c. *Industrial Sales, Output and Productivity, Prewar Area of Germany 1949–1944*, United States Strategic Bombing Survey. Includes estimated value of construction for the armed forces.

d. 1940–1942, *Rise and Fall of German War Economy 1939–1945*, Wagenfueher; 1939 extrapolation based on data contained in *Industrial Sales, Output and Productivity*.

e. *The Gross National Product of Germany, 1936–1944*, United States Strategic Bombing Survey.

f. Residual.

g. From data compiled of the Machine Report Unit of the Speer Ministry.

shows, such expenditures are estimated to have increased from 11 to 46 billion RM, accounting in 1942 for about a half of total war expenditures, as defined in the German budget. Unfortunately, budget data showing in detail the uses of these funds are not available. On the basis of such information as can be pieced together, however, we can obtain an approximate idea of how the nonmilitary portion of the war budget was used. In the first place, it appears that some of the projects included in "war expenditures" were essentially peacetime public works projects, and that such activities continued in rather substantial volume until 1943. For example, highway construction and the construction of public buildings is reported to have declined only moderately prior to 1943.[24] As will be indicated in Chapter VIII, interference of the war effort with Nazi social aims was kept at a minimum prior to Stalingrad.

Second, and related, the general administrative expenses of the government during this period — indeed, throughout the war — were extremely large. According to the estimates collected by the Bombing Survey, total administrative payrolls of German civilians averaged some 12 to 13 billion RM annually during the period 1939 through 1944.[25] Of the total volume of war expenditures (which averaged 25 billion RM annually, 1939–1942) not directly associated with paying and equipping the armed forces, probably almost half represented administrative payrolls. During the years 1941 and 1942, administrative payrolls amounted to about 8.5 per cent of the output available to Germany, and nearly 10 per cent of the output of goods and services produced in Germany. By contrast, during the years 1943 and 1944, government civilian payrolls in the United States accounted for only about 6 per cent of the nation's total output.[26] Part of the huge cost of administration in Germany, of course, was associated with the occupation of the conquered countries.

Third, it appears that a considerable part of the output taken from other nations did not contribute directly or indirectly to the output of military goods, i.e., was not taken out of the occupied countries.

During the period 1940–1942, total government expenditures in the occupied areas amounted to around 44 billion RM in 1939 prices, accounting for approximately one fifth of total war expenditures, and about 45 per cent of the "Other war expenditures" shown in Table 26. These government expenditures measure practically all of the estimated net economic contribution of other countries.

The proportion of the 44 billion RM total which went directly for the equipping of the armed forces was very modest; through the year 1942, Wehrmacht industrial purchases in the occupied areas totalled

24. United States Strategic Bombing Survey interrogation of Walter Fey, construction statistician, Planning Board, Ministry for Armaments and War Productions.

25. *The Gross National Product of Germany, 1936–1944.*

26. 1951 National Income Supplement, Department of Commerce, appendix tables I and II.

only about 7 billion RM, or less than 15 per cent. Purchases of combat munitions amounted to only 4 billions.

Part of the contribution of the occupied areas went for the building of fortifications and other military installations. The total cost of these projects can be only very crudely estimated. The Organization Todt, which was responsible for their construction, in 1943 employed about 900,000 workers in the occupied areas and in Italy.[27] The associated volume of construction might have been around 3 billion RM, at an annual rate, if the foreign construction workers were as productive as German workers.[28] Considering that the productivity of foreign workers was in general lower than German workers, and that construction employment outside of Germany was supposed to have reached its peak in 1943, it appears improbable that German-sponsored construction could have totalled over 5 billion RM during the period 1940–1942.

Not counting the feeding or housing of German troops, we may put total "military aid" (military goods and military construction) supplied by the occupied countries at not more than 12 billion RM, or a quarter of the total estimated contribution of the occupied areas.

The total net amount of goods actually taken out of the occupied nations, apart from goods and services supplied directly to the Wehrmacht, appears to have been relatively small. From 1940 to 1942, the clearing balance, which was used mainly to finance the excess of German imports over exports and to pay foreign governments for the services of laborers conscripted for work in Germany, increased only by some 6 or 7 billion RM.[29] Of this sum, about 2 billion was used to finance the import surplus.[30] In total this "economic aid" accounted for less than 15 per cent of the total foreign contribution, and it increased output available to Germany by only around 2.5 per cent annually.

"Military and economic aid," as defined, together amounted to around 15 to 20 billion RM during the period under review, or two

27. *Effects of Strategic Bombing,* p. 58.

28. For total volume of work, see *Effects of Strategic Bombing,* p. 55; for employment, *Effects of Strategic Bombing,* appendix table 45.

29. Memorandum on Foreign Contributions, Research Office for Military Economy.

30. Memorandum on Foreign Contributions; and Report of Central Statistical Office, *Deutschland: Der Aussenhandel nach Ländern 1936– Juli 1944.*

fifths of the total net contribution of the occupied areas. The remaining portion, it must be assumed, went mainly for the maintenance of the occupying forces and for general administrative expenses connected with the occupation. According to some reports, the
operation of the central governments in the occupied areas was substantially financed through occupation funds.[31]

France's total net contribution during this period amounted to
approximately 22 billion RM — 45 per cent of the total contribution
of the occupied countries. Wehrmacht industrial purchases amounted
to around 3 billion RM, and another 3 billion was used to finance the
import balance and labor services. Including a generous allowance
for military construction in France, it does not appear that she supplied more than two fifths of her total contribution in the forms of
"military and economic aid." A substantial amount appears to have
gone for the operation of the French government, i.e., represented
an internal transfer.

The contributions of all the occupied countries for the entire war
period amounted to about 78 million RM.[32] Of this sum, approximately 35 billion was supplied by France; 12 billion by the Netherlands; 9 billion by Belgium; and 7 billion by the Eastern Occupied
Areas.[33] France, Belgium and the Netherlands together supplied almost three quarters of the total contribution.

Total deliveries of industrially produced goods to the armed forces
amounted to 12 billion RM, of which 6.5 billions was munitions.[34]
Approximately 13 billion RM went for the financing of the export
surplus of the occupied countries and for payment for foreign labor
services.[35] Germany's excess of imports over exports from the occupied countries totalled 5 billion RM, while value of German exports
to all other countries exceeded imports by about 3 billion RM.[36]
Sweden, Rumania and Italy received a considerably larger volume
of goods from Germany than they supplied to her.[37]

31. USSBS interrogation of Professor Hettlage, financial advisor to Ministry
for Armaments and War Production.
32. Memorandum on Foreign Contributions.
33. Memorandum on Foreign Contributions.
34. Data compiled by Machine Report Unit, Ministry of Armaments and
War Production.
35. Memorandum on Foreign Contributions.
36. *Deutschland: Der Aussenhandel nach Ländern, 1936–Juli 1944.*
37. *Deutschland . . . 1936–1944.*

Including the total cost of military and related construction, estimated at about 8 billion RM, total "military and economic aid" comes to 33 billion RM for the whole war period. It amounted to just over two fifths of the total net contribution of the areas outside of Germany's 1939 boundaries. Excluding the payments out of occupation funds for foreign laborers conscripted for work in Germany, "military and economic aid" totals about 25 billion RM, or 3.5 per cent of the German national product during the period of the occupation. On the other hand, approximately 45 billion RM of the total net contribution was not taken out of the occupied areas.

These estimates do not pretend to provide any definitive answer as to what Germany really got out of the occupation; they only suggest that a substantial portion of the total transfer did not contribute very much to Germany's economic war effort. In several important respects they understate the economic value of the occupation. In the first place, only part of the value of the services of foreign labor is taken into account. Secondly, the approach leaves out of account the acquisition of particular resources which were in extremely short supply in Germany, including alloys, bauxite, and petroleum.[38]

In other respects, contribution of the occupied areas, even when measured in terms of "military and economic aid," may be considerably overstated. While military necessity undoubtedly would have required the maintenance of substantial occupation forces, it also appears that economic exploitation was in itself quite an expensive undertaking. As of June 22, 1951, the number of troops engaged in the occupation totalled around 1 million.[39] Documentary evidence suggests frequent difficulties in keeping the plants in the occupied areas in operation, and the delivery of the goods on schedule. These problems were generally solved by increasing the number of German civilian and military "supervisory" personnel, and this constituted a real drain on Germany, for throughout the war military manpower was undoubtedly her scarcest resource. Thus for Germany the occupation was not a highly profitable enterprise.

38. Germany's wartime raw material situation is discussed in Chapter V.
39. *Panzer Leader,* General Heinz Guderian, London, 1952, pp. 150 and 151.

3. MUNITIONS PRODUCTION IN THE UNITED KINGDOM
AND IN GERMANY

The low level of German munition output during the period 1939–1942 is strikingly shown by a comparison of her output with Britain's. Before turning to such a comparison it is useful to indicate the approximate difference between the size of the two economies.

Prior to the war, according to Colin Clark's estimates, Britain's total national output was about 70 per cent of Germany's.[40] Civilian employment in Britain was about 60 per cent of the number employed in Germany; real output per worker was 15–20 per cent greater.[41] The difference in over-all productivity was probably mainly associated with the higher industrial concentration of the British labor force. Available data indicate that there was no major difference in productivity in industry between the two countries.[42] Britain's industrial employment was about 70 per cent of Germany's.[43] The same ratio is found in comparing employment in the metal and chemical industries (the munitions industries) and the steel output of the two nations.[44] The relative economic potentials of Germany and Britain, therefore, and Germany's earlier start in munitions output might be expected to indicate a considerably larger volume of munitions output in Germany.

The relative increase in total available output between 1938 and 1942 and the contraction in home consumption and investment was about the same in both nations. The increase in total output available to Britain, after allowance for lend lease, was about two-fifths per cent or about the same as Germany's[45] increase in total domestic output and external contributions. In both nations, the level of domestic consumption and investment declined almost 25 per cent (measured in constant prices). Britain's 1942 government expendi-

40. *Conditions of Economic Progress*, pp. 63, 101.
41. *Conditions of Economic Progress*, pp. 63, 101.
42. L. Rostas, "Industrial Production, Productivity and Labor Distribution in Britain, Germany and the United States, 1935–1937," *Economic Journal*, Vol. XIII (April 1943).
43. *Effects of Strategic Bombing*, p. 202; and *Statistics Relating to the War Effort of the United Kingdom*, Cmd. 6564, His Majesty's Printing Office, 1944.
44. *Statistics Relating to the War Effort of the United Kingdom*.
45. *National Income and Expenditure of the United Kingdom, 1939 to 1946*; and (for deflators) *London Economist*, April 13, 1946, and May 5, 1946.

tures (including lend lease) represented, as did Germany's, more than half of her total available output.[46]

We now compare the munitions output in the two nations. The estimates of total munitions production for the United Kingdom are those compiled by the Planning Division of the War Production Board, after some fairly minor adjustments to make the items included in it and the German series approximately comparable.[47] Included in munitions production are tanks, trucks, and other armed forces vehicles, aircraft, naval vessels, weapons, and ammunition. It was not possible to adjust for some types of communications equipment not included in the German figures. It appears unlikely, however, that this source of error understated the German total relative to the British total by more than 5–10 per cent annually. The factor used for converting the British pound figures to marks was based on several independent estimates — which were in close agreement — of the relative prices of industrial products in the two countries.[48]

Table 27. Munitions production in Germany and the United Kingdom

	Index numbers (1939 = 100)		Billions of marks	
	Germany	U. K.	Germany	U. K.
1939	100	100	8.3	2.9
1940	145	335	12.0	10.9
1941	146	489	12.1	16.0
1942	193	760	16.0	24.8

Sources: See Table 26 for the German estimates. The U. K. estimates were obtained from "World Munitions Production, 1938–1944," Planning Division, War Production Board, July 15, 1944 (the study has been declassified). For the purpose of comparing absolute levels of output, a conversion factor of 1:14 was used. Approximately the same ratio was used in the Planning Board's study. In his comparison of industrial output in Britain and Germany, Rostas used a ratio of 1:17:08 ("Industrial Production, Productivity and Labor Distribution in Britain, Germany, and the United States," *Economic Journal*, 1943). Correcting this for price changes from 1935–1939 indicates a ratio of about 1:15. For a similar comparison, an unpublished study of the German Planning Board also used a ratio of 1:14.

46. *London Economist*, April 13, 1946, and May 5, 1946; and Table 26.
47. *World Munitions Production, 1938–1944*, Planning Division, War Production Board, July 15, 1944.
48. See Table 27, *Sources*.

In Britain, as Table 27 shows, total munitions output increased six and one-half times between 1939 and 1942, representing in 1942 one quarter of Britain's total gross national product. During the same period in Germany, however, munitions output hardly doubled, and as a proportion of total output reached only 11 per cent in 1942.

Even more surprising is the relationship between their absolute levels of output. Table 27 shows that Britain's munitions production was much below Germany's in 1939, but the tremendous acceleration in her munitions output between 1939 and 1940 almost closed the gap. Monthly or quarterly munitions production data for this period are not available, but the trends in their respective outputs make it not unlikely that during 1940, and probably not long after Dunkirk, the British were outproducing the Germans. In the following two years, the British margin over German munitions output became very substantial; in 1941 it was a third, and in 1942, a half.

Although this comparison is subject to a considerable margin of error, the general impression given is confirmed by an examination of each country's output of specific types of military production. It is impossible to take quality differences in individual types into account, but it is unlikely that they could substantially change the general tenor of the comparisons. The British and German annual production data for a number of important classes of munitions are shown in Table 28.

In terms of the quantity of resources directed into their production, aircraft were the single most important type of munitions in both Germany and Britain. From 1939 until 1942, about 35 per cent of total munitions expenditures of each went for the procurement of aircraft.[49] As Table 28 shows, Britain led Germany in total aircraft production by 40 per cent in 1940, by 70 per cent in 1941, and by 50 per cent in 1942. This comparison exaggerates Britain's lead over Germany because it does not take into account the larger percentage of heavier types of aircraft produced in Germany. Even in terms of weight of aircraft produced, however, Britain outproduced the Germans by 30 per cent over the three-year period.

Since Germany's strategy depended much more heavily on large

49. "World Munitions Production" and "Index of German War Production," Planning Board, Ministry of Armaments and War Production, June 1941.

Table 28. Output of particular types of armaments in Germany
and the United Kingdom, 1940–1942

	1940 Germany	1940 U. K.	1941 Germany	1941 U. K.	1942 Germany	1942 U. K.
Military aircraft	10825	15050	10775	20100	15550	23670
Bombers	4000	3720	4350	4670	6540	6250
Fighters	3105	4280	3730	7065	5215	9850
Others[a]	3720	7050	2695	8365	3795	7570
Armored vehicles						
tank	1640	1400	3790	4845	6180	8610
Other[b]	500	6000	1300	10500	3100	19300
Trucks (1000's)	88	113	86	110	81	109
Weapons:						
Artillery (20 mm. and over)	d	4700	11200	16700	23200	43000
Small arms (1000's)						
Infantry rifles	1350	80	1360	78	1370	594
Infantry machine guns	170	30	320	46	320	1510
Ammunition: (million rounds)[c]						
Heavy (75 mm or over)	27	7	27	14	57	25
Light (20–75 mm)	d	3	8	9	42	25
Small arms (under 20 mm)	2950	540	1340	1120	1340	2190
Naval armaments:						
Heavy guns (75 mm and over)	d	620	300	740	1020	1060
Light guns (20–75 mm)	d	860	380	1730	1070	2740
Torpedoes	d	940	14200	1900	11000	3900

Source: *Statistische Schnellberichte zur Rüstungsproduktion*, February 1945. Survey of Armaments Production, Ministry of Armaments and War Production, January, 1945. Statistics Relating to the War Effort of the United Kingdom; Effects of Strategic Bombing on the German War Economy.

a. Includes naval, reconnaissance, transport and other.

b. Includes armored cars, armored half-trucks, armored infantry and gun carriers.

c. Excludes naval ammunition.

d. Data not available.

ground armies than Britain's, it is to be expected that with reference to ground force munitions, at least, she outproduced Britain. In the period 1939–1942, nearly 60 per cent of her munitions expenditures went into the production of tanks, armored vehicles, trucks, weapons and ammunition, compared with about 35 per cent for Britain.[50] It is true that in weapons and ammunition — with the exception of artillery — German output greatly exceeded Britain's. On the other hand, in the production of tanks and other armored vehicles, weapons which were supposedly the key to German blitzkrieg successes, and in the production of trucks the British were substantially ahead of the Germans. During the three years, 1940, 1941, and 1942, the British produced nearly 30 per cent more tanks than the Germans. In terms of tank weight Britain's margin was smaller, but the data for such a comparison are not available. In the same period British armored vehicle production was seven times that of Germany. Britain's lead in truck production was more modest; about 30 per cent in each of the years.

Because data for the total tonnage of German naval ships completed during this period are not available, it is not possible to make an exact comparison with the British data. But on the basis of the official German data for the numbers of various types of vessels built, and some data on their standard displacement weights, we were able to make rough estimates of the total tonnage of naval vessels completed.[51] A comparison of these with the more exact British data shows that in the three years, 1940, 1941, and 1942, the British completed about twice as much tonnage as the Germans.[52] In 1942, naval vessels and equipment represented about one quarter of total U. K. munitions output.[53]

Because of her greater reliance on large ground armies, a larger proportion of the German effort, of course, had to be devoted to non-munitions items, e.g., food and clothing for the troops. But the general conclusions suggested by comparing the relative increases and absolute levels of munitions output are not substantially altered by considering a wider range of war production. Table 26 shows that total sales of German industry increased no more percentagewise in the period 1939–1942 than did munitions output alone. The propor-

---

50. "World Munitions Production" and "Index of German War Production," Planning Board, Ministry of Armaments and War Production, June 1941.

51. *Statistische Schnellberichte zur Kriegsproduktion,* Planungsamt, Speer Ministry, for number of vessels completed. Minutes of Meetings of Zentrale Planung, April 1942, for average weights.

52. *Statistics Relating to the War Effort of the United Kingdom.*

53. *World Munitions Production,* War Production Board, July 15, 1944.

tion of the German national output represented by industrial armed forces purchases averaged only about 16 per cent, and was only slightly above the proportion in Britain taken by munitions alone. In 1942 the munitions share alone of the British gross national product was larger than the share accounted for by total Werhmacht purchases in Germany.

For the year 1942, we can compare British and German armed forces' expenditures on all types of home production except for the item of food. During this year, approximately 2550 thousand pounds were spent by the British forces on nonagricultural products produced in the United Kingdom.[54] The corresponding figure for Germany was 28 billion marks.[55] In Britain these expenditures amounted to 55 per cent of government outlays and 35 per cent of gross national product. The percentages for Germany were 30 and 20 respectively. Valued in marks, the total for Britain was more than 25 per cent above Germany's. As we might expect, this was less than Britain's lead in munitions production alone, but nevertheless, with the resources available to Germany, we should have expected to find their relative positions in war production reversed.

4. A COMPARISON OF GERMAN MUNITIONS PRODUCTION WITH INTELLIGENCE ESTIMATES

In comparison with munitions output in Britain, a country with a substantially smaller economic potential than Germany, Germany's production was surprisingly small. The contrast is even greater in comparing the German record with intelligence estimates — which were essentially estimates of Germany's economic capabilities.

A comparison of the intelligence estimates prepared by the Ministry of Economic Warfare with actual output for the period 1939–1942 is shown in Table 29. During the first three years of the war, the estimates ran 50 to 100 per cent above actual output. In 1942, a sharp rise in German munitions output brought actual production within range of the estimates. Tank production appears to be the only munitions item which the Ministry of Economic Warfare underestimated, and this was true only after 1940.

For their comparisons of Axis and Allied production strength the

54. *World Munitions Production,* War Production Board, July 15, 1944.
55. See Table 26.

Table 29. Comparison of the estimates of the ministry of economic warfare
with actual German production of various types of war goods
(estimates as a percentage of actual)

	1939	1940	1941	1942
Fighter aircraft	180	155	145	130
Bombers	200	145	150	115
Tanks	225	140	90	95
Oil	a	210	145	165
Artillery	a	125	145	135

Sources: *Effects of Strategic Bombing on the German War Economy* and *An Appraisal of Pre- and Post-Raid Intelligence*, U. S. Strategic Bombing Survey.
a. Data not available.

Planning Division of the United States War Production Board estimated the total munitions output of the principal belligerents. Their estimates of German munitions expenditures which were derived from estimates of government expenditures, and the actual data are shown in Table 30. As the table shows, the estimates substantially overstated both the rise and the level of actual munitions expenditures. From 1939 to 1942, they overstated the average level of expenditures by more than 100 per cent and the rise in expenditures by nearly 100 per cent.

The Planning Board's figures showed that in 1941 munitions production in the United States was about a half that of Germany's.[56] Actually, during this year it was about three quarters as large as

Table 30. German munitions expenditures
(billions of marks)

	War Production Board estimate	Actual
1939	14.2	8.3
1940	23.6	12.0
1941	27.9	12.1
1942	39.8	16.0

Source: World Munitions Production, 1938–1944; War Production Board; and Table 27.

56. Table 26, and Raymond W. Goldsmith, "The Power of Victory — Munitions Output in World War II," *Military Affairs*, Vol. X, No. 1, Spring, 1946.

Germany's, and in 1942, the first year of American participation in the war, $2\frac{1}{2}$ times the German level.

5. POSSIBLE EXPLANATIONS FOR THE LOW LEVEL
OF MILITARY OUTPUT

In the first four years of the war, Germany's output of munitions was small compared with her total national output, with munitions production in Britain, or with the output ascribed to her by Allied intelligence. Military output was also small during this period, according to one German statistician, in comparison with Germany's military production record of World War I.[57]

What are the various factors which could have imposed such a low limit on German munitions output? First, there is the possibility of a shortage of particular types of resources, e.g., specialized labor, certain raw materials, or plant capacity. A second explanation might be Nazi inefficiency in the conduct of the war production program. Finally, if not limited by such factors, the explanation might be simply that the German leaders did not think that a larger effort was required. Each of these hypotheses will be examined in the following two chapters.

57. Rolf Wagenfuehr, *The Rise and Fall of the German War Economy*, p. 2.

V *A Resources Limitation?*

Although Germany's general resource position would have supported a much higher volume of military production, there is the possibility that her effort was limited by a series of specific shortages. Based on the experience of this country and that of Britain, we might expect to find these shortages crop up first in industrial capacity, then in raw materials, and finally in manpower, which is undoubtedly the ultimate limiting factor on a nation's war effort. We shall now briefly examine the situation with respect to each of these possibilities.

INDUSTRIAL CAPACITY

The volume of construction and of machinery production as well as of total employment in these industries, for the period 1939–1942, is shown in Table 31.[1] The volume of construction fell sharply throughout the period, in 1942 reaching about 40 per cent of the 1939 level, while machinery production, on the other hand, increased steadily. Approximately the same relationship holds for employment in the two industries. These divergent movements are indicative of the changing nature of investment during this period, of an increasing concentration on the building and equipping of war factories.

The composition of Germany's wartime investment cannot be described precisely since the Germans themselves did not make de-

1. Unlike the capital formation series presented in the last chapter, these data include public as well as private capital goods, and refer to the current changing boundaries of Greater Germany rather than to a single geographic area.

Table 31. Net value of output and employment in the construction
and machinery industries
(billions of marks, thousands of employees)

	Volume of construction[a]	Employment	Volume of machinery output[a]	Employment
1939	12.8	2,530	6.3	867
1940	8.3	1,721	7.6	935
1941	6.9	2,012	8.8	1,045
1942	4.7	1,445	10.1	1,100

Sources: *Die deutsche Industrie*, a report prepared by the Planungsamt in 1944; data prepared by Wirtschaftsgruppe Machinenbau; and Kriegswirtschaftliche Kraftebilanz for 1939, 1940, 1941, and 1942.

a. In 1939 prices.

tailed estimates for the years after 1939. However, on the basis of scattered information, it is possible to indicate the changes in the several main components. There was, in the first place, a substantial, though an uneven, curtailment of nonwar types of construction. Private residential construction fell by 50 per cent during 1940, and by 1942 was down to 25 per cent of the 1939 volume.[2] Nonindustrial business construction fell less during the early war years, but was practically eliminated in 1942.[3] Until 1942, the curtailment of public nonwar construction was more gradual than that of private. In 1940 and 1941, a large number of public and Nazi party buildings were still under construction, and highway building was still an important component of total construction, possibly 20 per cent.[4] It was not until 1942 that Speer, Minister of Armaments and War Production, was able to persuade Hitler to stop unnecessary public construction.[5]

By 1942, with the sizable curtailment of these types of expenditures, the building of military and industrial facilities remained the major portion, about 80 per cent, of total public and private investment.[6] During this year, the volume of investment in factories, the

2. *Effects of Strategic Bombing,* Appendix Table 39, p. 231.

3. *Wochenbericht des Planungsamtes,* No. 33, Ministry for Armaments and War Production.

4. *Wochenbericht des Planungsamtes,* No. 33, Ministry for Armaments and War Production.

5. "Transcript of Fuehrer's Conferences," October, 1942.

6. Memorandum on investment outlays, prepared in Planungsamt, March 1944.

power industry, and the railroads was more than 4 billion marks, about the same as in 1939.[7] Investment was notably large in aircraft, oil, and electric steel facilities.

Was productive capacity a limiting factor on armaments output during this period? With regard to factory space, there is no indication that this was a bottleneck in the war production program. The United States Strategic Bombing Survey interrogated a number of German officials on the importance of plant space as a limitational factor in armaments output, and agreement was practically unanimous that until 1944, at least, there was no problem of a shortage of buildings.[8]

A major part of the explanation for this is to be found in the enormous capacity of the German construction industry, an industry which had expanded greatly during the prewar years, and whose output in 1939 amounted to more than 10 per cent of the gross national product.[9] The substantial curtailment of construction activity during the war years was due almost entirely to a shrinkage of demand; capacity far exceeded requirements placed on the industry. The construction labor force at the beginning of the war was much larger than could be used in later years. Nor is there any indication of a shortage of building materials. The prewar capacity for producing these materials was much above wartime needs. The only item which could have presented a problem was steel, which we shall discuss later.

Another reason why the factory space problem could be easily solved was that many types of armaments production did not require specially designed structures. This was particularly true with regard to aircraft assembly, where all that was needed was protection from the weather. As far as the structures themselves were concerned, conversion from civilian to armaments production in many cases could be made easily.

If Germany was faced with a capacity problem, we should expect to find it in machinery and not in industrial structures. During the first years of their respective war efforts, the United States and Britain were faced with very serious machinery and machine tool

7. Memorandum on investment outlays, prepared in Planungsamt, March 1944.
8. *Effects of Strategic Bombing,* chapter V.
9. See Table 31.

problems. In striking contrast, however, there is no evidence that a shortage of machinery or machine tools ever presented a serious problem in Germany.

With notable exceptions in electric power, oil and electric steel, German industry was generally characterized by excess capacity. The Ministry of Armaments and War Production estimated that in the spring of 1942, outside of the basic industries (where multishift operations are prescribed by technical conditions), 90 per cent of all industrial workers worked on the first shift, 7 per cent on the second, and 3 per cent on the third.[10] This means that with an average working day of about 8 hours (see Table 41) excess capacity in industry as a whole amounted to around 50 per cent. Even in armaments plants, such as small arms and artillery, only 10 per cent of the employees worked on a second shift, and a negligible fraction on a third.[11] In the aero-engine industry, where a serious capacity problem existed according to German officials, 25 per cent of the employees were engaged on a second shift and 10 per cent on a third.[12] The machine tool industry worked 10.2 per cent of its employees on a second shift, and practically none on a third.[13]

What was the machine tool situation? If machine tools were really short, we should expect to find greater and greater degree of utilization of the machine tool stock as the war progressed, i.e., an increasing number of employees per machine tool. The data, however, show no evidence of this. In Table 32 the annual machine tool inventory has been divided by the total number of employees in the industries using machine tools to give the annual ratio of workers per machine tool. The ratio is nearly constant for the years 1940, 1941, and 1942. Nor can it be argued that machine tools were highly utilized throughout the period. Using Britain as a basis of comparison, we find that in this period the average German worker was provided with twice as many machine tools as the average British worker.[14]

The major reason for Germany's lack of general machinery or machine tool shortage is to be found in the large capacity of her machine-producing industries. One indication of this is the sizable

10. According to a calculation of the Technical Office of the Speer Ministry.
11. *Effects of Strategic Bombing*, p. 43.
12. *Effects of Strategic Bombing*, p. 43.
13. *Effects of Strategic Bombing*, p. 43.
14. *Effects of Strategic Bombing*, p. 44.

Table 32. Employees per machine tool
in the industries using tools

July 1939	2.44
July 1940	2.26
July 1941	2.29
November 1942	2.32

Source: Calculated from data prepared
by the *Wirtschaftsgruppe Maschinenbau*,
and employment figures in *Beschäftigung
der Industrie* compiled by the *Statistisches
Reichsamt*.

volume of machinery exports. In the year 1938 the exports of this industry amounted to 750 million RM, 17 per cent of the industries total output, and 14 per cent of Germany's total value of exports for this year.[15] During the war years exports declined, but even as late as 1942, 10 per cent of the total volume of domestic machinery and machine tool production was exported.[16] Another indication of ample capacity is the fact that during the war a large part of the industry could be directly converted to munitions production. In 1942, nearly 30 per cent of the total production of machinery, heating-equipment, and railroad-equipment industries was munitions items.[17] Finally, the capacity of the machinery-producing industries was not fully utilized. In the machine tool industry (the only part of the machinery industry for which the data are available) only 10 per cent of the workers were employed on a second shift.[18]

To the extent that Germany used special-purpose machine tools, some temporary bottlenecks were inevitable whenever armament designs were appreciably changed. Such tools, as a rule, could be used only for a single type of operation and were outmoded whenever finished commodities were redesigned. Interrogations of German officials and transcripts of the meetings of the Central Planning Board indicate a dozen or so cases when armaments production was significantly slowed up for this reason. But unlike the United States, a major machine tool problem did not arise because special-purpose

15. From data prepared by *Wirtschaftsgruppe Maschinenbau*.
16. From data prepared by *Wirtschaftsgruppe Maschinenbau*.
17. *Effects of Strategic Bombing*, p. 48.
18. *Effects of Strategic Bombing*, p. 42.

machine tools were not widely used in Germany. In the years 1939–1942, when their production was pushed in order to reduce the need for skilled labor, special-purpose machine tools constituted only 5 to 8 per cent of total machine tool production.[19]

The major problem which the German authorities faced with regard to their machinery and construction industries was not to increase output but to restrict it. There was a constant and strong tendency to produce capital goods not necessary for war. The insatiable demand was due partly to a tax system which favored the ploughing back of earnings and partly to the industrialists' concern over inflation, which provided a powerful incentive to convert assets into real forms.[20] This, incidentally, was another manifestation of the fear of inflation which had so greatly hindered the Nazi rearmament in the prewar era.

In order to eliminate unnecessary orders, a system for screening machine tool orders was established in 1940, and in 1942 it was extended to machinery in general. The controls were not very successful, however; production of practically every individual category of machinery remained at a high level through 1943.[21] To some extent this was due to the fact that the firms themselves initially determined their needs for machine tools, and also to the fact that the screening process was very poorly administered. For example, machinery orders were frequently based on unrealistic war production plans, and when these were scaled down, there was no provision for reexamining the original orders. It also might be noted that the agency responsible for the screening process, the Economic Group for Machinery, was not entirely unsympathetic to the machinery industry or to its customers. The head of this organization, Karl Lange, had been for many years director of the machinery trade association.

Dr. Todt, appointed General Plenipotentiary for the construction industry in 1938, believed that during the years 1939, 1940, and 1941 both war and nonwar construction activity were much above Germany's needs. His advice to Hitler in 1940, in sharp opposition to the demands of the armed forces and the industrialists, that Germany

19. From data prepared by *Wirtschaftsgruppe Maschinenbau.*

20. From a report on German War Finance prepared by Hettlage, Financial Advisor to the Speer Ministry.

21. Detailed machinery production data prepared by *Wirtschaftsgruppe Maschinenbau.*

needed no new capacity to carry out an expansion of armaments production, won him the post of Minister of Weapons and Munitions Production. How much larger construction activity would have been were it not for Todt's efforts, we do not know. It should be noted, however, that industrial construction was maintained at the 1939 level through 1940 and 1941, and that public nonwar construction was still being carried on during these years on a sizable scale.

Germany had no serious problem of a shortage of either factory space or industrial equipment. To the extent that there was a capacity problem, it was a problem of restricting the output of the construction and machinery industries. This is not to deny that instances of shortages of particular types of equipment can be found. But such cases could hardly provide more than an insignificant part of the explanation for Germany's small war output during the first three years of the war.

RAW MATERIALS

What is the possibility that the supply of raw materials was the critical factor. In view of the weaknesses in Germany's raw material base at the beginning of the war, this possibility requires serious consideration. No attempt will be made to give a comprehensive picture of Germany's raw material situation during this period. Our only interest is to see if one or more raw materials could have been the limiting factor in war output. Accordingly, materials like textiles, agricultural raw materials, or oil which could have only remotely affected munitions output will not be included in the discussion.

1. MATERIALS WITH WHICH GERMANY WAS WELL SUPPLIED

A. *Chemicals*

While the production of nitrogen, the chief wartime chemical, did not increase very much during the war,[22] during the period 1939–1942 there was no question of a shortage for war uses. This was because military consumption amounted to less than 10 per cent of

---

22. Average monthly output rose from 76 thousand tons in 1939 to 80 million tons in 1942. *Statistische Schnellberichte zur Kriegsproduktion*. Planungsamt, Ministry for Armaments and War Production.

total consumption during these years. The bulk of Germany's nitrogen was used for fertilizers. Output of the other principal chemicals — methanol, carbide, soda, chlorine and sulphuric acid — did not come up to the production plans made before and during the war.[23] There is no evidence, however, that war production was retarded in the period before 1943 because of a shortage of any chemical product.

B. *Rubber*

A delay in the completion of the synthetic rubber program inaugurated before the war resulted in a temporary shortage during 1940. With natural rubber imports at about one fifth of the prewar level, total rubber supplies dropped 40 per cent below the 1939 amount, necessitating a depletion of stocks and conservation measures.[24] During the year, however, a large plant at Schkopau came into operation, and in 1941 synthetic production, totaling 69,000 tons, plus natural rubber imports equalled the prewar annual rate of consumption.[25] In 1942, Germany was able to begin exporting rubber to the Continental countries.[26] With the exception of the brief period at the beginning of the war, there is no evidence that Germany was short of rubber for military or other essential uses.

C. *Aluminum and Zinc*

In the capacity of its aluminum refining industry, Germany was very favorably situated, being, in 1939, the world's largest producer.[27] It is true that her own ore resources were insignificant, but Continental sources proved ample. During the first year of the war, supplies from Yugoslavia, Italy, Hungary, and Greece matched total prewar imports, and after 1940, with the acquisition of the large French output, total supplies increased considerably.[28] The large capacity and abundant ore supplies permitted a tremendous increase in aluminum ingot production during the war. Between 1939 and 1942, production rose by nearly 50 per cent.[29] This was sufficient not only to satisfy uses in which aluminum was practically indispensable,

---

23. *Statistische Schnellberichte zur Kriegsproduktion,* Planungsamt.
24. *Effects of Strategic Bombing,* p. 84.
25. *Effects of Strategic Bombing,* p. 84.
26. *Effects of Strategic Bombing,* p. 84.
27. *Statistische Jahrbuch,* 1941/1942, p. 79*.
28. *Monatliche Rohstoffübersichten,* Statistisches Reichsamt, Abtg. VIII.
29. *Statistische Schnellberichte zur Kriegsproduktion,* Planungsamt.

i.e., aircraft, but also to allow aluminum to be substituted for other metals, especially copper. Aluminum consumption rose from 180 thousand tons in 1939, which was high even by comparison with United States consumption, to 290 thousand tons in 1941, and 385 thousand tons in 1943.[30]

Domestic output of zinc and imports from Spain, Sweden, Italy, and the Balkans proved ample for requirements. Supplies in 1942 were 40 per cent above the 1939 rate and metal stocks were substantially larger than when the war began.[31] All annual reports from 1940 through 1944 of the Referate for Metals list zinc in the "abundant" category.

2. MATERIALS WITH WHICH GERMANY WAS NOT WELL SUPPLIED

If the 1939–1942 record of munitions production is to be explained by a lack of raw materials, the bottlenecks might be expected to occur in steel, ferroalloys, other metals, or in coal. We shall consider first Germany's position in the metals copper, lead, and tin, and then Germany's most important raw material problem, steel and ferroalloys. Coal will be brought into this discussion.

A. *Copper, Lead, and Tin*

The German experience with copper shows most clearly how well a nation can manage in wartime with very limited supplies of a "strategic" material. Despite all the indications that Germany's copper position would become very serious in a long war, and despite the fact that there was a substantial reduction in copper supplies during the war, there is no evidence that the production of armaments was ever seriously embarrassed by a shortage of copper. Hitler's conference with his economic advisers, the reports of various agencies charged with the direction of the war production, or interrogations of German officials contain very few references to copper. When copper was mentioned, it was to express satisfaction with the metallurgists' attempts to find substitutes, or to express surprise over the great success of a scrap drive.

The solution of the copper problem called for drastic measures on the side of both the supply and the demand. Since Germany's domes-

---

30. *Statistische Schnellberichte zur Kriegsproduktion,* Planungsamt.
31. *Statistische Schnellberichte zur Kriegsproduktion,* Planungsamt.

tic ore output could provide only about one tenth of her metal consumption, and since the principal prewar sources of imports were overseas, special means of obtaining supplies had to be found. Along with special efforts to maintain European ore and metal imports, the Germans seized stocks of metal in all forms from occupied countries and started an energetic salvage drive at home.[32] One lucrative source of copper was the French high-tension electric lines. France was divided into copper salvage districts, and the Germans went from district to district, removing copper lines. The French were permitted to replace them with steel lines when it was deemed necessary. The domestic salvage drive, which included among other things the collection of bells, provided for about 15 per cent of total supplies during the years 1941, 1942, and 1943.[33]

Consumption was reduced by substituting other metals for copper wherever possible. Steel in shell casings, and aluminum and zinc in electrical products, were the principal substitute materials. An extreme example of the success of substitution measures is to be found in the case of locomotives. At the beginning of the war the manufacture of a locomotive required 2.3 metric tons of copper — by 1943, the amount used had been reduced to 237 kilograms, or by 90 per cent.[34]

The success of these measures in improving Germany's copper stock position is shown by Table 33. As the table shows, total copper supplies fell about 30 per cent in 1939 and increased only slightly

Table 33. Copper supplies, consumption and stocks, 1938–1943[a]
(thousands of metric tons)

	1938	1939	1940	1941	1942	1943
Total supplies	460	312	318	329	344	314
Consumption	448	324	292	372	238	221
Stocks[b]	194	183	209	167	265	373

Source: *Statistische Schnellberichte zur Kriegsproduktion*, Planungsamt.
a. Includes scrap, reclaimed and captured stocks.
b. End of year.

32. Report of Referate for Metals, dated July 1944.
33. Report of Referate for Metals, July 1944.
34. Interrogation of Karl-Otto Saur, Head of the Technical Division of the Speer Ministry.

during the following years. Consumption of copper was reduced during every year of the war with the exception of 1941, when controls were relaxed. Especially impressive is the fact that in the years 1942 and 1943, when the index of war production was climbing rapidly, copper consumption was nearly one third below the 1939 rate. Economies in copper use permitted a sizable increase in metal stocks; from 1939 to 1943 they doubled. A report of the Referate for Metals, dated July 1943, stated that stocks and that part of current supplies considered "safe" were sufficient to cover requirements until 1948.

For lead and tin, the story was substantially the same: seizure of supplies in the occupied countries, scrap drives in Germany, and substitution of other metals whenever possible. As with copper, these methods were successful with the other important nonferrous metals; not only were requirements met but the stock position was improved during the course of the war.

American and British intelligence experts, basing their views on German prewar experience or on the wartime experience of their own countries, were unaware of what Germany could do by way of metal scrap drives or by economizing on the use of scarce metals. The British Ministry of Economic Warfare estimated that from the beginning of 1940 until the end of 1942, Germany's copper stocks had fallen from 200 to 75 thousand metric tons;[35] whereas actually they rose from 183 to 265 thousand metric tons. It was also supposed that Germany's stock position in lead and tin had steadily deteriorated during this period; the decline in lead stocks was put at 70 per cent, that of tin at 50 per cent.[36] The German data show that lead stocks remained about constant, and that tin stocks doubled between the beginning of 1940 and the end of 1942.[37]

B. *The Steel Situation*

A shortage of steel presented a real problem, and there was scarcely a meeting between Hitler and his economic advisers in which

---

35. United States Strategic Bombing Survey, *An Appraisal of Pre- and Post-Raid Intelligence,* p. 37.

36. *An Appraisal of Pre- and Post-Raid Intelligence,* pp. 38–39.

37. *An Appraisal of Pre- and Post-Naval Intelligence,* pp. 38–39.

the steel situation was not discussed.[38] Indeed, one gets the impression from the transcripts of these meetings, that, from the beginning of the war until 1943, a steel shortage dwarfed all other economic problems.

It is necessary, therefore, to examine the steel situation rather carefully, looking first at the problems the Germans encountered in attempting to increase steel output, and then at the efficiency of the allocation system; finally, we shall attempt to determine how short steel really was.

1. *Steel Production, 1939–1942.* As indicated in an earlier chapter, Germany's steel position on the eve of the war was not satisfactory. Steel capacity, it is true, was quite large. In 1939, Greater Germany, including Austria and Czechoslovakia, possessed an annual steel capacity of approximately 26 million tons of crude steel and 22 million tons of pig iron.[39] By comparison, British crude steel capacity was in that year about 15 million tons,[40] and Russian about 19 million tons.[41] But in steel input items, Germany was less fortunate; for the preponderant share of ferroalloys and iron ore, she had to depend on imports. In 1939, German mines could supply only about 30 per cent of the ore which would have been necessary to operate the steel plants at full capacity.[42] Nearly all of the ferroalloys had to be imported, and a substantial portion came from overseas countries.

---

38. Transcripts of the Fuehrer's Conferences, 1940, 1941 and 1942.

39. Estimated Steel Capacity, 1939 (millions of metric tons)

	Pig iron	Crude steel
Germany proper	19.5	22.5
Austria	0.8	0.7
Czechoslovakia	1.9	2.5
	22.2	25.7

Source: "Übersichten über die Eisenschaffende Industrie, 1939," a report prepared for the Hermann Goering Works.

40. Statistics relating to the War Effort of the United Kingdom, Cmd. 6564, His Majesty's Printing Office.

41. According to the German Statistical Yearbook, 1939–1942 edition, p. 75*, in 1939 Russian crude steel output was 18,796 metric tons.

42. Based on 1939 pig iron production, ore consumption, and domestic ore production.

The German leaders were well aware of this heavy dependence on foreign ore and ferroalloys. In fact, this was a major reason why they feared Germany's entanglement in a large-scale war.

The steel situation from the beginning of the war until after the fall of France indicated that such anxiety was warranted. From the middle of 1939, when plants were operating at capacity levels, to the Spring of 1940, the output of rolling mill products and crude steel production fell by nearly 20 per cent. Pig iron production was better maintained, but only by drawing down stocks of iron ore. The loss of steel output during this period was due partly to the closing down of plants in the Saar, because of their proximity to the front, but mostly to a lack of iron ore.

In 1940, with iron ore supplies from France, Belgium, Luxembourg, Spain, and overseas sources reduced to a mere trickle of the prewar amount, Germany's total iron ore imports dropped to 40 per cent. Practically all of them came from Sweden.[43] Table 34 shows

Table 34. Domestic output and imports of iron ore, iron content
(millions of metric tons)

	Domestic production[a]	Imports	Total supplies
1938	4.2	11.6	15.8
1939	4.7	10.0	14.7
1940	5.7	5.8	11.5
1941	5.5	14.4[b]	19.9
1942	4.8	14.0[b]	18.8

Source: "The Role of Foreign Ores in the German Iron Industry," a report prepared by Dr. Rohland, Head of the Main Committee for Iron Production, an agency under the Ministry for Armaments and War Production; *Statistische Schnellberichte zur Kriegsproduktion*, February 1945, Planungsamt.
a. Prewar area of Germany.
b. Includes output in areas annexed to Germany in 1940.

that total ore supplies in 1940, including domestic output which was at its wartime peak, were about 30 per cent below the prewar rate. Had the allies been able to cut off Swedish ore supplies, as was feared in Germany, the German steel industry could not have op-

43. Sweden supplied 85 per cent of Germany's iron ore imports during 1940.

erated at more than 50 per cent of capacity during 1940 without depleting ore and scrap stocks.[44]

In 1940, after the fall of France, Germany's steel situation was much improved. Occupation of France, Belgium, and Luxembourg gave Germany at least 16 million tons of additional steel capacity.[45] With a 26-million ton capacity in Germany proper, total capacity available to Germany amounted to around 42 million tons. Thirty million tons of this lay in Greater Germany, which included the annexed territories of Alsace-Lorraine and Luxembourg. The other 12 million tons were in the Occupied Areas of France, Belgium, and the Netherlands.

Much more important than additional steel capacity was Germany's direct acquisition of the Lorraine-Luxembourg-Minette iron ore deposits and a resumption of ore imports from the Occupied Areas of France and from Spain and North Africa. As Table 34 shows, with these sources of supply, Germany's total iron ore supplies increased from 11.5 million tons (in iron content) in 1940 to nearly 20 million tons in 1941.

As a result of her newly acquired steel capacity and ore supplies, Germany's steel output rose after 1940, but not by nearly as much as might be supposed. Table 35 shows the total amount of steel production at Germany's disposal, including output in the Occupied Areas, averaged about 31.5 million tons during 1941 and 1942. This represented only 6.5 million tons more output than Germany had at the beginning of the war, and was 10 million tons short of the total steel capacity of this area.

What prevented a fuller utilization of capacity in the period after 1940: a shortage of ore, of ferroalloys, or some other resource?

It may seem that ore was the critical factor since, even after the annexation of Alsace-Lorraine and Luxembourg and the resumption of ore imports from France, Spain, and North Africa, Germany's ore supplies were still only 20 per cent above the prewar amount and were less than the growth of steel output. This presumption, however, is contradicted by the fact that early in 1942 the less productive mines in Southern Germany were being closed down. The

44. D. Rohland, "The Role of Foreign Ores in the German Iron Industry." Files of United States Strategic Bombing Survey.
45. Estimates of *Reichsvereinigung Eisen*.

Table 35. Crude steel output in Greater Germany and the occupied areas,
1941 and 1942
(millions of tons)

	Greater Germany[a]	Occupied areas	Total
Total 1941	28.23	3.59	31.82
1st Quarter	6.89	0.92	7.81
2nd Quarter	7.12	0.90	8.02
3rd Quarter	7.13	0.88	8.01
4th Quarter	7.09	0.89	7.97
Total 1942	28.74	3.38	32.13
1st Quarter	6.42	0.75	7.17
2nd Quarter	6.85	0.81	7.66
3rd Quarter	7.42	0.86	8.28
4th Quarter	8.05	0.97	9.02

Source: *Reichsvereinigung Eisen*, and *Statistische Schnellberichte zur Kriegsproduktion*, February 1945.
a. Includes, in addition to the prewar area of Germany, the Protectorate Alsace-Lorraine, Luxembourg, and Upper Silesia.

total amount of ore mined in Germany proper during 1942 was about 10 per cent less than in 1941.[46] These facts confirm the opinion of German steel experts that the supply of ore was adequate and did not limit steel output.[47]

Germany's ferroalloy situation involved a heavy dependence on foreign sources for ores. It was the opinion of many experts both in Germany and abroad that the supply of these metals was one of the weakest spots in Germany's raw material position. The Foreign Economic Administration in the United States and the Ministry of Economic Warfare in Britain believed that preclusive buying of such metals as Turkish chrome or Portuguese tungsten would bring about a curtailment of German steel production sufficiently great to reduce German armaments output substantially.

Examination of Germany's ferroalloy supply situation at the beginning of the war indicates that there was some basis for this view. Of

46. *Effects of Strategic Bombing*, Appendix Table 66, p. 247.
47. "The Achievements and Difficulties of the Reichsvereinigung Eisen and the Iron Industry," a report prepared by Hans Hahl, a steel expert associated with the Technical Department of the Ministry of Armaments and War Production; "The Role of Foreign Ores in the German Iron Industry," a report prepared by Dr. Walther Rohland, Head of the Main Committee for Iron Production.

the seven important alloys, only three — vanadium, manganese, and silicon — were produced in large quantities in Germany. In 1939, Germany was practically self-sufficient in vanadium, about 70 per cent self-sufficient in manganese, and 50 per cent in silicon. For her chrome, nickel, molybdenum, and tungsten requirements, however, she had to rely on continued access to Continental sources or on her accumulated metal reserves. As we saw in Chapter II, at the beginning of the war Germany possessed a supply of only one of these four scarce alloys sufficient for more than twelve months' estimated requirements.

Despite such a gloomy picture, however, German steel production was never seriously embarrassed by a shortage of alloys.[48] This was in some measure due to the acquisition of supplies not counted on at the beginning of hostilities. Occupation of Norway gave Germany the output of the Petsamo nickel mines in Finland; capture of Nikopol and Krivoi Rog in the Ukraine gave her manganese. She was able to import chrome from the Balkans and Turkey, and tungsten from Spain, Portugal, and Japan.

These sources of supply, although important, would not have been sufficient by themselves to have prevented a very critical ferroalloy shortage. However, the Germans were able to prevent such a shortage and to keep supplies adequate for requirements by a number of ingenious and energetic measures. Stringent regulations were issued for the conservation of ferroalloys. Careful segregation and utilization of alloy scrap was required and steel plants were frequently inspected and heavy penalties were imposed for wasting scrap. Equally important were technical measures taken to reduce the requirements for alloys. These took the form of developing less highly alloyed steels in which loss of quality was partially compensated for by heat treatment. Finally, the more readily available alloys were substituted for those in shorter supply. In meeting the problems posed by this

48. This is the unanimous opinion of a number of studies on German wartime steel production. Some of the reports consulted were the following: "New Processes in the Steel Industry introduced during the Second World War," by Dr. Rohland; "Rationalization of the Steel Industry," a report prepared by Dr. Rohland, Karl Saur, head of the Technical Division of the Ministry of Armaments and War Production, and Hermann Kellermann, manager of a steel plant; and "German Iron and Steel Industry, Ruhr and Salzgilter Areas," a study prepared after the war by a group of British steel experts. The following discussion is based on these sources.

shifting alloy situation, German metallurgists were exceedingly ingenious, substituting one alloy for another in ways considered impossible before the war. Vanadium, obtained from vanadium-rich
Thomas slags, was relatively abundant throughout the war and became the principal alloying material. For molybdenum, on the other
hand, Germany had to depend almost entirely on stocks accumulated
before the war, and after 1942 its use had to be practically eliminated. The supply situation for other metals varied from time to
time throughout the war and required continuous adaptation of
alloy processes. At the beginning of the war, the efforts of metallurgists were concentrated on finding substitutes for chrome, nickel,
and molybdenum. Later manganese became very short, while nickel
and chrome became more plentiful. When chrome again became
scarce because of irregular deliveries from Turkey, capture of
Nikopol put manganese in the "relatively abundant" category.

These measures of conservation and substitution, as well as the new
sources of supply, meant that not only could the demands of the
steel industry be satisfied, but stocks of alloys were maintained at a
relatively high level throughout the war. This is shown in Table 36,

Table 36. Number of months' alloy consumption
requirements covered by existing stocks
and domestic output

	September 1939	November 1943
Manganese	18.2	19.0
Nickel	6.0	10.0
Chrome	8.0	5.6
Molybdenum	17.0	7.8
Tungsten	10.0	10.6

Source: From a report of the Ministry of Armaments
and War Production, dated November 12, 1943.

which compares the stock situation in 1939 with that in 1943.

The possibility that Germany could so successfully solve her ferroalloy problem was entirely dismissed by Allied Intelligence. According to the British Ministry of Economic Warfare, by the end of 1943
German stocks of chrome, tungsten, molybdenum, and nickel had
been exhausted.[49] If this had been the case, Germany's steel produc-

49. Report of the Ministry of Economic Warfare, dated August 1944.

tion and indeed her whole economic war effort would have been badly crippled.

The fact that Germany did not suffer seriously for lack of chrome, nickel, molybdenum, tungsten, and also copper, even when these materials were in extremely short supply, suggests that in general measures to deny an enemy access to certain strategic materials can prove of only limited value. The extent to which conservation can be practiced and substitution improvised under the pressure of wartime necessity is seldom fully appreciated and cannot be gauged in advance.

Neither the iron ore or ferroalloy supply, then, can be considered as limiting factors in German steel output. Instead, the limiting factor proved to be Germany's most important natural resource — coal. In 1939, Germany was the world's third largest coal producer, with an output of 234 million tons, nearly as high as Britain's, and slightly more than half the production of the United States.[50] During the war, this output was increased by the annexation of foreign territory, particularly Silesia. As Table 37 shows, with the annexed territories German coal production increased from 240 million tons in the coal year 1938–1939 to 340 million tons in 1942–1943, a total rise of 40 per cent. Total supplies available to Germany (including

Table 37. Coal production in Germany and occupied territories, 1938–1943[a]
(millions of metric tons)

Coal year ending March	Production in Greater Germany			Production in occupied areas	Grand total
	Prewar Germany	Annexed territories[b]	Total		
1938–1939	232.3	8.0	240.3	92.5	332.8
1939–1940	233.7	34.0	267.7	96.9	364.6
1940–1941	239.5	76.0	315.5	87.3	402.8
1941–1942	241.5	76.4	317.9	89.9	407.8
1942–1943	250.3	90.1	340.4	89.3	429.7

Source: *Statistischer Bericht*, Reichsvereinigung Kohle.
a. Broun coal included in terms of hard coal equivalent.
b. Approximate; includes production of Alsace-Lorraine, Czechoslovakia, Austria, and Upper Silesia.

50. *Statistisches Jahrbuch*, 1941–1942, p. 101.

output of the occupied countries) in that year (1942–1943) were 430 million tons, or 80 per cent greater than those available in the coal year ending March, 1939.

In spite of Germany's large coal output during the war, German steel experts were agreed that coal was the limiting factor in steel production.[51] According to reports prepared by official agencies and transcripts of Hitler's conferences with his economic advisers, Germany was faced with a coal shortage from the winter of 1940 on. By the fall of 1942, the shortage was regarded as serious. In a report given to the Central Planning Board at that time it was stated that unless coal supplies could be increased curtailments of power, aluminum, and chemical output would be necessary during the following winter.[52] What was regarded as the most immediate and important consequence of the shortage, however, was that it made a scheduled expansion of steel output impossible: "supplies of iron ore and ferroalloys have with great difficulties been assured, but unless the coal problem is solved there can be no increase in steel output." [53] For the proposed goal of 2.65 million tons of finished steel per month — a 25 per cent increase above current output — it was stated that coal supplies of the steel industry would have to be increased by one million tons per month, or about one quarter.[54]

In view of Germany's large coal resources, how was the coal shortage itself explained? One of the explanations given by the Germans runs in terms of a general coal shortage caused by a large, and to some extent unforeseen, growth in the demand during the war.[55] First was the fact that in acquiring Western Europe's industry, Ger-

51. "Rationalization of the Steel Industry," the report prepared by Dr. Rohland referred to in footnote 48; interrogation of Karl Saur, Head of the Technical Division of the Ministry of Armaments and War Production; interrogation of Paul Pleiger, Head of the Hermann Goering Works; report prepared in the Ministry of Armaments and War Production, "The Economic Situation 1943–1944."

52. Transcripts of the Minutes of the Meetings of *Zentrale Planung,* November 1942.

53. Transcripts of the Minutes of the Meetings of *Zentrale Planung,* November 1942.

54. Transcripts of the Minutes of the Meetings of *Zentrale Planung,* November 1942.

55. A general coal shortage is given much emphasis in a report of the German Business Cycle Research Institute, "The German Economy in War and in Peace."

many also acquired the problem of meeting its coal deficit. In 1938 those European countries without adequate resources of their own imported about 60 million tons of coal, about half from Germany and Silesia and the other half from Great Britain.[56] During the war, Germany had to take over in part, at least, Britain's role as a principal supplier of European coal.

A second reason for the large increase in demand is that coal was the backbone of practically all of German industry. It was the principal raw material in the growing synthetic oil, rubber, and chemical industries; it was the main source of electric power; and it formed the basis for Germany's metallurgical industries.

A sizable increase in the demand for coal does not in itself prove, however, that there was a real shortage. There is, in fact, good reason to believe that this opinion of a serious general coal shortage was greatly exaggerated. For if there were a critical coal shortage, such as Britain was experiencing at the time, we should expect to find, as in Britain, a severe curtailment of nonessential coal consumption. But this was not the case. The German coal consumption data show that consumption in households and commercial establishments increased about 20 per cent during the first two years of war and that it remained nearly at this level until 1943.[57] This is hardly compatible with the notion of a serious coal shortage.

It is true that some government officials urged a sharp reduction of nonessential coal consumption before 1943, but evidently Hitler did not believe that the situation warranted such a measure. During a meeting of the Central Planning Board in September 1942, for example, Speer pointed out what Britain had done by way of economizing on coal consumption, quoting from one of Churchill's speeches on the British coal situation. When he proposed an appeal for a voluntary reduction in household fuel consumption, however, he was informed by the Propaganda Ministry that no space was available in the newspapers.

Such evidence makes us very skeptical that a general shortage of coal was holding back steel production. Another explanation appears more plausible, emphasizing not a general coal shortage, but rather a specific shortage of those types suitable for coking. Coking plants

56. *Statistisches Jahrbuch*, 1941–1942, p. 193*.
57. *Statistischer Bericht*, No. 12, Reichsvereinigung Kohle.

required particular types of hard coal, and a shortage of such coal is entirely consistent with the idea that Germany was not troubled by a general coal shortage.

During the war, the supply of coking coal increased very little while the demand mounted rapidly, not only because of the needs of an expanded steel industry but also because coking coal was required in the synthetic oil and rubber industries. Between 1939 and 1942, the output of coking coal in Greater Germany increased from 48 million tons to 54 million tons, or 12 per cent.[58] Imports from the Occupied areas in the latter year amounted to 2.5 million tons, bringing total supplies up to 56.5 million tons, 13 per cent greater than 1939.[59] During the same period, with a 15 per cent increase in iron and steel output,[60] a doubling of synthetic oil output,[61] and a fivefold increase in synthetic rubber output,[62] the demand increased enormously.

Assuming that steel capacity could not be more fully utilized because larger coke supplies were not available, the cause of this shortage of coke remains to be investigated. That coking plant capacity was not the bottleneck is indicated by the fact that coke works in Belgium and France were never fully utilized.[63] Lack of transportation facilities caused some trouble late in 1942, but this was soon remedied and, in any event, it would not explain why more coke was not produced before the winter of 1942–1943. The only satisfactory explanation, and the one given major emphasis by the Germans, is a shortage of mine labor.[64] This was caused mainly by the drafting of large numbers of German coal miners during the war. Up to the spring of 1942, about 100,000 coal miners had been taken into the armed forces; this represented more than 15 per cent of the total number of coal miners in 1939.[65] Although a much larger number of foreign workers had been put to work in the coal mines, their

58. *Statistische Schnellberichte zur Kriegsproduktion*, Planungsamt, 1943.
59. *Statistische Schnellberichte zur Kriegsproduktion*, Planungsamt, 1943.
60. *Statistische Schnellberichte zur Kriegsproduktion*, Planungsamt, 1943.
61. *Statistische Schnellberichte zur Kriegsproduktion*, Planungsamt, 1943.
62. *Statistische Schnellberichte zur Kriegsproduktion*, Planungsamt, 1943.
63. Evidence presented before *Zentrale Planung*, November, 1942.
64. Report of the Reichsvereinigung Kohle, dated October, 1943; Minutes of Meetings of *Zentrale Planung*, July–December, 1942; Dr. Rohland, "The Creation and Organization of the Reichsvereinigung Eisen."
65. *Kriegswirtschaftsliche Kraftebilanz*, 1943.

productivity was much lower than that of the native Germans. According to one estimate, the average foreign worker mined only about 60 per cent as much coal per day as the average German mine worker.[66] Whether this was due to reluctance or inability to produce more, we cannot say.

If a shortage of miners limited coal, and hence steel output, why were not more adequate measures taken to solve the mine labor problem? The most obvious solution would have been to defer mine workers from military service; yet this was not done until 1943. Another measure which would have helped considerably once the coal emergency developed would have been returning to the mines workers who had already been taken into the armed services. In 1942, the total deficit of coal miners was put at 107,000, about the same number as had been drafted up to that time.[67] Still another solution for the coke problem itself would have been the transfer of workers from other types of coal mining to those mines producing coking coal. As we have seen, Germany could have afforded to close down some of her other bituminous mines in order to increase the output of coking coal. All of these measures were in fact proposed by various government officials, but were not undertaken during the period up through 1942, which we are considering. The only positive steps taken consisted of raising mine wages in order to attract more German labor into the mines, and recruiting foreign laborers. Until Sauckel's new foreign labor policy was instituted during the fall of 1942, this recruitment was largely on a volunteer basis.

The German coal and steel experts themselves offer no explanation for the failure to undertake much fuller measures to solve the coal manpower problem. One report on the subject prepared by Dr. Rohland, head of the Main Committee for Iron and Steel Production, concludes with the statement that "since an expansion of steel production was absolutely dependent on more coal, the lack of an energetic policy to put more laborers in the coking-coal mines was incomprehensible." [68] One possible reason for the lack of such a policy is simply that there was no specific steel shortage at this time. If more steel had been urgently needed in direct military uses, it is

66. *Effects of Strategic Bombing,* p. 94.
67. Meeting of *Zentrale Planung,* October 1942.
68. Dr. Rohland, "The German Coal Problem," 1943 (Files, U. S. S.B.S.).

not likely that the measures advocated by Dr. Rohland and others to increase the supply of coke would have been neglected.

This review of German steel production problems from 1939 through 1942 makes us skeptical, therefore, that there really could have been serious concern over increasing steel output. The way the steel allocation system was operated also casts suspicion on the seriousness of the shortage.

2. *The Steel Allocation System, 1939–1942.* In Chapter II, it was shown that from the beginning of 1937, Germany's steel production was not sufficient to cover the total public and private demand. During the year 1937, an ever mounting overload of orders threatened to reduce steel distribution to chaos, and to interfere with the rearmament program. The government, therefore, took initial measures to bring order into the distribution system and to channel more steel into priority uses. All outstanding orders were cancelled and it was decreed that new orders should be certified by the Ministry of Economics, under the general supervision of the Four-Year Planning Office. However, even before the outbreak of war this method of controlling steel distribution had proved ineffective. By 1939 the accumulation of orders was much larger than when controls had been set up; even top priority users like the synthetic oil industry were complaining about the long delays in delivery promised supplies.

With the beginning of the war, the steel industry was placed under an even greater strain. Together with the demands of the armed forces, steel requirements for the civilian economy were also substantially higher than they had been before the war. The mobilization plan drawn up in July 1939, for example, stated requirements at 650,000 tons per month for the armed forces and a like amount for the civilian economy and for export.[69] By the first quarter of 1940, military requirements had risen to 980,000 tons per month, 50 per cent more than the prewar figure, and requirements for civilian economy were up by 20 per cent.[70] In the face of these rising demands, steel output fell continuously from September 1939 until the middle of the following year. After the conquest of France, German

---

69. "The Raw Materials Situation as of July 1, 1941," Economic and Armament Office, Supreme Command of the Armed Forces.

70. "The Raw Materials Situation as of July 1, 1941."

steel supplies increased substantially but not by as much as requirements. In the middle of 1941, total requirements were stated at about
2.8 million tons per month, or one million tons more than current
production. Despite the pressing need for the adoption of a workable allocation system, very little was done in this direction until much later in
the war. In 1939, a very crude sort of a priorities system was inaugurated, and with few modifications it was used until the fall of
1942. At first there were only two priority designations: S (*sonder-
stufe*) and SS (*sondersonderstufe*). It was intended that these would
be given only to steel users producing armaments and urgently
needed industrial facilities (synthetic oil works, for example). It was
soon discovered, however, that nearly all orders reaching the steel
plants were stamped either "S" or "SS." To remedy this situation,
"SSS" and "SSSS" designations were created for the most urgent
steel uses. The creation of these categories was followed by a general
priorities "inflation" in which the priority number given to a particular manufacturer was little more than license to hunt for steel. It
will be recalled that the United States was experiencing a similar
priorities "inflation" in its own war production program, and at
about the same time.

In the first part of 1942, the first winter of war with Russia, it
was generally agreed that the chaos in steel distribution would cripple
the war production effort unless decisive measures were taken. At
that time, the backlog in steel orders amounted to ten to fifteen
million tons, and steel delivery periods of 12 to 18 months were not
uncommon.[71] While some plants were forced to close down for lack
of steel, others had been able to hoard a supply of 12 to 15 months.[72]
All through the war, indeed, many businessmen tried to hoard steel
as a hedge against inflation.

The initiative to remedy the situation was taken by Albert Speer,
newly appointed Minister of Armaments and War Production. In a
letter written to Hitler in March 1942, Speer condemned the existent
steel distribution system, pointing out that the scramble for steel had

71. Report from Speer to Hitler, March 1942, predicting an economic crisis
if the defects in steel distribution were not corrected.
72. Report from Speer to Hitler, March 1942.

led to such an exaggeration of needs that it was impossible to obtain an accurate picture of requirements; that in spite of the professed shortage manufacturers were in general fabricating less steel than they received;[73] and that a much lower percentage of steel was going for war needs than in World War I. Speer stated that without a more efficient steel distribution system, he could not take the responsibility for the war production program.

As a first step towards a more workable scheme, Speer proposed the creation of an over-all board and subordinate organization to coordinate production planning with raw material allocation. In it were represented Speer's Ministry of Armaments and War Production, the Economics Ministry, acting in the interest of the civilian economy, Goering's Four-Year Planning Office, and the Armed Forces. Hitler issued a directive setting up such an organization under the name of *Zentrale Planung* (Central Planning Board). Hitler did not name a director (it was characteristic of him to resist delegating full responsibility on such a vital matter to any single cabinet minister); in fact, however, Speer quickly appointed himself to this position, and indeed this was the opening wedge for his eventual assumption of control over the entire German economy.

At the first meeting of *Zentrale Planung* in April 1942, a three-point policy was agreed upon. First, the total amount of steel allocated for a given quarter was not to exceed expected output of that quarter. Second, the armaments industry was to be given precedence over all other steel claimants. Third, steel production itself was to be pushed to the limit.

The working out of the actual details of a new allocation system was left to Kehrl, head of the Raw Materials Division of the Armaments Ministry. This proved to be a difficult task because a workable allocation system required a degree of coordinated economic planning not heretofore practiced, and because little thought had been previously given to allocation techniques. Indicative of the latter was Kehrl's complaint before *Zentrale Planung* that the Iron and Steel Section of the Four-Year Planning Office had not even assembled

73. During the third quarter of 1940, for example, plants working for the armed forces requested 11.4 million tons of steel (by quote weight), had 8.8 million tons put at their disposal, and only used 7.1 million tons of this during the period. "The Raw Materials Situation as of July 1, 1941."

data on "quota weights," i.e., the amount of steel required to produce a Tiger tank, an 88 mm gun, a particular type of truck, etc.

It was not until late in 1942 that the new steel allocation system was put into operation. Until then, the quarterly distribution of steel to the major claimants was decided upon in *Zentrale Planung*. During the interim period, this organization was a debating society where each major claimant defended his request for steel, and where personal prestige and political shrewdness weighed heavily in the outcome.

The twenty-second meeting of the Board may be cited as a typical performance. At the beginning of the meeting the stated requirements of all the major claimants were put together and it was apparent that the total was much greater than the most optimistic estimate of steel production for the following quarter. All parties agreed that the allocations would have to be cut, but the question of where to begin resulted in an immediate deadlock. This was finally broken when General Thomas offered to make some concessions for the army if Cejke of the Air Ministry would do likewise. Following this, representatives of the transport system, the coal industry, and the power industry reluctantly agreed to bargain. When a settlement was reached, Speer and Fieldmarshal Milch combined against Minister of Economics, Funk, who was a match for neither of them, and forced him to make drastic concessions. Finally, when everything appeared to be settled, one claimant let it be known that he had been left out entirely. Exhausted from the previous struggle, the others agreed to a proposal of Speer that they take care of the omitted claimant by a uniform percentage cut in all quotas.

Though there is little doubt that even this method of reckoning the quotas was superior to the previous priorities confusion, it was a far cry from making rational decisions on the composition of Germany's war effort. Nor was the first principle established by *Zentrale Planung* — that total allocations for a given quarter should not exceed the estimated production — adhered to. During every quarter of 1942, the total amount of steel allocated exceeded production by about 15 per cent.[74] The result was that at the end of the year the

74. Meeting of *Zentrale Planung*, January, 1943.

steel industry was faced with an even greater backlog of orders than when the agency was established.[75]

3. *Was Armaments Production Limited by a Steel Shortage?* Having examined German steel production and steel allocation for the years 1939–1942, we are now in a position to consider directly the major issue — can the steel situation itself explain why Germany did not have a larger armaments production during this period? A variety of evidence points to the conclusion that it cannot. First, no great effort would have been required to raise the production of steel since a substantial increase could have been obtained by so simple an expedient as adding more labor in the coking coal mines. Yet the practical problems involved in increasing steel output did not receive top-level attention until the summer of 1942, and it was not until early in 1943, with the adoption of the emergency steel plan (Eisenschnellplan), that real steps were taken to increase the output of coking coal.[76] The fact that this was not done earlier suggests that a steel shortage did not really seriously disturb Germany's leaders. Second, even if Germany's total steel supplies could not have been increased, there is ample indication that more could have been channeled into the war industries. The ineffective priorities system and the resulting chaos in steel distribution until the end of 1942 make it very unlikely that such a system could have given the war industries the largest possible amount of steel. This is confirmed by reference to the types of uses into which steel was actually going during this period.

In an economy attempting to realize the largest possible munitions production from the steel at its disposal, we should expect to find a rapidly diminishing portion going into various general uses, and an ever increasing amount used for war plant construction and armaments. This, however, was not the case with Germany. Table 38 shows the quota rights issued quarterly to various military claimants (including requirements for construction of synthetic oil and chemical plants) and to other claimants. The data show that from the first war year, when the German economy was hardly on a full war foot-

---

75. In October 1942, a new steel allocation system was inaugurated, but as it actually did not become effective until the first quarter of 1943, discussion of it does not belong to the period now under consideration.

76. Meeting of *Zentrale Planung*, April 1943.

Table 38. Quarterly allocation of steel rights to major claimants
(thousands of metric tons per month)

Year and quarter	Total armed forces including war plant construction		Other domestic uses		Exports		Total	
	Quantity of steel rights issued	Per cent of total	Quantity of steel rights issued	Per cent of total	Quantity of steel rights issued	Per cent of total	Quantity of steel rights issued	Per cent of total
1939								
4th	859	49	732	41	173	10	1764	100
1940								
1st	924		760		200		1884	
2nd	915		769		200		1884	
3rd	908		792		258		1958	
4th	1024		849		330		2203	
Average	943	48	792	40	247	12	1982	100
1941								
1st	1058		848		352		2258	
2nd	1033		891		451		2375	
3rd	1167		897		455		2519	
4th	932		974		403		2309	
Average	1047	44	902	38	415	18	2365	100
1942								
1st	1153		965		525		2643	
2nd	1174		1078		525		2777	
3rd	1100		777		340		2217	
4th	1254		1007		350		2611	
Average	1170	46	957	37	435	17	2562	100

Source: OKW Wehrwirtschafts v. Rüstungsamt, "The Raw Materials Situation as of July 1, 1944"; Planungsamt, "A Statistical Survey of the Quantity of Steel Rights Issued."

ing, through the third war year, the amount of steel allotted for military purposes increased by barely one fifth, and that as a percentage of total steel rights issued it actually declined.[77]

77. These data, it is to be noted, refer not to actual steel consumption but to steel quotas issued. Comparison of these figures with such steel consumption figures as are available indicates that while they exceeded total steel consumption by around 30 per cent, the percentages going to major claimants were about the same in both sets of figures.

It is also difficult to reconcile the notion of a real shortage with some of the marginal purposes for which steel was being used. Reference has already been made to the fact that through 1941 construction of public and party buildings still had not been eliminated. It was only in April 1942 that Speer was able to convince Hitler that Germany could not afford steel for such projects. As we have also noted, the desire of industrialists to have their assets in real forms resulted in a much higher level of machinery production, particularly of machine tool production, than Germany required or the Ministry of Armaments and War Production wanted. Speer's efforts to curb machine tool production were not successful until much later in the war. Other examples of nonessential steel uses are to be found in the field of consumer durables. As late as 1942, many of these items still had not been added to the forbidden production list. One of them — haircurlers — occasioned a stormy debate between Hitler and Goebbels, on the one side, upholding German womanhood, and Speer, on the other, arguing that no unessential use of steel should be spared.[78] While these marginal items probably did not consume an important percentage of total steel supplies, their mere existence is a significant indication of the slack that still existed in the German economy in the third year of war.

Probably the most convincing evidence that more armaments could have been produced in the years 1939–1942 with the steel available during that period is the record of what actually happened later. Armaments production did rise very rapidly from the beginning of 1943 through the middle of 1944 and with very little increase in total steel supplies. As Table 39 shows, with only slightly more steel, Germany was producing about two and one-half times as much armaments during 1944 as she produced in 1941.

Thus, whether we look at the problems involved in raising steel output, in the steel allocation system, in the actual uses to which steel was being put during this period, or in the armaments which Germany produced with practically the same total steel supplies during a later period, it is difficult to reconcile the evidence with the belief held by many Germans that it was a general lack of steel which held armaments production back during the first three years of the war.

78. Minutes of the Fuehrer's Conferences, January, 1943.

This still leaves the question, however, of whether the limiting factor might not have been high-grade steels suitable for munitions manufacture. We have already seen that insofar as ferroalloys could have been the bottleneck, this problem was solved. How about capacity for the production of high-grade steel? It is true that electric steel capacity, a principal means of producing highly alloyed steel, was in short supply throughout the war. The Four-Year Plan made very little provision for the construction of electric steel furnaces, with the result that a major expansion had to be undertaken during the war period. From 1940 until 1944 electric steel capacity was more than doubled.[79]

Table 39. Indices of total steel supplies and armaments output
(1941 = 100)

	1941 (entire year)	1944 (January–July)
Total steel supplies	100	102
Armaments output	100	247

Source: Steel supplies: Data compiled by Reichsvereinigung Eisen. Armaments output: *Indexziffern der deutschen Rüstungsendfertigung*, Planungsamt.

It is not true, however, that construction of electric furnaces was the only means of alleviating the shortage of high-grade steels. Under the pressure of wartime needs, techniques for raising the quality of inferior grades of steel and economies in the use of high-grade steel were found which previously had not been considered.[80]

Two processes were discovered (the so-called "HPN" and "Alto") for raising the quality of Thomas (Bessemer) steel to that of Siemens-Martin (open hearth) steel. The principal innovation of the "Alto" process consisted of adding aluminum to the charge. By 1943, about 10 per cent of Thomas steel (itself about 50 per cent of the total steel output) was being produced by these methods. Processes were also introduced enabling higher quality carbon and alloy steels to be produced in the Siemens-Martin furnaces.

The introduction of these methods considerably eased the shortage

79. Data prepared by Reichsvereinigung Eisen.
80. The following discussion is taken from a monograph by Dr. Rohland, "Rationalization of the German Steel Industry."

of high-grade steels. By way of example, in the second half of 1943, 80 per cent of the ammunition previously made from Siemens-Martin could be produced from the improved Thomas steel. In the same year most of the ball bearings, for which it had been earlier thought that electric steel was indispensable, were being made out of superior grades of Siemens-Martin steel.

It was also found that for many uses inferior grade steel was as satisfactory as high-grade. For example, the quality of steel used in automobile frames was lowered with no significant effect on the serviceability of the vehicles, according to the German steel experts. Lowering the quality of steel for armor plate was accomplished with less than a 5 per cent decline in surface hardness. In gun barrels, the substitution made the weapon slightly less safe, but its effectiveness was not otherwise reduced.

It is very difficult to ascertain the extent to which the new processes and the substitution of inferior grades eased the shortage of high-grade steels, or to determine how short these steels really were. There are several factors, however, which make a genuine shortage unlikely, at least in the period before 1943. One is that the measures described above, for the most part, were not introduced before 1942. Had the Germans been really concerned over a shortage of high quality steels, it is not unlikely that these would have been found earlier. Another is that French and Belgian capacity for the production of high-grade steel was only partially utilized before the middle of 1943. Dr. Rohland, head of the Main Committee for Iron and Steel Production, complained bitterly at a meeting of *Zentrale Planung* in July 1942 that with all the talk of a shortage of electric steel, various plants in Belgium and France were for no good reason at a standstill.[81] Finally, the sizeable increases in electric steel capacity occurred not in the period 1939 through 1942, but afterward. The necessity for large-scale construction was not recognized as a task of paramount importance until the formulation of the Steel Emergency Plan in March 1943.[82] When the war ended, electric furnaces were still in the process of construction.

Our study of the principal materials used in armaments production indicates, therefore, that while ferroalloys, steel (particularly

81. Evidence presented before *Zentrale Planung*, July 1942.
82. Meeting of *Zentrale Planung*, April 1943.

high-grade steel), and copper presented the Germans with serious supply problems, they were not limiting factors in armaments output and cannot be used to explain why German armaments output remained relatively low throughout the first three years of the war. Having found that neither industrial capacity or raw materials can provide us with the explanation, we now turn to an examination of the third possibility — labor.

V I   *A Resources Limitation? (continued)*

LABOR

A third possible factor limiting armament output is the supply of labor. The major changes in Germany's manpower situation between 1939 and 1942 are summarized in Table 40. The three most significant developments were these: First, from 1939 through 1942, 8 million men were taken into the armed forces; in the latter year 22 per cent of the male population was in military service. Second, in this period 3.8 million foreigners and prisoners of war were added to the civilian labor force, accounting in 1942 for about 15 per cent of the total labor force. Third, despite the addition of foreign labor, the civilian labor force in 1942 contained 3.8 million fewer men and women than in 1939, a loss of nearly 10 per cent.

What is most surprising, there was no increased mobilization of German labor to offset the losses to the armed services. During this period, the Germans added only about 400,000 persons to their own working force, a figure which just about corresponds to the natural growth in the working population. Employment of women, a most important labor reserve in the United States and Britain, actually declined.

Nor was the supply of labor significantly increased by lengthening working hours. As Table 41 shows, the workweek in the whole of German industry in March 1942 averaged 48.7 hours, one hour longer than in 1939. Even in the production-goods industries, where one might expect to find the greatest evidence of a labor shortage, the average workweek for skilled labor only increased from 50.5 hours

Table 40. Total labor force, 1939–1942[a]
(millions)

	1939	1940	1941	1942
German civilian labor force	39.11	34.89	33.43	31.49
Men	24.49	20.51	19.24	17.03
Women	14.62	14.39	14.19	14.46
Foreigners and prisoners of war	0.30	1.15	3.07	4.13
Total civilian labor force	39.51	36.04	36.50	35.63
Armed forces				
Total mobilized	1.71	6.26	7.66	9.68
Active strength	1.71	6.05	7.33	8.60
Total Germans mobilized	40.92	41.15	41.09	41.17
Men	26.20	26.76	26.90	26.71
Total Germans and foreigners				
mobilized	41.12	42.30	44.16	45.30
Total German population	79.53	79.92	80.32	80.71
Men	38.84	39.00	39.17	39.34
Women	40.69	40.92	41.15	41.38
Percentage of German population				
mobilized	51.5	51.5	51.5	51.0
Men	67.5	68.5	68.5	68.0
Women	36.0	35.0	34.5	35.0

Source: Data for civilian labor force and total mobilized from "Kriegswirtschaft Kraftebilanz: Vorkriegsgebiet (Von der Reichsgruppe Industrie Abgestimmte Zahlen des statistischen Reichsamtes, Abteilung VI)," and "Kraftebilanz," 1939 and 1942, Statistisches, Abteilung VI. Figures for active strength of armed forces taken from "Zusammenstellung uber die personnelle und materielle Rüstungslage der Wehrmacht," OKW.

a. Old Reich, Austria, Sudetenland, Saar, and Memel.

in 1939 to 52 hours in 1942. Statements in the German press to the contrary, the 60-hour week was far from the general rule in German industry.

We cannot explain Germany's failure to increase the mobilization of her own labor force over this period because of an already high degree of mobilization in 1939. In Chapter III it was shown that the degree of labor mobilization in that year was not significantly greater than in 1933 or 1925, the other two years for which complete labor force data are available. The number of gainfully employed men and women in relation to the total population of working age was practically unchanged in all three years. If the calculation could be ex-

Table 41. Average weekly hours worked by wage earners in production and consumption goods industries, by sex and skill, selected periods 1929-1942[a]

| Year and month | All industries | All wage earners | Production goods[b] | | | |
| | | | Male | | Female | |
			Skilled	Unskilled	Skilled	Unskilled
1929	46.0	46.3	–	–	–	–
1933	42.9	43.0	–	–	–	–
1935	44.4	45.9	–	–	–	–
1937	46.1	47.3	–	–	–	–
1938	46.5	47.8	–	–	–	–
1939, Mar.	47.6	48.2	50.2	49.5	47.2	46.8
Sept.	47.8	48.8	50.7	50.9	46.2	45.7
1940, Mar.	47.6	48.5	50.7	49.7	46.7	43.9
Sept.	49.2	49.9	52.3	52.6	47.9	44.7
1941, Mar.	49.1	49.9	52.4	51.4	47.2	44.8
Sept.	49.5	50.3	52.8	52.3	46.1	44.5
1942, Mar.	48.7	49.6	52.2	50.4	45.1	43.6
Sept.	48.7	49.5	52.0	51.2	43.8	42.9

| Year and month | All industries | All wage earners | Consumption goods[b] | | | |
| | | | Male | | Female | |
			Skilled	Unskilled	Skilled	Unskilled
1929	46.0	45.7	–	–	–	–
1933	42.9	42.9	–	–	–	–
1935	44.4	42.6	–	–	–	–
1937	46.1	44.5	–	–	–	–
1938	46.5	44.9	–	–	–	–
1939, Mar.	47.6	45.9	48.1	47.9	46.5	46.8
Sept.	47.8	43.5	46.6	47.9	42.5	43.7
1940, Mar.	47.6	43.8	46.9	47.5	43.1	44.3
Sept.	49.2	45.9	49.4	49.2	45.3	45.0
1941, Mar.	49.1	45.8	49.7	49.2	44.8	44.4
Sept.	49.5	45.9	50.0	49.4	44.7	44.1
1942, Mar.	48.7	45.0	49.2	48.8	43.8	43.2
Sept.	48.7	44.8	49.9	49.2	42.9	42.5

Sources: 1929-38: *Statistisches Jahrbuch*, 1939-40, p. 384; 1939-44: *Ergebnisse der amtlichen Lohnerhebungen für März* 1944, Statistisches Reichsamt, Abteilung Sozialstatistik.

a. Data for 1929-1938 are annual averages. Data for 1939-1944 are monthly averages.

b. Data not available for years 1929 through 1938.

tended to 1942, it would be found that the relative size of the labor force then was no greater than in 1925.[1]

It is of some interest to compare Germany's experience in labor mobilization during this period with Britain's. The percentage of the nonagricultural population of working age in the nonagricultural labor force was about the same in both countries in 1939. In Germany, the figure was 85 per cent for men and 35 per cent for women, compared with 82 per cent and 35 per cent, respectively, in Britain.[2] From 1939 through 1942, however, Britain added about 1.6 million workers to her labor force, or about four times as many as Germany (see Table 42). During the same period the number of women in the

Table 42. Number of gainfully occupied men and women in Germany and Great Britain, 1939 and 1942

(millions)

| | 1939 | | 1942 | |
	Germany	Great Britain	Germany	Great Britain
Men	26.2	14.7	26.7	15.2
Women	14.6	6.3	14.5	7.4
Total	40.8	21.0	41.2	22.6

Source: For Germany see Table 40; for Britain see "Statistics Relating to the War Effort of the United Kingdom."

British labor force increased by more than one million, or 18 per cent; whereas in Germany, fewer women were employed in 1942 than in 1939.

Until March 1942, responsibility for the recruitment of civilian labor rested primarily with the Ministry of Labor. In spite of the shrinkage of the labor force during the first three years of the war, this agency evidenced little interest in conscripting more German

1. Since the population figures for 1942 are not broken down by age groups, it is not possible to calculate exactly the size of the working population (14 years and over). On the basis of some rough extrapolations from the 1939 figures, however, it turns out that the percentages of the working population in 1939 and 1942 were about the same.

2. British population data from report of Registrar General. In computing the nonagricultural population it was assumed the agricultural population contained 1.3 million men and 1.4 million women. German population data from *Statistisches Jahrbuch*, 1941–1942, p. 33.

civilian labor. Yet it could have taken almost any steps it chose, since its powers were practically unlimited. In February 1939 a government decree gave the Ministry, through its regional offices, the authority to conscript all adults for work of national importance for an indefinite period of time.[3] And during the war years its powers were extended even further. Whatever may have been the purpose of these decrees, however, they were seldom used by the Ministry to press more Germans into the labor force. According to a report of one governmental agency, the 1942 labor force would have been just as large if the decrees had not been issued and if the Labor Ministry had not existed.[4]

The policy with regard to employment of women was still dominated by the Nazi belief that woman's primary duty was to raise children. Such female conscription measures as were issued applied to unmarried women or to childless wives. Thus, in 1939 labor service was made compulsory for all unmarried women between the ages of 17 and 25.[5] Subsequently, the term of service was extended from six months to one year, and the measure was extended to childless wives and widows.[6] These measures, however, may have been intended as much to encourage women to marry as to bring more women into the labor force. As a conscription measure, they do not appear to have been very effective; in September 1942, only about 200,000 women were in the compulsory labor service.[7] No attempt was made to encourage women with children to seek employment; on the contrary, liberal soldiers' dependency allowances, together with other benefits, encouraged women to withdraw from the labor force to domestic life.

In March 1942, the powers of the Labor Ministry were transferred to Fritz Sauckel, newly appointed Commissioner for the Mobilization of Labor. Sauckel was a prominent Nazi party member; his strong party ties are indicated by the fact that on assuming power the administration of his program was transferred from the Reich regional labor offices to the local party chieftains — the Gauleiters.

3. *Reichsgesetzblatt*, 1939, I, 126.
4. Report of the Statistisches Reichsamt on "Labor Utilization," dated January 1943.
5. "Labor Utilization," January 1943.
6. "Labor Utilization," January 1943.
7. "Labor Utilization," January 1943.

This change of administration, at least for the period 1939 through 1942, had no effect on the mobilization of German labor. Sauckel stated his aims in a directive dated 20 April 1942.[8] To satisfy the needs of the armaments industry, some reliance was to be placed on a further combing out of workers from unessential industries, but the main source of additional manpower was to be foreign labor. Nothing was said about measures to bring more of the German population into the labor force. In fact, with respect to women, Sauckel's views were explicitly to the contrary:

> Examining this very difficult problem and after getting thoroughly acquainted with the fundamental opinion of the Fuehrer as well as of the Reichsmarshal of the Greater German Reich and my own most careful inquiries and their results, I must absolutely reject the possibility of having an obligatory service decreed by the State for all German women and girls for the German War and Nutrition industry.
>
> I only ask for confidence in me as an old fanatical district chief of the National Socialist party and to believe that this could be the only possible decision.[9]

In his solicitude for the health and well being of German mothers, Sauckel went even further, declaring that the most urgent task after satisfying the needs of the armament industry was the conscription of 400,000 to 500,000 Polish and Russian girls for domestic service in German homes! [10]

Sauckel's major interest, and the principal reason for his appointment, was to organize an energetic drive for the conscription of foreign workers. Until the middle of 1942, even the methods for recruiting foreign labor were, by later standards, moderate. Compulsory conscription methods were used only in Poland, Russia, and Greece. In the occupied countries of Western Europe, it was hoped that a sufficient number of workers could be obtained by offering high wages and promising better living conditions.

Soon after his appointment, Sauckel introduced compulsory methods of conscription for the Western countries. At first the compulsion was indirect; plants were closed down in the occupied territories, and workers refusing employment in Germany were not allowed un-

8. *Nazi Conspiracy and Aggression*, III, 50–53.
9. *Nazi Conspiracy and Aggression*, III, 52–53.
10. *Nazi Conspiracy and Aggression*, III, 52.

employment relief or issued food ration cards. Later, such methods were succeeded by outright conscription; in the East, all able-bodied men and women were taken; in France and the Lowlands, workers were called up by age groups. By the end of 1942, Sauckel's new labor policy had added about 1.6 million foreign workers to the German labor force.[11]

Except for the number of people engaged in public service, there were no pronounced shifts in the distribution of the labor force. In the nonpublic sector, employment was best maintained not in industry but in agriculture. Agricultural employment declined about 500,-000 during the first two years of the war, but by 1942 it was back to the prewar level. This was possible because agriculture was the major recipient of foreign labor. In 1942 nearly one fifth of the agricultural laborers were foreigners (chiefly Poles and Russians), and about one half of the foreign workers in Germany were employed on farms.[12]

The decline in employment in industry, transport, and power combined was about 15 per cent, a somewhat larger reduction than the reduction in civilian employment as a whole. In industry proper, it was somewhat less, about 10 per cent.

While the proportion of the total labor force employed in industry was no greater in 1942 than in 1939, there was, however, a noticeable change in its composition; that is, there was a fairly pronounced increase in the number of employees engaged directly or indirectly in war manufacturing, and a substantial decline in other types of manufacturing employment. The numbers employed in the basic industries increased slightly from 1939 to 1942, and in the metalworking industries the increase was about 20 per cent.

Employment in occupations not essential to the war effort generally declined more than other types of employment, but there were important exceptions, still leaving in 1942 a substantial labor reserve in the civilian economy. The most successful combing out of unessential workers occurred in wholesale and retail trades. Between 1939 and 1942, as Table 43 shows, such establishments released more than one million workers, about 30 per cent of the total number employed

11. Report of the Statistisches Reichsamt on "Labor Utilization," dated January 1943.

12. *Kriegswirtschaftliche Kräftebilanz* for 1942.

Table 43. Distribution of the civilian labor force, 1939–1942[a]
(thousands of workers and percentages)

	May 1939		May 1940		May 1941		May 1942	
Agriculture	11224	28.5	10699	29.7	10734	29.4	11227	31.5
Total industry	18637	47.3	16432	45.6	16863	46.2	15881	44.6
Manufacturing	10945	27.7	9980	27.7	10344	28.2	9943	28.0
Handicraft	5335	13.5	4230	11.7	4207	11.4	3503	10.1
Transport	2124	5.4	2018	5.5	2103	5.7	2227	6.2
Power	231	0.6	204	0.6	207	0.6	206	0.6
Commerce and finance	4602	11.7	3966	11.0	3820	10.4	3323	9.3
Trade	3020	7.6	2595	7.2	2492	6.7	2024	5.8
Other	1582		1371		1328		1299	
Public administration	2359	5.9	2552	7.1	2669	7.5	2865	8.0
Professional	1008	2.5	902	2.0	922	2.5	868	2.4
Domestic servants	1573	4.0	1489	4.1	1488	4.0	1461	4.1
Total civilian labor force	39515	100.0	36042	100.0	36499	100.0	35627	100.0

Source: Compiled from "Kriegswirtschaft Kraftebilanz; Vorkriegsgebiet (Von der reichsgruppe Industrie abgestimmte Zahlen des statistischen Reichsamtes, Abteilung VI)," and "Kraftebilanz," 1939 and 1942, Statistisches Reichsamt, Abteilung VI.

a. Old Reich, Austria, Sudetenland, Saar and Memel.

at the beginning of the war. On the other hand, the number of domestic servants declined only by 100,000 from 1939 to 1942; less than the percentage decline in total employment. Nor were large numbers of German domestics replaced by foreigners. In 1942, 97 per cent of the domestics were of German nationality.[13]

The extent to which Germany redistributed her labor force in favor of war-essential occupations can be better appreciated by comparing her experience in this respect with Britain's. Because of some gaps in the 1942 German employment date, our comparisons are for the years 1939 and 1943.

For the comparison, the German data has been classified to agree as closely as possible with the groupings presented in the British White Paper.[14] The three major categories used are intended to

13. *Kriegswirtschaftliche Kraftebilanz* for 1942.
14. "Statistics Relating to the War Effort of the United Kingdom."

divide the various occupational groups according to their importance to the war effort. The comparison in absolute as well as in relative terms is shown in Table 44.

Table 44. Mobilization of manpower in Great Britain and Germany, 1939–1943
(1939 = 100)

	Great Britain			Germany		
	Employment (thousands)		Index	Employment (thousands)		Index
	1939	1943		1939	1943	
Group I						
Metal, chemical, and allied industries	3106	5233	169	5778	6863	118
Group II	5530	5632	102	18419	19227	104
Agriculture	1113	1118	100	11224	11301	101
Mining	873	818	94	766	903	118
Government services	1385	1786	129	2894	3879	134
Electricity, gas, and water	232	200	86	231	206	89
Transport	1273	1191	94	1624	1799	111
Manufactured foods, beverages, and tobacco	654	519	79	1680	1139	68
Group III	10477	6779	65	14969	10757	72
Construction and civil engineering	1310	726	55	2534	1256	50
Textiles, clothing, and shoes	1754	1154	66	2769	2111	76
Other manufacturing	1444	968	67	2475	1833	74
Distribution	2887	2009	70	3428	2156	63
Other services	1882	1422	76	2181	1959	90
Domestic service	1200	500	42	1582	1442	91
Armed forces	557	5068	910	1710	11235	655
Total	19670	22712	116	40876	48082	118
Total excluding armed forces and agriculture	18000	16526	92	27942	25546	115

Source: Great Britain: "Statistics Relating to the War Effort of the United Kingdom." German: "Kraftebilanz," 1943, Betriebzahlung, 1939, and a compilation prepared by the Planungsamt in 1944.

Aggregate employment changed about the same in both nations; total employment, including the armed forces, increased about 15 per cent between 1939 and 1943, and a nonagricultural civilian employment declined about 10 per cent. As pointed out, civilian employment was maintained in Britain by internal mobilization, in Germany, by the importation of foreign labor.

But the British went much further than did the Germans in transfering workers into occupations essential to the war effort. As Table 44 shows, employment in essential (Group I) industries was relatively higher in Germany in 1939; but Britain expanded employment in these industries nearly 70 per cent from 1939 to 1943, whereas in Germany the increase was only 20 per cent. In 1943, about one third of the British nonagricultural civilian labor force was employed in essential industries; in Germany, just over one quarter. On the other hand, employment in the industries least essential to the war (Group III) contracted 35 per cent in Britain and 28 per cent in Germany. The combing out of workers in the distributive trades went somewhat further in Germany, but Britain was much more successful in releasing workers from domestic service and other service trades. By 1943, the number of domestic servants in Britain had been reduced by over 60 per cent; in Germany, by less than 10 per cent.

When we consider either the number of Germans mobilized or changes in the distribution of the labor force, therefore, there is little doubt that until the beginning of 1943, at least, the German economy possessed substantial labor reserves. From this it follows that her small armaments production during the first three years of the war cannot be explained by a general shortage of labor.

It also seems likely, though the evidence is less clear on this point, that a shortage of skilled labor was not very important in impeding armament production during this period. For example, there was no large-scale program for training and recruiting additional skilled labor. In 1936 a program for the training of skilled workers had been inaugurated. The labor offices of each district were assigned a quota of apprentices to be trained in a given period, and they were instructed to give special priority in filling apprenticeships. The success of the program is indicated by a tripling in the number of apprentices between 1936 and 1939.[15] During the first three years of the war, however, the training program was not appreciably expanded. In 1942 the number of apprentices was no greater than it had been in 1939.[16]

Another indication that the Germans were not greatly concerned

15. Data compiled by Statistisches Reichsamt, Files, SBS.
16. Data compiled by Statistisches Reichsamt, Files, SBS.

about a shortage of skilled labor is the fact that in calling workers into the armed forces no differentiation was made between skilled and unskilled labor. Blanket deferments were given for workers in certain types of high priority production, but the type of production rather than the degree of skill was made the principal criterion. Before 1942, the process for obtaining a deferment of a skilled worker from the draft was extremely complicated, and deferments were rarely granted (see Chapter VII).

An examination of Germany's production performance during the first three years of the war discloses a startling fact: the small output in munitions. To solve this mystery, we began by inquiring whether there was an economic explanation, whether Germany's war output was limited by the amount of resources available to her. In Chapter V it was found that industrial facilities were by no means a limiting factor, and it was shown that although a number of German officials believed that war production was held up by a lack of certain raw materials, no real basis for such beliefs could be found. In this chapter it was seen that a lack of labor certainly could not have prevented a greater munitions output; the German economy possessed adequate labor reserves throughout the period 1939 through 1942. In short, armaments output was not limited by the quantity of available resources.

Far from solving the mystery of Germany's low volume of war production, a number of other puzzling features have been added to it. The volume of unessential investment permitted during this period; the neglect of simple measures required to increase steel production; the primitive method used for allocating steel with the resulting quantities of steel going into nonwar uses; the small increase made in the working day; the lack of an energetic training program for skilled labor; the failure to transfer labor from domestic service and other unessential occupations — all of these features of the German economy require some explanation. They certainly point to a different picture of the economy than the much advertised characterization "total war."

The next two chapters offer an explanation for the surprising degree of slack found throughout the German economy.

V I I *The German Economic Administration, 1939–1941*

During the war the German economy was often characterized by British Intelligence as a "taut string." This summed up a widely held view that Germany, even in the early part of the war, was mobilized so completely and in so well balanced a way that any loss of a day's labor anywhere in the economy — on a farm, in a munitions plant, in a clothing factory — would be equally damaging to the war effort. The conclusions of the previous chapters indicate no such state of mobilization, but instead a large degree of slack throughout a number of sectors of the economy. How is this to be explained? One possible explanation is that the Nazi economic administration was so inefficient that it could not effectively mobilize the nation's resources. Another is that the German war leaders did not demand a very much larger economic effort than that which was actually put forth. In Chapter VIII we shall discuss the aims of the war leaders, and in this the efficiency of the administration.

That the first explanation — the inefficiency of the economic administration — is not altogether implausible has been amply indicated in previous chapters. In the prewar years, the failure to draw up a comprehensive and integrated plan for war production; the unbalanced raw material preparation; the inability to channel raw materials into desired sectors of the economy; and the large percentage of public expenditures budgeted for nonwar purposes, all cast suspicion on the efficiency of the direction of the war effort. The same is true, during the war period, of the way in which the Germans handled their "major economic problem" — the steel shortage.

No attempt will be made to supply a detailed description of the German economic administration.[1] To obtain a general idea of how the system worked, a broad outline of the administrative set-up is sufficient; and we shall limit ourselves in this chapter to the period up until February, 1942, when Albert Speer was appointed Minister of Armaments and War Production. The period after 1942, the so-called "Speer period," will be discussed in Chapter IX.

I. THE ECONOMIC AGENCIES

The basic principle for Germany's system of economic controls up to 1942 was established by the May 1935 Defense Law.[2] Schacht's Economics Ministry was made responsible for the preparation of the economy for war, and Schacht appointed himself general plenipotentiary for the economy. The control of the armaments industry itself rested with the War Economy and Armament Office (*Wehrwirtschafts und Rüstungsamt*), an organization under the Ministry of War, with General Thomas at its head.

The inability to separate the economy into "war" and "civilian" sectors resulted in a struggle between the civilian and military agencies that was to continue through most of the war. General Thomas thought that his organization could not carry out its responsibilities without some voice in general economic matters; Schacht demanded that all economic activities be placed under his direction. This conflict was intensified by basic policy disagreements. Thomas wanted a large-scale program for building up the basic industries — an "arming in depth" — and a highly disciplined economy. Schacht believed that Germany could not afford such a lavish undertaking, and favored as little government regulation of industry as possible.

In 1936, Goering's Office of the Four-Year Plan was created. Without solving the question of who was going to control the economy, another party was added to the dispute. In 1940, Hitler established yet another agency, the Ministry of Armaments and Munitions, responsible only to him. During the early part of the war, therefore,

1. For a fuller description of the German Economic Administration, see Franz Neuman's *Behemoth,* (New York, 1944).
2. A copy of this secret decree was found in the files of the Speer Ministry.

the German economy was under the control of four independent organizations: the Economics Ministry, the War Economy and Armaments Office, the Four-Year Planning Office, and the Ministry of Armaments and Munitions.

A. *The Ministry of Economics*

During the period of the 1930's, the whole of German industry was organized on the so-called leadership principle. The territorial and functional organizations of business, which had been highly developed under the Weimar Republic, were taken over by the State under the direction of the Ministry of Economics and membership in them was made obligatory. Every business was compelled to belong to a National Group (set up on a functional basis) and a Chamber of Commerce (organized territorially). In principle the Groups and Chambers were to be agents of the government and assist in preparing the economy for war. Actually, in the prewar period they simply continued to carry on, with the support of the government, typical trade association activities — the establishment of uniform cost accounting systems, advising members on foreign trade regulations, specifying the size of fees and discounts, regulating certain types of competition, etc.

The principal administrative organs of the Ministry of Economics were the *Reichstellen*. Originally established as Supervisory Boards to administer import controls, they could easily be taken into the wartime economic administration. At the beginning of the war, there were 27 *Reichstellen*, each controlling a specific group of raw materials. For the particular commodities under its control, each *Reichstelle* was empowered to set production quotas, regulate stocks, and supervise distribution to the user industries.

In 1939, the Minister of Economics was entitled Commissioner General for the Economy, and his responsibilities, besides the general supervision of business and control of raw materials, were substantially expanded to include the Ministry of Labor, the Ministry of Food and Agriculture, the Office of the Reich Forest Master, and the Office of the Price Controller. This in effect gave him complete control over all sectors of the economy except that of war production.

In November 1938, when Schacht was forced to resign from the government, Goering temporarily assumed the position of Minister of Economics. Before retiring from the Ministry, he staffed the key positions with his own men and sponsored Walter Funk, economic editor of the party paper, to head it. It is obvious that the purpose of Goering's move was to appoint a weak man to be nominally in charge of the Ministry while he retained real control for himself in his capacity as Plenipotentiary for the Four-Year Plan. Funk himself was not respected by any of Hitler's inner circle and was an inconspicuous figure during the war years. The voluminous transcripts of Hitler's conferences with his economic advisers do not indicate Funk's presence at a single meeting.

B. *The Armed Forces' War Economy and Armament Office*

The Armed Forces' War Economy and Armament Office was created in 1934 as the economic planning staff of the Ministry of War. The Minister of War was not a Secretary of National Defense, in the American sense, with the three services under his command. On the contrary, the commanders-in-chief of the army, navy, and airforce also had cabinet rank and reported to Hitler. Because these three branches of the service were especially opposed to the establishment of any central procurement agency, the War Economy and Armament Office had very limited powers. It gathered statistical data, prepared economic intelligence on foreign countries, and acted as an expediting agency for the forces when called on to do so.[3]

In the years preceding the war, there was a major struggle for power within the high command. Blomberg, as Minister of War, thought that he should enjoy full responsibility in preparing the military forces for war; von Fritsch, Commander-in-Chief of the Army, was convinced that this was his duty as commander of the most important armed service; Goering, as Commander of the Air Force, did not want to lose power to either of them. In February 1938, Goering succeeded in implicating both von Fritsch and Blomberg in scandals, whereupon they were dismissed. The Ministry of War was abolished, and in its place Hitler established the Supreme Command of the Armed Forces (*Oberkommando der Wehrmacht*) with Keitel at its head. This, however, did not give the armed forces a unified command. Keitel was merely Hitler's Chief of Staff, a liaison agent

---

3. General Thomas, *Basic Facts for a History of the German War Economy,* Files, United States Strategic Bombing Survey.

between Hitler and the armed forces. Hitler, as Commander-in-Chief of the Armed Forces, interested himself almost exclusively with the Army. The air force and navy remained practically autonomous organizations, as they had been under Blomberg. The inability of the OKW to provide central direction for the armed forces was most conspicuous in economic matters. As in peacetime, the army, navy and airforce handled their procurement activities separately.

When OKW was formed in 1938, it took over the Armed Forces' War Economy and Armament Office. Although this organization became somewhat more important in war than it had been in peacetime, its success in coordinating the procurement activities of the three branches of the service was distinctly limited.

During the war the Office continued under the direction of General Thomas, one of the conspirators in the 1938 plot against Hitler, and an outspoken critic of his economic rearmament policy. Thomas was greatly opposed to Germany's entry into war before the economy could be adequately prepared through a tremendous "rearmament in depth" (to use his favorite expression). Once war had begun, he advocated such Spartan measures as elimination of unnecessary civilian consumption, a substantial lengthening of the working day, introduction of multiple shifts, and the drafting of women. His attitude did not make him popular with Hitler or the Nazi leaders; according to his own testimony, Thomas saw Hitler only two or three times during the war.[4] He was dismissed from the OKW in July 1943 and imprisoned after the July 1944 assassination plot against Hitler.

C. *The Four-Year Planning Office*

In 1936 Goering was appointed Plenipotentiary for the Second Four-Year Plan. The major aim of the Plan, as we have seen, was to prepare Germany's raw material position for the demands of war. During the first several years at this post, however, it seemed that Goering was going to go farther and assume responsibility for the direction of the entire economy. Immediately after his appointment to this post, Goering took over Schacht's strategic departments (such as foreign trade); later he was instrumental in effecting Schacht's dismissal. After Schacht left the Ministry of Economics, Goering

4. General Thomas, *Basic Facts for a History of the German War Economy.*

gained control over the Ministry, appointing his own men to the key posts. And as we have seen, a few months later, when Goering resigned from the Ministry, he secured the appointment of a man of his own choice. At the beginning of the war, Goering became Plenipotentiary for the War Economy and Chairman of the Economic General Council, which was to be the top-level coordinating body. During wartime, however, Goering was Germany's economic dictator in name only, and was interested only in retaining authority over the economy.

D. *The Ministry of Armaments and Munitions*

Hitler's dissatisfaction with the handling of economic matters by military officials led to the establishment of the Ministry of Armaments and Munitions in February 1940. Its jurisdiction was strictly confined to matters relating to munitions for the army. Even in this its powers were limited, for in setting up the Ministry, Hitler did not take away any of the army's procurement functions.

The director of the Ministry, Fritz Todt, was also Inspector General for Water and Power, Inspector General for Roads, Plenipotentiary for Building, and head of the Organization Todt (whose chief activity was the construction of fortifications). Todt was more interested in his construction work than becoming involved in disputes with General Thomas, the army procurement agencies, or Hitler and Goering. According to Speer, then one of his assistants, Todt spent only one or two days a week in Berlin; the rest he spent inspecting work on the Atlantic defenses, the building of roads in Norway and Russia, the construction of the superhighways in Germany, etc.[5]

2. THE SYSTEM OF ECONOMIC CONTROLS IN OPERATION

The management of the German economy can be divided into five separate functions: first, fiscal policy and price control; second, procurement of war material; third, control of civilian production; fourth, control of resources, raw materials, labor, and investment; and fifth, over-all coordination.

5. Letter from Speer to Hitler, dated July, 1944, Files, United States Strategic Bombing Survey.

A. *Government Finance and Price Control*

After 1939, when Schacht's repeated predictions of financial collapse had failed to materialize, and he had left the government, Germany began to rely more and more on deficit spending. It appears that Hitler and Goering themselves had become converted to the "new theory of public finance" at a somewhat earlier date, but not until after Schacht left did Germany begin to rely on public deficits as a principal source of war finance.

Table 45. Reich expenditures, tax receipts, and annual deficit,[a] fiscal year beginning April 1
(billions of marks)

	Expenditures	Taxes[b]	Deficit
1938	31.8	18.2	10.5
1939	52.1	24.2	19.2
1940	78.0	27.5	38.9
1941	101.0	32.3	49.8
1942	128.6	42.7	59.0
1943	153.0	38.0	85.2

Source: Wolf, *Geld-und Finanzprobleme der deutschen Nachkriegswirtschaft.*
a. Central government only, does not include state and local.
b. Includes custom receipts.

Table 45 shows that the Reich's annual deficit rose from the modest figure of 10.5 billion marks in the fiscal year 1938–1939 to 85.2 in 1943–1944, by which time the total debt had risen to 252 billion marks, or about twice Germany's national income. The other expanding source of public revenue was forced loans and occupation levies on conquered countries. Tax receipts provided a continuously narrowing portion of total public revenues; about one half in the fiscal year 1939–1940, and one quarter in the fiscal year 1943–1944.

According to Professor Hettlage, financial adviser to the Speer Ministry, the Ministry of Finance continuously urged higher personal and business taxes, but was opposed by the Ministry of Economics, Goering, and by Hitler himself, who, Hettlage said, was unwilling to impose greater sacrifices on the masses of the people.[6] In the summer of 1944, a taxation scheme for "total war" was prepared, but Hitler decided to delay announcement of it. Finally in March 1945, as the war was about to end, a system of steep tax rates was put into effect.

Thus, the Nazis made two fundamental errors in fiscal policy during their regime: on the one hand, they maintained very high tax rates in the early years when recovery from the depression was the primary aim, and on the other, when the problem was one of curtailing private consumption, they relied too much on deficit spending. (Perhaps their mistake was in not having a Keynesian-minded Plenipotentiary for Public Finance, like von der Nahmer, during the depression, and in keeping a conservative like Schacht during the war — with Hitler himself determining the total volume of public expenditures.)

In order to maintain price stability, the Germans relied mainly on direct controls. General price controls were initiated as early as 1936, when there was a general price freeze, and it was decreed that no increase could be granted without the approval of the Price Commissioner. Subsequently, some advances were allowed, mostly because imports became more expensive, but on the whole the level of prices was remarkably stable. This is shown by Table 46. Although there was some trading at prices above the legal maxima, German wartime

Table 46. Cost of living and wholesale price indices, 1936–1943
(1936 = 100)

	Wholesale prices	Cost-of-living index
1939	102.5	101.5
1940	105.5	103.5
1941	107.5	106.0
1942	110.0	108.5
1943	111.5	110.0

Source: From a report prepared by the Planungsamt, "Report on the German Economic Situation, 1943–1944."

6. Report prepared by Hettlage on "German War Finance" for United States' Military Government Officials.

officials agree that black market operations did not assume significant proportions during the war.[7]

One important group of commodities, military goods, was exempt from the Price Commissioner's authority and their prices were determined by the procurement officials in the armed forces. The cost-plus system, which was the method of price fixing until 1942, was subjected to a good deal of criticism on the grounds that it tended to make munitions procurement more and more expensive, and that it did not encourage manufacturers to adopt efficient production procedures.[8]

B. *Procurement*

The procurement of war material is one of the most vital functions of an economic high command. Associated with it are the translation of military strategy into armed forces' requirements, the determination of weapon designs, the selection of the particular plants to produce the various types of armaments, and immediate responsibility for seeing that production orders are filled. Three aspects of German procurement methods, which are of particular interest, will be discussed: first, the method for determining armed forces' requirements, second, the coordination of procurement activities, and third, the relations of procurement organizations with industry.

1. Determination of requirements. A rational method for the determination of the material needs of the armed forces requires a high degree of cooperation among the branches of the armed forces, and between them and the civilian agencies which control munitions production. Lack of cooperation of the first type is analogous to the members of a family deciding independently on the shares of the family income each intends to spend. Lack of cooperation of the second type is analogous to a family planning its expenditures without regard to its income or its bank balance.

In the pre-Speer period in Germany, we find practically no com-

7. Report by Dr. Alfred Jacobs, chief of division of social statistics, Central Statistical Office; and Hettlage, report on "German War Finance," Files, United States Strategic Bombing Survey.

8. The loudest objections were voiced by Speer and by Hettlage, Speer's financial adviser. FIAT and United States Strategic Bombing Survey interrogation reports.

munication between the armed forces and civilian agencies, and very little among the separate branches of the armed forces. According to Speer and General Thomas, those agencies responsible for the general direction of the economy — the Four-Year Planning Office and the Economics Ministry — were never consulted in the formulation of requirements.[9] This, of course, corresponded to Hitler's precepts on the proper duties of military leaders and the leaders of the economy. The formulation of requirements was left entirely to the three military commands. Each command determined its needs independently and was responsible only to Hitler. General Thomas, head of the OKW's War Economy and Armament Office, has stated that the cardinal defect of the system was that his Office had no voice in drawing up or in modifying the material requirements for the three services; that they came to him only after encountering difficulties in securing the necessary labor, raw materials, or industrial facilities.[10]

The method for determining requirements within the army itself has been criticized on the ground that there was little communication between those planning military strategy and the officers responsible for drawing up requirements.[11] The Army General Staff interested itself in requirements only insofar as it decided the size and make-up of the army, or the food, ammunition, gasoline, and spare-part requirements for particular field operations. The actual planning of the army's needs was done under the direction of the Chief of Army Equipment and Commander of the Replacement Army, who headed army procurement, and reported not to the Chief of Staff but directly to Hitler.

A major reason for this lack of liaison was that supply officers were regarded as mere technicians and as inferior to officers responsible for the planning and execution of military campaigns. The War Academy was not open to technical officers; they were rarely assigned to command staff positions; and a long tradition extolled the fighting man and belittled the rear echelons.

2. Coordination of armed forces procurement. The armed forces operated as independently in the actual procurement of war mate-

---

9. Thomas, "Basic Facts for a History of the German War Economy"; Speer's letters to Hitler; Speer's diary.

10. Speer's letters to Hitler; Speer's diary.

11. Speer's letters to Hitler; Speer's diary.

rial as they did in determining their requirements. Army procurement was directed by Colonel General Fromm, Chief of Army Equipment and Commander of the Replacement Army. Nominally, Fromm was under the Army Commander; actually, he reported directly to Hitler, by-passing both the army and OKW general staffs. Aircraft design, procurement, and distribution were centralized under a General Luftzeugmeister, General Milch, who was Deputy Air Force Commander. Until March 1944, when the production of fighter planes was brought under the Speer Ministry, Milch's organization was practically autonomous, having, according to General Thomas, as little as possible to do with the War Economy and Armament Office, and free of the influence of Hitler, who was mainly preoccupied with the Army.[12] Naval procurement was relatively unimportant and neither Thomas nor Hitler showed much interest in controlling it.

The Armed Forces' War Economy and Armament Office played only a secondary role in procurement. In the first place, it was responsible for the production of such ordnance items as were used in common by the army, navy and airforce. This group of items was kept as small as possible by the forces themselves. For calibres of rifles nominally identical, for example, it was the practice of each of the services to specify slight differences in order to retain the right of procurement, and also to avoid competition for ammunition stocks. Supplies other than munitions used in common, food and clothing being the most important, were procured and distributed by the army.

A second responsibility of the War Economy and Armament Office in procurement was the supervision of the Armament Inspection Offices (*Ruestungsinspektionen*), the economic field offices of the high command. These regional offices were responsible for seeing that the armaments plants had the necessary labor, raw materials, and power to carry out their orders.

The Armament Inspection Offices did not place contracts, and they had no power to determine the order in which contracts should be serviced. In 1940, according to Thomas, industry was flooded with war orders which would have taken several years to execute.[13]

12. Speer's letters to Hitler; Speer's diary.
13. Speer's letters to Hitler; Speer's diary.

Thomas testified that his attempt to end this chaos by instituting a priorities system for the servicing of orders was a complete failure because the Inspection Offices had no powers of enforcement.

During the years 1939 through 1941, therefore, there was little coordination of the purchasing activities of the army, navy and airforce. The principle of procurement was essentially one of competing for supplies.

3. *Procurement agencies in their relation to industry.* A major reason, according to Speer and his associates (particularly Saur and Schieber), for the low level of war production during this period was that the armed forces procurement officials had no industrial experience.[14] This opinion was shared by Thomas except with regard to the staff of his own office.[15] When Speer later became Minister of Armaments and War Production, one of his first moves was to substitute his own technical experts for these military officials, and he regarded it as a major reason for his success.

Variants of the following quotation appear in Speer's memoranda to Hitler, his speeches to German industrialists, his personal diary, and reports which he wrote for American and British officials after the war:

> After 1933, the Wehrmacht was therefore forced to build up administrative organizations which could deal with industrial problems in detail and on as large a scale as the lessons of the First World War required. These organizations quickly developed into the huge War Production and Armaments Board of the OKW, with approximately 3,000 persons, the Army Ordnance Board with 8,000 persons, the Quartermaster General for the Air Force with 5,000 persons, the Naval Armaments Board, and the Ordnance Inspections. These organizations, consisting of officers and civil service officials, conducted purely theoretical deliberations on rearmament, and became so large that they managed only to keep each other busy. They committed what might be called mental incest, and when Germany's rearmament got actively under way, all the mistakes which later led to the surprisingly low level of armaments production were already present in embryo. . . . Even after the outbreak of war, our armament production remained far below that of the years 1917–1918, although industry had since made considerable progress and should have been capable of greater production. The great administrative organizations of the Wehrmacht were

---

14. United States Strategic Bombing Survey interrogations of Speer, Saur and Schieber; Speer's letters to Hitler; Speer's diary.

15. Speer's letters to Hitler; Speer's diary.

incapable of exploiting the available capacity. Highly qualified personnel had found better pay in industry and were not called on for their
cooperation.[16]

An outspoken critic of long-range economic planning because he
believed planners were inevitably second-rate bureaucrats, Speer
envied Russia and particularly the United States in having to im-
provise their wartime economic organizations (the English, he believed, were as tradition-bound as the Germans).[17]

Speer probably exaggerated the importance of low-calibre procurement staffs in accounting for Germany's small munitions production.
In comparison with other factors which will be discussed later, it
seems to have been of secondary importance. Nevertheless, a review
of some of the procurement practices shows that there was a real
basis for his views.

The Air Ministry was probably the worst offender in its dealings
with industry. In accounting for the low aircraft production during
the first several years of the war, a number of German officials have
attached considerable importance to numerous changes in designs and
in models which prevented the utilization of mass production techniques.[18] Requirements were initiated in the Air Staff, an organization composed mostly of young combat heroes appointed by Goering.
The membership of the Air Staff was frequently changed, and it is
said that each new officer thought it his duty to introduce a few
changes, at least, in aircraft designs.[19] Furthermore, during the period
1939–1942, there were frequent changes in the basic decision as to
whether Germany should build up a fighter or a bomber force, and
these were reflected in orders to industry.

A perhaps exaggerated example of the lack of appreciation for
industrial problems is illustrated by the experience of the Henschel
Aircraft Company. In 1940, when this company was engaged in the
production of the JU 88, the Air Ministry ordered it to change to
the HS 129. Production tooling was about half completed when the

16. Report written by Speer on "The Industrial Mobilization of Germany for
War Production."

17. Letter to Hitler dated 20 July 1944.

18. "Rationalization of the German Armament Industry," a symposium of
essays prepared by a number of German technical experts. Files, United States
Strategic Bombing Survey.

19. "Rationalization of the German Armament Industry."

contract was canceled, and the company told to make preparations for producing the JU 188. When the JU 188 was about to come into production, the Air Ministry again changed its mind, and substituted the Me 410. The story does not end here. The company was about 80 per cent tooled up for production when a new order directed Henschel to produce instead the JU 388. These planes had only started to flow off the production line when the Air Ministry decided to give up the bomber program. During the remainder of the war the Henschel plant manufactured wings for the JU 88, a night fighter.

German statisticians have estimated that in 1942 there was a loss of 20 per cent in total aircraft production simply because of frequent design changes, which prevented the industry from getting into serial production.[20]

Another indication that the Air Force was not expert in its dealings with industry was its famous "court-martial" system of procurement which probably owe its origin to Goering himself. Manufacturers were commanded to deliver a specified quantity of aircraft or air armaments within a specified period of time. If successful, there was usually a rather impressive ceremony at which the plant manager was presented with a medal; if not, he was court-martialed. In the latter case the defendants invariably laid the blame on failure to receive promised laborers, tools, materials, or components, and were usually acquitted. Needless to say, however, this system hardly made for good relations in industry.

Incompetent procurement practices were not confined to the air force. The army has been severely criticized on two general grounds.[21] First, it has been stated that armaments designs (particularly in tanks and armoured vehicles) were introduced without consulting industry as to the production problems involved. This often resulted in expensive delays for redesigning equipment, large losses of production in order to make minor improvements in performance, and a general failure to achieve the economies of large-scale output. A second criticism was that the Army's insistence on "German" standards of technical perfection required a dispropor-

20. From a study on aircraft production made by the Planungsamt, Files, United States Strategic Bombing Survey.
21. "Rationalization of the German Armament Industry."

tionate use of resources achieving such perfection only at the cost of a much smaller output. Saur, head of the Technical Department of the Speer Ministry, was fond of the following illustration:

> It is a valid law that with 60 per cent expenditure one can have 90 per cent success, but in order to have 100 per cent success one must have 100 per cent expenditure. The attempt should never be made to achieve the last 10 per cent since the expenditure is too great.[22]

We may conclude that German military procurement, 1939 through 1941, suffered from several major defects. Each branch of the service was engaged in its own procurement activities with little central direction. As a result, requirements were formulated with little attention either to the nation's total resources or to attaining a balanced use of resources among the branches of the forces. Finally, their procurement methods hampered firms from producing efficiently.

C. *Control of Civilian Production*

Control over the production and allocation of civilian goods was the responsibility of the Ministry of Economics and the Ministry of Food and Agriculture, both of which were under Funk, Commissioner-General for the Economy. According to Speer and his confederates, Funk's policies were heavily to blame for Germany's failure to mobilize her economy during this period. Specifically, Funk was said to have been more interested in protecting the German standard of living than of channeling resources from the civilian to the war sector of the economy.[23] Aggregate civilian consumption actually rose in 1939 and fell only moderately during 1940 and 1941. The real decline did not come until 1942, when consumption was reduced 10 per cent below the 1941 level, bringing it down to nearly the depression level.[24] Although Funk's critics, notably Speer, blamed him for failing to accomplish this reduction earlier, Funk, himself, was only a puppet. Major policy matters like this were decided at a much higher level by Hitler, Goering, and the Nazi Party.

Besides this failure, Funk's Economics Ministry was criticized on

22. "Rationalization of the German Armament Industry."
23. Speer's letters to Hitler; Speer's diary; and reports written by Wagenfuehr, Kehrl, and Schieber.
24. See Appendix, section 1.

two other grounds:[25] first, because it failed to cooperate with the war agencies in curtailing production of goods using scarce materials, and second because it was said to be inefficient in converting civilian industries to war production. Speer gives these two charges against Funk as the main reasons for his taking over from the Economics Ministry the supervision of a number of consumer goods industries in 1943.[26] At practically every one of Hitler's conferences with his economic advisers, Speer protested that one factory or another — a factory making furniture, one producing cooking utensils, a toy factory in Thuringia — could not be converted to war work because of objections of the Economics Ministry or of the local Gauleiters. Speer's attempt to curb the production of radio tubes for civilian uses because of a serious shortage for radar and other communications equipment became a major issue in which the Economics Ministry was backed by the Propaganda Ministry and by Sauckel.[27] The second criticism applied not only to the Economics Ministry but also to the armed forces procurement agencies. Speer claimed that these organizations permitted plants to work on war orders, while still continuing to produce civilian goods, preventing the economies of large-scale production for both types of output. He also denounced the Economics Ministry for not closing down many small consumer-goods manufacturing establishments altogether, and concentrating output in the most efficient plants. When Speer later tried to do this himself, he ran into the powerful opposition of the Gauleiters, the local party chieftains, interested in protecting the business firms in their own districts.

D. *Control of Resources*

Having discussed the government controls over the production of civilian goods and armaments, we now examine the methods used for controlling resources — raw materials, labor and investment. Our primary interest is to learn how the direction of resources was integrated with decisions on output of end products.

1. Raw Materials. The production and distribution of raw materials was directed by the *Reichstellen* (discussed above) and like

25. Written statements of Albert Speer on "The Industrial Mobilization of Germany for War Production," Files, United States Strategic Bombing Survey.
26. "The Industrial Mobilization of Germany for War Production."
27. Record of the Fuehrer's Conferences, October, 1942.

organizations, nominally under the Ministry of Economics. The Ministry, however, did little by way of supervising or coordinating their work. Each *Reichstelle* instituted its own priority procedures, inventory regulations, material conservation policy, methods of production control, etc.

The efficiency of the controls varied from one *Reichstelle* to another. For iron and steel, the Reich Board continually issued more priority of quota rights than there was steel, with the result that no manufacturer could be sure that he would receive the quantity originally allotted to him. For nonferrous metals, on the other hand, regulation was more successful. Energetic salvage drives, strict regulations specifying which metals could and could not be used in various end products, and tight controls over their distribution prevented what otherwise might have been a very serious problem.

The *Reichstellen,* however, comprised only one link in the whole process of raw material allocation, and the major defects in raw material allocation lay in the manner in which the system as a whole operated. This can be illustrated by tracing the procedure by which armament plants obtained their raw materials. First, individual plants reported their raw material requirements for the ensuing three-month period to the procurement agency under which they held their contracts. This agency then prepared a consolidated requirements statement for the War Economy and Armament Office. On this level, the system can be severely criticized on the grounds that plants invariably exaggerated their needs and the procurement agencies further exaggerated them on the premise that all armed forces' requirements would later be cut by a uniform percentage. General Thomas cites as an extreme example the 1940 requirements for copper, which in total exceeded the entire world's output.[28] The air force program "Elch" provides another example of inflated requirements. Under this program, from August 1941 until March 1943, total aircraft production (measured by weight) was to be increased about 30 per cent. To accomplish this, the Air Ministry demanded an 85 per cent increase in aluminum supplies, a 100 per cent increase in magnesium, and a 65 per cent increase in the total number of workers employed by the aircraft industry.[29] After the War Economy and

28. "Basic Facts for a History of the German War Economy."
29. The details of this program were found in the files of the Air Ministry.

Armaments Office received the statements of estimated material needs from the three branches of the service, it negotiated with the Economics Ministry for material supplies. Neither of these organizations had the means or the power to go back and examine the details of the requests to see if they were reasonable; rather, according to General Thomas, discussions were carried on in terms of global quantities of steel, copper, aluminum, etc. Disagreements — and these were not infrequent — were arbitrated by the Four-Year Planning Office or directly by Hitler. The process did not end here, however, for these decisions only informed the *Reichstellen* how they were to distribute the materials; the actual distribution to the plants was their responsibility. And if, as in the case of iron and steel, the distribution controls were inefficient, the plants had no assurance they would obtain the steel allotted to them and the entire allocation procedure then became a sheer farce.

As a necessary consequence of such a system, it was only by accident that individual producers received their raw materials in the proper proportions. For example, an ammunition producer might obtain the quantities of copper, coal and other materials necessary to execute a contract but find himself short of the needed steel, while another producer might have satisfied his steel requirements but be held up for a lack of copper. General Thomas stated that cases of this sort were very common, but that his Office could do little to remedy the situation.[30]

To make matters even worse, production programs were frequently modified or canceled after the raw material allocations had been made. In such cases, plants frequently did not cancel their orders for scarce materials, operating on the principle that at a later date these would be difficult to obtain.

2. *Labor.* Until 1942 responsibility for the recruitment and placement of labor rested with the Labor Ministry. Although this Ministry was placed under the Plenipotentiary for the Economy in 1939, no real control was exercised over it by Funk. The transfer of the control over labor to Sauckel in 1942, therefore, cannot be said to have divorced labor from production controls, for these two never had been united. This was a basic defect of German economic organization throughout the entire war.

30. "Basic Facts for a History of the German War Economy."

Most of the friction between the Labor Ministry and the civilian and military agencies responsible for production arose through the activities of the so-called Comb-out Commissions. Supervised by the local Labor Offices, these Commissions had the power to remove excess labor from any plant, both in essential and nonessential industries. This was especially resented by the armed forces and Todt's Ministry of Armaments and Munitions (established in 1940), who complained that the Labor Offices had no right to tell manufacturers under their jurisdiction how to run their plants. In the spring of 1941 Todt set up his own investigating commissions which to a considerable extent only duplicated the activities of the Comb-out Commissions and provided no solution at all. In the civilian goods industries the energetic efforts of the Comb-out Commissions released more labor than would have been the case if the task had rested entirely with the Economics Ministry. And in this case their interference in production policy was desirable for the war effort.

These combing-out operations were only one phase of the Labor Ministry's general responsibility for satisfying war industries with the necessary manpower. In the early years of the war several decrees gave the Labor Ministry extraordinary powers in this regard. In 1939 it was decreed that workers in a number of industries could not leave their employment without the consent of the local Labor Office, and that no industry could hire a laborer unless he was referred by a Labor Office.[31] A 1942 decree gave the Labor Offices complete control over the hiring and dismissing of workers in all occupations.[32]

Labor was assigned to the armaments industry by application of the plants to the appropriate Labor Office. As long as there was sufficient labor locally — and this was generally the case during the early war years — the system functioned smoothly. When the local exchange could not make the necessary number of workers available, the War Economy and Armament Office asked the Ministry of Labor to arrange for a transfer of workers from some other district. It was here that Thomas and later Speer ran into difficulties. For there was not always agreement on whether the demand for labor was urgent enough to make relocation necessary, and there were disputes on

31. *Reichsgesetzblatt,* 1939, I, p. 444.
32. Report of Statistisches Reichsamt on "The Labor Situation in 1943."

which industries had the first claim on released labor. The question of who should establish the priorities was not settled until 1943, when Hitler restricted Sauckel's powers to control the supply of labor, leaving Speer alone responsible for its distribution.

Besides the fact that labor and production policies were poorly coordinated, a second and hardly less serious defect was that there was no real attempt to relate military manpower requirements to manpower requirements of industry. Unlike the system used in the United States during the war, the calling up of military manpower in Germany was done by the armed forces themselves, with little consultation with outside organizations. The draft system was based on the theory that the military should have first claim on all available manpower, the armaments industries satisfying their needs with those who were left. For workers engaged in high priority production, blanket deferments were granted on occasion, but generally key personnel could be deferred from the army only with great difficulty.

To keep an employee from being drafted, the firm first had to apply to its economic chamber. If the application was approved there, it would go to the local military command which would communicate with the local Labor Office to see if a replacement could be found. If the Labor Office replied in the negative, a commission headed by a military officer would investigate the case and arrive at a decision. According to Schmelter, head of the Manpower Utilization Branch of the Speer Ministry, such deferments were very rare before 1942 and plants lost many of their key personnel to the army.[33] In February 1942, armaments plants were given authority to designate "reserved workers," and submit the list for approval to the Armament Inspectorates. Men in key positions were deferred indefinitely, and specialized workers could not be called up prior to an eight weeks' notification.[34]

In spite of the fact that before 1942 there was no real coordination between the determination of military manpower requirements, the recruitment of a civilian labor, and the planning of production, there were surprisingly few complaints of labor shortages during this period. Records of the meetings of *Zentrale Planung* or the transcripts of Hitler's conferences with his economic advisers contain

33. From a report prepared by Schmelter on "Manpower Utilization."
34. From a report prepared by Schmelter on "Manpower Utilization."

very few references to labor difficulties. This was not due to any positive merits of this system of government economic organization, but simply to the fact that Germany still had ample labor reserves. At a later date, as we shall see, the flaws in the organization became more apparent.

3. *Investment.* Two general methods were used to control investment during the war: bans prohibiting certain types of unessential investment, and direct supervision over the activities of the construction and machinery industries.

Investment bans had been instituted as early as 1933, not as a move towards preparing for war, but as a part of the compulsory cartelization program. Cartel arrangements have generally attempted to limit expansion of capacity, but only with some difficulty since when an industry succeeded in earning monopoly profits the individual members found it to their own advantage to increase capacity. A law on compulsory cartels in 1933 sought to remove this "danger" by giving the Ministry of Economics the power to prevent the establishment of new enterprises or the enlargement of capacity of existing firms in those industries where large excess capacity threatened ruinous competition.[35] In following years the prohibition was applied to such diverse industries as cement, glass containers, rolled-wire products, cigarettes, and graphic printing.

During the war, this long-tried method of investment control was used to prohibit investment in industries deemed unessential to the war effort. In 1939, 45 branches of industry, one branch of insurance, and three branches of trade were affected by investment bans.[36]

It soon became apparent, however, that this type of investment control was inadequate for wartime needs. The problem was one of determining the needs for capital goods, buildings, and machinery, firm by firm, and allocating them accordingly. Building activity was supervised by the General Plenipotentiary for the Construction Economy, Todt. Control of machinery production and distribution rested with the Economic Group for Machine Construction, an agency of the Ministry of Economics.

The inability of these authorities, especially in machinery, to re-

35. For an extended discussion of this subject see Samuel Laurie, *Private Investment in a Controlled Economy.*

36. Laurie, *Private Investment in a Controlled Economy.*

duce the output of capital goods to the desired extent was discussed in Chapter V. It is necessary here to say something about their relations with the organizations responsible for armaments production. From the beginning of the war there were sharp disagreements between Todt and the armed forces' procurement agencies over the necessity for constructing additional capacity in the armaments industry, especially army armaments. In January, 1940, Todt recommended to Hitler that the armed forces should make better use of existing facilities, rather than carry out a large contemplated expansion. Partly because Todt's recommendation corresponded with Hitler's own ideas, and partly because Hitler was dissatisfied in general with the army procurement agencies, Todt was appointed Minister of Weapons and Ammunition. This, however, did not settle the dispute as to who was to have the final word on building new armaments plants. Even within the Ministry's limited jurisdiction, ground force munitions, Todt's powers were uncertain, and he had no authority over the production policies of the navy or air force. His appointment had the effect of dividing responsibility on the key decision of the desirability of building new plants among personalities whose views and interests were basically antagonistic.

In the case of machinery, the sides in the conflict between the armed forces and the government director of the industry were reversed. As we have indicated in Chapter V, Lange represented the interests of the industry in desiring to sell as much machinery as possible. Officials like General Thomas, on the other hand, wanted to curb machinery output in order to save scarce materials and convert a greater part of the industry to munitions production.

E. *Top-level Coordination*

At the beginning of this discussion we pointed out that rational economic planning required centralized decisions on the use of the economy's resources. We may now ask how was this possible in the German wartime economic administration? As we have seen, decisions on war production were independently made by the three branches of the armed forces; the production of civilian goods was controlled by another group of agencies under the Ministry of Economics. Control over resources was under the authority of still other organizations. Furthermore, the leaders of these organizations did not comprise a personally harmonious group. Who then made the top-level decisions? Was there an economic high-command?

At the beginning of the war this was a hotly contested issue between the armed forces and Goering's Four-Year Planning Office. General Thomas believed that it was impossible for the armed forces to run the war sector of the economy without having a voice in the control of resources. For this reason he believed that his organization and the Ministry of Economics should cooperatively direct the economy. Goering, however, wanted neither a strong Ministry of Economics nor the usurpation of his powers by the armed forces. Goering won the dispute, formally at least, partly because of Hitler's long-standing prejudice against military meddling in economic affairs and against civilians concerning themselves with military matters, and partly because Hitler had no respect for General Thomas. In September 1939, top-level economic powers were given to an Economic General Council, with Goering as Chairman.

The Economic General Council, however, was an organization only on paper. According to Speer and Thomas, it met only a few times during the war and exercised none of its powers.[37] As a matter of fact, later in the war, when Speer was Minister of Armaments and War Production and exercised almost complete control over the economy, he was not even a member of the council.

Nor was the Four-Year Planning Office the top-level coordinating body. Aside from settling some disputes on raw material questions, the Four-Year Planning Office did not participate in the decisions of other civilian or military economic agencies. This may have been due to Goering's preoccupation with the Air Force or to Hitler's unwillingness to have a powerful economic dictator at this time. All accounts agree, however, that Goering's position as Plenipotentiary for the War Economy was a fiction.[38]

Since none of these agencies provided the economy with top-level direction, the only remaining possibility to be considered is Hitler himself. And it must be admitted that until Speer became Minister of

37. Speer's Memoranda and Thomas' "Basic Facts for a History of the German War Economy."
38. "Basic Facts for a History of the German War Economy."

Armaments and War Production in 1942, Hitler, in fact, directed the economy, as he did the armed forces. This is not to say that as head of the nation Hitler only had a hand in determining the broad economic objectives. His role in the economic administration went much further than that. Hitler made countless day-to-day decisions on all sorts of economic matters, many of which another dictator would have left to his subordinates. And however gifted Hitler may have been as a military strategist (a subject we will leave to the military historians), his talents as an economic director were distinctly limited.

In the first place, Hitler did not appear to comprehend the essence of economic thinking, namely, that the production of various types of commodities compete with one another for the use of resources. Rather, his thinking simply ran in terms of maximum performance for every industry. This is well illustrated by a conversation between Hitler and Speer shortly after the latter became Minister of Armaments and War Production. At the time Speer asked Hitler how he was to decide on priorities in case army, navy and air force requirements could not be simultaneously executed. Hitler told him that this was no problem; that Speer simply had to see that a maximum amount of everything was produced.

Hitler's second weakness as an economic planner we have already alluded to — his great concern with details and an incomprehensible disinterest in general matters. One will look in vain through the thousands of pages of Hitler's conferences on economic matters to find expression of views on such subjects as whether more laborers could be released from the civilian goods industries; whether too much steel was going into nonwar uses; or whether one half of total munitions expenditures should be used for the air force. What will be found, instead, is a tremendous concern with all the details of army supply problems, and Hitler's *ad hoc* decisions on countless immediate issues, such as the melting down of church bells of great historic interest, the closing of toy factories in Thuringia, high-grade steel for the Tiger tank program, the building of a new power plant in the Ruhr, etc. Most of all, the reader will find evidence of Hitler's fastidious interest in weapons designs. Next to being a military genius, Hitler prided himself most on being a great technical expert. Speer reports that Hitler inspected every piece of army equipment, and all changes in designs had to be approved by him personally.[39]

Hitler himself made the final decision on every detail of army requirements. According to Speer his decisions were based on two considerations: the 1917–1918 supply figures which Speer claimed that Hitler knew in detail, and intuition on the maximum quantities of the various types of armaments which Germany might be able to produce.[40]

This study of the administration of the German war economy indicates, first, that the use of resources was planned and directed by at least ten independent organizations, with no effective leadership or coordination. This fact alone would have prevented a wise use of resources, regardless of what the ultimate economic objectives may have been. Armaments production, for example, should be planned by a single organization balancing the demand for war production as determined by the general war strategy against the nation's supply of resources. But in Germany, the air force, the army, and the navy determined their needs independently. The Labor Ministry had a hand in armaments production insofar as it had ultimate responsibility for the placement of labor. The Economics Ministry came in through its responsibility for allocating raw materials. The General Commissioner for Building had a voice in determining where additional capacity was needed. Hitler's *ad hoc* decisions on all sorts of matters relating to armaments production further subdivided responsibility.

A number of aspects of Germany's war effort can be understood only in terms of this "system" of decision-making. As a prime example, how can it be explained that throughout the war between 40 and 50 per cent of all German munitions expenditures went for aircraft and air armament? [41] In Britain, the proportion of resources devoted to air power was no more, and in the United States it was much less.[42] And certainly air power did not have nearly the place in Germany's over-all war strategy that it had in that of the Allies.

39. "The Industrial Mobilization of Germany for War," Files, United States Strategic Bombing Survey.
40. "The Industrial Mobilization of Germany for War."
41. *Indexziffern der Deutschen Rüstungsendfertigung,* Planungsamt, 1944.
42. "Wartime Production Achievements," report of the War Production Board dated October 9, 1945, and "World Munitions Production," War Production Board, July 15, 1944.

If during the war someone had actually proposed to Hitler that about the same amount of resources be used for equipping the air force as the army, it is very unlikely that he would have agreed to such a suggestion. For all of his military campaigns Hitler's strategy relied primarily on ground force operations, in particular on panzer operations. After the failure of Goering's plan to cripple Britain by strategic bombing, Hitler regarded air power as of only secondary importance in Germany's over-all military strategy: to provide air-ground support for his armies, and to protect the homeland. But there is no evidence that Hitler ever concerned himself with the question of whether a disproportionate amount of resources was going into the aircraft industry; it is more likely that this came about as a result of Goering's personal position and nothing more.

A second conclusion of this chapter is that the economic administration in several of its important functions was inefficient, notably in the procurement of war material and the allocation of raw materials. In procurement, frequent changes of weapons designs, insistence on the highest quality of technical perfection, and general ignorance of industrial problems on the part of procurement officials, prevented a maximum utilization of the capacity and labor employed in the armaments industry. In raw material distribution the chaos in steel distribution itself could have supplied an important part of the explanation for the low level of armaments production during the first several years of the war. Moreover, the whole system of raw material distribution operated in such a manner that it was impossible for manufacturers to get their materials in the needed proportions.

Granted that the efficiency of the Nazi bureaucracy in economic matters fell far short of that attributed to it by the outside world, the question still remains whether this alone can explain the limited mobilization of the German economy during this period. This question cannot be answered until we have found what sort of economic performance the Nazi leaders really demanded. If a large-scale mobilization of the economy was demanded, then we have no reason to doubt that it was prevented by an inefficient economic administration. If not, then we may be able to explain not only the small war output which the Germans obtained from their economy, but also why they were satisfied with their chaotic system of economic controls.

V I I I   *"A Peacelike War Economy"*

This chapter examines the hypothesis that Germany's failure to produce more armaments was a failure of the German leaders to demand a greater economic effort. We shall begin by summarizing Hitler's war plans insofar as they affected economic preparations.

1. HITLER'S WAR PLANS

Hitler's decision to go to war with Poland in September 1939 represented just one more step in his long-range plan of conquest. This plan contemplated the satisfaction of Germany's territorial desires not by a major war, but by a series of blitzkriegs against the smaller European nations. In each case, the "enemy" was to be conquered, by force or by intimidation, so speedily that the democracies could be presented with a *fait accompli* before they had time to intervene. To carry out this plan, a large-scale war effort was not envisioned. Fifty or sixty well-trained divisions and an air force of several thousand planes were regarded as sufficient. As a further precaution it was the task of the Propaganda Ministry to create the illusion of a much more powerful military force. Russia was immobilized, temporarily at least, by a Pact concluded a few days before the outbreak of hostilities.

When the conquest of Poland was planned in the spring of 1939, it was assumed that, as at Munich, the British and French would again back down. The directive for "Case White" stated:

> Our policy aims at confining the war to Poland, and this is considered possible in view of the internal crisis in France and British restraint as a result of this.[1]

1. *Nazi Conspiracy and Aggression,* VI, 935.

In his speech before the military commanders on August 22, 1939, Hitler again expressed the opinion that the probability of Allied intervention was small, that Britain was unprepared and that France was unwilling to enter a major war.[2]

After Poland had been conquered, Hitler expected that Britain and France would regret their declaration of war on Germany and withdraw as gracefully as they could. When, however, it became apparent that they were not going to "listen to reason," Hitler found himself involved in a major war, the very thing he had planned and hoped to avoid. It was feared, especially by the General Staff, that a war with France and Britain would mean a war of attrition, a repetition of World War I. Given the weaknesses in Germany's economic potential, both Hitler and the military leaders strongly feared that such a war would result only in defeat. Moreover, they were more immediately concerned that France and Britain, remembering the experience of World War I, might take the initiative in occupying Belgium and Holland. It was believed that from there they could destroy the Ruhr by aerial and artillery attack, if not by actual invasion. When the German armies were occupied in Poland, the military leaders staked everything on the hope that the Allied Armies would not be able or willing to march into the Lowlands. After the conquest of Poland this was still regarded as an imminent danger. The Memorandum and Directives for the Conduct of the War in the West, dated 9 October 1939, stated:

> As long as neutral Belgium and Holland remain as protective zones in front of the Ruhr, attack by aircraft is still somewhat difficult, bombardment by long-range artillery impossible. But, in the event of the cessation of Belgian-Dutch neutrality, the military boundary would be withdrawn to a distance which would bring at least the South-West Ruhr zone within the Range of super-long-range guns, and Dusseldorf even within the range of long-range batteries. From this moment the Ruhr, as an active factor of the German war-economy, would either drop out, or at least be crippled. There is no means of replacing it.[3]

Hitler's speech before the military commanders in November suggests more than aerial and artillery bombardment:

> We have an Achilles' heel: the Ruhr. The progress of the war depends on the possession of the Ruhr. If England and France push through

2. *Nazi Conspiracy and Aggression*, VII, 584.
3. *Nazi Conspiracy and Aggression*, VII, 805.

Belgium and Holland into the Ruhr, we shall be in the greatest of danger. That could lead to a paralyzing of the German power of resistance. . . . *If the French army marches into Belgium in order to attack us, it will be too late for us.*[4]

That these fears were real is evidenced in the fact that until the actual invasion of France, the Germans worked feverishly on the construction of the Siegfried Line. From 1938 until May 1940, two billion reichsmarks were poured into the building of these defenses.[5] Even after the offensive began, the building of fortifications was not discontinued. The directive for the invasion of the Lowlands stated: "Finally at every hold-up, even during the big attack, construction of a defensive line in the rear will be begun, using the materials which otherwise would serve to reinforce the West Wall." [6]

During the Autumn of 1939, therefore, the Germans were not very happy about their prospects in either a long or a short war, if the Allies took the initiative. Many of the military leaders were of the opinion that there was only one sensible alternative: Germany had to make peace with the Allies even if the terms were not favorable. Although Hitler had to admit that he was wrong in assuming that France and Britain would back down, as they had at Munich, he could not accept such a recommendation, if for no other reason than it might well mean the possibility of his downfall.

Hitler's counterproposal was to make a daring attack — initially set for November 23 — through Belgium and Holland to seize these countries before the Allies could. In a speech before the military commanders in November he stated that such action was very risky, but he saw no other alternative, as he put it, to "victory or defeat." [7] Hitler listed four factors in Germany's favor: first, the superior fighting quality of the German soldier; second, the superiority of the German armies in men and equipment; third, the pact with Russia which prevented for the time being a two-front war; and finally, to use his own words, "As the last factor I must name my own person in all modesty: irreplaceable. Neither a military nor a civil person could replace me. . . . I am convinced of the powers of my intellect and of decision. Wars are always ended only by the destruction of

4. *Nazi Conspiracy and Aggression*, III, 578 (author's italics).
5. *Bericht von Westwall*, a document found in the files of the Speer Ministry.
6. *Nazi Conspiracy and Aggression*, VII, 814.
7. *Nazi Conspiracy and Aggression*, III, 575ff.

the opponent. Everyone who believes differently is irresponsible." [8]

The optimism of "this Austrian corporal" was not shared by the Generals. Military leaders like von Brauchitsch, Commander-in-Chief of the Army, Halder, Chief of the Army General Staff, Admiral Canaris, head of OKW Intelligence, Generals Witzleben and Beck, Commanders of Army Groups, and General Thomas, head of the War Economy and Armaments Office, were firmly convinced that it would be folly to attack. In his book, *To the Bitter End,* Gisevius reports a historic meeting between von Brauchitsch and Hitler on 6 November 1939:

> Yesterday the expected conference between Brauchitsch and Hitler had taken place. There was a sharp clash when the general expressed his fears about the offensive. All his strategic arguments were repulsed; Hitler did not even listen to his political arguments. At last the commander-in-chief brought up one of his heavy guns — which he should not have done. Brauchitsch declared to Hitler that the morale among the troops was so poor that they could not risk such a daring enterprise.
>
> That was the last straw. Hitler worked up the usual fit of rage. . . .[9]

As in 1938, there was talk between these and other officials (Gisevius being one of them) of a conspiracy to seize Hitler and make peace with France and Britain. According to Gisevius, Thomas, and Halder, the Allied countries were informed of the plotters' intentions through neutral channels.[10] Gisevius also states that several of the plotters (not the Generals) went as far as warning Holland and Belgium, as well as France and Britain, of the impending invasion. The last of these famous warnings, Gisevius reports, was given to the Dutch ambassador on May 9, the night before the invasion. The Commander of the Dutch armies, however, refused to order the blowing up of the dikes. The Dutch had been warned so many times that they thought this was simply a part of the "war of nerves." [11]

It is probably true that the prognostications of the Generals were as much influenced by their hatred of Hitler as by an objective appraisal of the situation. Nevertheless, it can be seen that there was

8. *Nazi Conspiracy and Aggression,* III, 576.

9. Hans B. Gisevius, *To the Bitter End,* p. 388. This conversation is also reported in a SHAEF interrogation of General Warlimont.

10. Gisevius, *To the Bitter End,* pp. 376–456; United States Strategic Bombing Survey interrogations of Halder and Thomas.

11. Gisevius, *To the Bitter End,* pp. 454–455.

some real basis for their pessimistic views. As far as military manpower was concerned, Germany's strength was not regarded as greater than the strength of her enemies; in the autumn of 1939 German Intelligence credited each side with about 100 divisions.[12] As for armaments, German Intelligence correctly assumed that she had a marked superiority in two types, antiaircraft and antitank guns, and that she was inferior in heavy infantry weapons (which were not, of course, so important).[13] As far as tanks and aircraft were concerned, the available German Intelligence documents do not contain estimates of French and British strength. Assuming, however, that German information did not seriously underestimate British and French strength in these weapons, there was no cause for optimism here. In the spring of 1940, according to Tissier, England and France together had about 3850 tanks[14] as compared to about 3500 for the Germans[15] (mostly the light Mark I and Mark II types). In September 1939, Germany had about 1450 modern fighting planes as compared to about 950 for Britain and France, and 800 bombers compared to their 1300.[16] In the following months it is extremely likely that the position of the Allies became even more favorable because in Britain, at least, aircraft production was increasing faster than in Germany. It is likely that the quality of German aircraft and tanks exceeded that of her enemies, although the evidence, particularly in regard to aircraft, is contradictory.[17] However, in estimating material strength of the enemy, it is reasonable to assume that German Intelligence attached much more weight to quantitative than to qualitative differences. The latter are more difficult to gauge, especially before the weapons have seen combat use.

It is clear, therefore, why the military leaders did not believe that a victory could be won simply from an overwhelming superiority of men and material. A victory clearly required something more, but

12. *Nazi Conspiracy and Aggression,* III, 397; IV, 1035.
13. *Nazi Conspiracy and Aggression,* III, 397; IV, 1035.
14. Pierre Tissier, *The Riom Trial,* 1942, London, p. 53. Tissier, it may be noted, credited Germany with 4000-6500 tanks.
15. *Effects of Strategic Bombing,* p. 163.
16. Figures for France and Britain, Tissier, *The Riom Trial,* p. 63; Germany, from the records of the OKL. Tissier credited Germany with 6265 first line planes at the time of the invasion, twice her actual strength.
17. Tissier, *The Riom Trial,* pp. 63ff.

what else could be counted on? The superior fighting quality of the German soldier? During the Battle of Poland, the General Staff and even Hitler were disappointed in the low morale of the German troops. What of the element of surprise? According to Halder and Thomas this was completely discounted by the Generals. The French and British had no reason to believe that Germany would respect the neutrality of Belgium and Holland. The fact that a German plane carrying a copy of the invasion plans was forced down in Holland was not likely to make them less suspicious of Germany's intentions.[18]

Therefore, until the spring of 1940, at least, there were two views on Germany's best course of action — Hitler's view and that of the Generals. It is almost certainly because of this fundamental difference of opinion, rather than the official reason, the weather, that the attack was again and again postponed. When Hitler planned the attack for November or December, he could hardly have expected sunny skies and dry roads.

Finally, in mid-December, the attack was definitely called off until spring. Why Hitler was able to impose his will on the Generals in May when he could not do so during the preceding winter is a matter of conjecture. Perhaps the failure of the Allied armies to take the initiative helped to convince the Generals that Allied military leadership was weak. Such a feeling was likely to be strengthened by Germany's speedy conquest of Norway. Undoubtedly they thought that tank operations could be more successful during the summer months. And perhaps, as Gisevius suggests, men like Halder, who earlier had boasted that they would refuse to give the marching orders, really did not have the courage of their convictions. When put to the test, it is unlikely that a German officer would have taken his "soldier's oath" lightly.

The actual strategy called for the weight of the attack to be directed not against the Lowlands, where it was expected, but through the Ardennes, where the terrain seemed to preclude the use of tanks. This plan was prepared and submitted directly to Hitler by von Manstein, Runstedt's Chief-of-Staff. Hitler decided to accept it in spite of the objections of von Brauchitsch and Halder, who were in favor of using the von Schlieffen 1914 plan of attack. To show their

18. Gisevius, *To the Bitter End*, p. 453.

displeasure they later removed von Manstein from his post and placed him in command of an army corps which did not take part in the attack.

The story of Germany's conquest of France is too well known to bear repetition. The German Armies marched into Holland on May 10. In a little more than a month the British had been driven from the Continent, the French Armies thoroughly defeated, and the Germans were marching victoriously through Paris. The cost of the operation, according to German figures, was 69,384 permanent casualties,[19] a small fraction of the number lost in the single Battle of Verdun during World War I.

If Runstedt's claims are true, the victory might have been greater if Hitler had not forbidden him to attack the British at Dunkirk:

> "To me," remarked the Field-Marshal rather ruefully, "Dunkirk was one of the great turning-points of the war. If I had my way the English would not have got off so lightly at Dunkirk. But my hands were tied by direct orders from Hitler himself."

> "This incredible blunder was due to Hitler's personal ideal of generalship. The Fuehrer daily received statements of tank losses incurred during the campaign, and by a simple process of arithmetic he deduced that there was not sufficient armor available at this time to attack the English. He did not realize that many of the tanks reported out of action one day could, with a little extra effort on the part of the repair squads, be made able to fight in a very short time * * * He, therefore, ordered my forces be reserved so that they could be strong enough to take part in the southern drive. . . ."[20]

Even though the Germans may have added to their success by attacking Dunkirk, there can be little doubt that the conquest of France was the most startling victory of modern times.

The Germans themselves were no less surprised than the outside world. According to all accounts, the speed of the German victory came as a complete surprise both to the General Staff and to Hitler. It may be assumed that Hitler had little idea that his "dangerous gamble" would bring his armies to Paris within a month. It also may be assumed that the victory made Hitler in his own estimation the greatest military strategist of all time. Even more than this, the con-

19. From the records of the *Heerespersonalamt*, files of United States Strategic Bombing Survey.

20. Milton Shulman, *Defeat in the West*, New York, 1948, pp. 42–43.

quest of France was indisputable proof to Hitler that future victories would be primarily a matter of his own military genius. Economic preparedness was to be a matter of secondary importance. It is this victory, more than anything else, which is the key to understanding why war with Russia and the United States did not convince the Nazis of the necessity of an all-out effort.

After the conquest of France, the next item on Hitler's agenda was the invasion of Britain. As early as July 16, 1940, a directive for the attack on Britain had been issued.[21] Several weeks later a large-scale attack on the British Air Force was ordered as a preparatory measure to actual invasion, and the date for the invasion itself (Operation Sea Lion) was tentatively set for September 21.[22] In mid-September, however, the attack was indefinitely postponed, and on October 12 it was called off until at least the spring of 1941.[23] Finally, in December 1940, Hitler decided that Operation Sea Lion would be postponed until after he had dealt with Russia.[24]

It would seem that the opportune time for the invasion of Britain was as soon as possible after the fall of France, before she had had time to recover from her defeat. Why did Hitler decide to call off the attack? The answer, according to a number of German military authorities, is that Germany had neither the sea power nor the air power to support an invasion effort of the size believed necessary.[25] The number of divisions which the Germans were prepared to carry and support across the channel was twenty-six.[26] It was recognized that the transporting of even this number of divisions was highly risky, given the tremendous British naval superiority. Moreover, the aerial battle over Britain showed the Germans that they had grossly overestimated their own air strength. Against these twenty-six divisions, however, German Intelligence credited Britain with thirty-nine full-strength divisions — a gross exaggeration.[27] According to Churchill, Britain actually had no more than two or three well-equipped divisions at the time.[28] When Hitler was presented with

21. *Nazi Conspiracy and Aggression*, III, 399.
22. Shulman, *Defeat in the West*, p. 47.
23. Shulman, *Defeat in the West*, p. 47.
24. *Nazi Conspiracy and Aggression*, III, 407.
25. Interrogations of Generals von Runstedt, Halder, and Thomas.
26. Shulman, *Defeat in the West*, pp. 48–49.
27. Shulman, *Defeat in the West*, pp. 48–49.
28. Shulman, *Defeat in the West*, pp. 48–49.

such "facts," he could not dispute the opinion of von Runstedt and others that the idea of an invasion was foolhardy. Even he had too much respect for British naval power to attempt such a venture.

Further, there was no desire to embark on massive aircraft and ship-building programs. The German economy had already been under the "strain" of war for a year. As the directive canceling the invasion stated, "At the same time, however, the German economy will be relieved of a burden. . . ."[29]

Long before the invasion of Britain was officially canceled, Hitler himself seems to have given up the idea. As early as August 1940, according to the testimony of German Generals at the Nuremberg Trials, Hitler was discussing the use of his armies elsewhere — for a conquest of Russia.

On August 14, General Thomas made the following comment in his *Basic Facts for a History of the German War Economy:*

> On August 14, the Chief of the War Economy and Armaments Office, during a conference with the Reichmarshal Goering was informed that the Fuehrer desired partial delivery to the Russians only until the Spring of 1941. Later we would have no further interest in completely satisfying the Russian demands. This allusion moved the Chief to give priority to matters concerning the Russian War Economy.

By November, 1940, there could no longer be any doubt of Hitler's intentions. A directive from the Fuehrer's headquarters dated 12 November 1940 stated:

> Political discussions have been initiated with the aim of clarifying Russia's attitude for the time being. Irrespective of the results of these discussions, all preparations for the East which already have been verbally ordered will be continued.

> Instructions on this will follow, as soon as the general line of the Army's operational plan has been submitted to, and approved by me.[30]

On December 5 the Chief of the Army General Staff submitted his plans to Hitler, and on December 18, 1940, Hitler issued a directive for the "Case Barbarossa."

> The German Armed Forces must be prepared *to crush Soviet Russia in a quick campaign* before the end of the war against England.[31]

29. Shulman, *Defeat in the West*, p. 52.
30. *Nazi Conspiracy and Aggression*, I, 797.
31. *Nazi Conspiracy and Aggression*, III, 407.

Preparations for the attack were to be completed by May 15, 1941. At the beginning of April, however, it became necessary to postpone the opening of the offensive because of a commitment to Mussolini in the Balkans (later Hitler learned that the loss of a month of good fighting weather in Russia was no small sacrifice). On April 30, Hitler made his final decision — "D" day was set for the twenty-second of June.[32]

While the operation against Russia was being planned, Goering proposed as an alternative an attack on North Africa and the Near East. His plan called for a three-pronged attack; through Spain to Gibraltar, through Italy to Tripolitania, and through the Balkans to the Dardanelles and the Suez Canal. The object of the plan was to defeat the British armies in Africa, to seal off the Mediterranean, and eventually to gain control of the Persian and Arabian oil fields. If Germany had undertaken this as a full-scale operation, it is highly probable that she would have been successful. Perhaps, as Goering believed, it would have even been enough to make Britain withdraw from the war. When Rommel was later sent to Africa, this grandiose plan had been forgotten; the purpose was to save the Italian armies from defeat. Even with only a few divisions, however, Rommel came very close to driving through El Alamein to Cairo and Alexandria. There is no evidence, however, that Hitler seriously considered this as an alternative to the Russian campaign. While he listened to Goering's proposals in January and February of 1941, he had already made up his mind to attack Russia.

In retrospect, there is no doubt that Hitler's decision to go to war with Russia was his greatest mistake. What decided him to undertake this venture? There are two possible interpretations. One is the line of reasoning which Hitler himself presented to the Japanese and to Mussolini, namely, that Russia had made impossible demands in the Balkans, that she had not lived up to her promises of ceasing Communistic propaganda in Western Europe, and, finally, that Britain could not be attacked while there was a danger of a "stab in the back" from Stalin.[33] Actually, none of the arguments appears very plausible. As for the first, Hitler had already decided on Barbarossa before negotiations had proceeded very far. On November 13, 1940,

32. *Nazi Conspiracy and Aggression,* III, 633.
33. *Nazi-Soviet Relations, 1939–1941,* United States State Department, 1947.

Hitler proposed a ten year's peace pact between Germany, Italy, Japan, and Russia.[34] The day before, however, he declared that preparations for war should be completed "irrespective of the results of these conversations."[35] On November 26, Stalin replied that he would agree to the pact providing Germany withdrew from Finland, gave Russia certain rights in the Dardanelles, and recognized Persia as belonging to the Russian sphere of influence. At this point negotiation ceased, and on December 13, the directive for the Operation Barbarossa was issued.[36] As for the second argument — that the Russians persisted in their Communistic propaganda — Hitler could have foretold this when he signed the Non-Aggression Pact in 1939. It is also difficult to believe that Hitler really thought there was danger of a Russian attack on Germany. This was entirely inconsistent with his own views on German military superiority. Why fear an attack from an "undisciplined mob of poorly equipped soldiers"? Even if 30 or 40 divisions were committed to an invasion of Britain, Germany still had another 100 to protect her homeland.

Another interpretation of Hitler's decision to attack Russia appears more plausible: that the Nazis had always hated Bolshevism, that they coveted Russian wheat, minerals, and especially oil, and, finally, that they believed that these could be acquired at a very small price.

Hitler was fully confident that the conquest of Russia required no more than a blitzkrieg. The testimony of German Generals indicates that Hitler hoped to conquer Western Russia in eight weeks, and fully expected to do so before the winter months of 1941.[37] The official "timetable for Barbarossa," issued April 30, 1941, contemplated "violent battles of the frontiers, duration up to four weeks. In course of the following development weaker resistance may be expected."[38] The Russian army was pictured as a large mass of men, poorly equipped, badly trained, and incompetently led.[39]

We know, in retrospect, that the Germans grossly underestimated Russian strength. Was this simply the result of bad technical, military, and economic intelligence on Russia? Although intelligence on

34. *Nazi-Soviet Relations, 1939–1941.*
35. *Nazi-Soviet Relations, 1939–1941.*
36. *Nazi-Soviet Relations, 1939–1941.*
37. Interrogations of Generals Thomas, von Runstedt, and Halder.
38. *Nazi Conspiracy and Aggression,* III, 634.
39. *Nazi Conspiracy and Aggression,* III, 627.

Russia was very poor, it was not this so much as the Nazis own pre-
conceptions which led to their error. According to General Thomas,
whose War Economy and Armament Office prepared estimates of
Russia's armament position, very little was known in Germany about
Russian industrial and military strength.[40] Further, Thomas states,
Hitler invariably used this as a pretext for arguing that the War
Economy and Armament Office's figures on Russian tank production,
weapon output, aircraft production, etc., were grossly overestimated.[41] The fact that General Thomas had a much higher opinion
of Russian industry than Hitler was another reason for the bad
relations between them. Hitler's own ideas on Russia closely corresponded with the Nazi "party line" which had always discredited
Russian technical and industrial achievements. On this aspect,
Wagenfuehr, an economist employed by the Speer Ministry, writes:

> Nor were people deterred in this view by the somber prospects of a
> war with the powerful Soviet Union. Since 1933, and even prior to
> that date, the ruling regime had done everything to minimize the
> economic achievements of the U.S.S.R. in the eyes of the Germans.
> Public opinion was systematically made to believe that the Soviet
> Union was hell, that its economic planning was nonsense and that its
> armaments were insignificant. There were enough "crown witnesses"
> for such allegations from the repatriated people whose reports, printed
> just as the German-Russian war began, stated that the Soviet army
> was clad in rags, that its armament was antiquated and lacking uni-
> formity and that altogether it was a wild undisciplined mob, to that
> professor at the biggest German university who wrote (under a pen-
> name) that it was proved conclusively that as a matter of principle
> everybody in the Soviet Union, with the sole exception of the com-
> missars, was starved: he exploited the public self-criticism of the Soviet
> papers to "prove" the completely neglected status of the Soviet in-
> dustry. Those who really knew the Soviet Union had their work made

40. The following statement of von Runstedt, commander of German armies
in Southern Russia, indicates how uninformed the Germans were on even
elementary intelligence: "I realized soon after the attack was begun that everything that had been written about Russia was nonsense. The maps we were
given were all wrong. The roads which were marked nice and red on a map,
turned out to be tracks, and what were tracks on the map became first-class
roads. Even railways which were to be used by us simply did not exist. Or
a map would indicate that there was nothing in the area, and suddenly we
would be confronted with an American-type town, with factory buildings and
all the rest of it." Interrogation of Field-Marshal von Runstedt, July 1945,
War Office.

41. Interrogation of General Thomas by Allied military personnel.

difficult; their unbiased reports were ridiculed or disappeared in secret safes.[42]

The Russo-Finnish war was confirmation to the Nazi leaders of all their general beliefs of Russian inefficiency. And, in fact, a good deal of German *military* intelligence was based on Russia's experience in this war. Practically every planning document for "Barbarossa" speaks of the poor showing of Russian tanks, the bad leadership of the Russian armies, the crudity of their equipment, etc.

Hitler's own appraisal of German strength, on the other hand, was based on the fact that Germany conquered the French and British armies, certainly the best in the world next to his own, in a month. Moreover, he never forgot that his own armies were led by the most brilliant military strategist the world had ever known. Hitler's confidence in an easy victory over Russia is best shown by the fact that after the offensive had been under way for only four weeks, he thought the war was practically won. Plans were made for demobilizing a large number of divisions and reconverting a substantial part of war industry to civilian production. Hitler's directive of July 14, 1941, stated:

> The military domination of Europe after the defeat of Russia will enable the strength of the army to be considerably reduced in the near future.[43]

Subsequently OKW issued an army reorganization plan which called for an increase in the number of motorized divisions by five, and a reduction in the number of infantry divisions by sixty-six.[44] How much of this demobilization scheme was actually carried out, we do not know. However, the mere fact that it was even contemplated at this date is astonishing. The economic demobilization, as we shall see, progressed far beyond the planning stage.

2. ECONOMIC OBJECTIVES, 1939–1942

It is the reaction of the Nazi leaders to their victory over France and Britain and the extreme confidence with which they entered the war against Russia which provide the basic explanation for the economic events of the period. With this background indicated, we

42. "Rise and Fall of the German War Economy," 1939–1945, pp. 16–17.
43. *Nazi Conspiracy and Aggression*, III, 635.
44. A copy of the demobilization plan was found in the OKW files.

now examine the type of economic effort the German leaders demanded for the invasion of France and for the campaign against Russia — first, the period September 1939 through December 1940; second, the period from January 1941 until the latter part of 1942.

Immediately before the war, statements of German high officials indicated that a tremendous economic mobilization was in the offing. Both Goering and Funk spoke of "a rigorous war economy with the sharpest limitation on consumption and civilian income." The men working in the homeland, it was said, should not "be any better off than the soldier." [45]

However, about the time such declarations were being made (immediately after the attack on Poland), Hitler was coming to the conclusion that the Allies would not remain in the war after Poland was conquered and that a large-scale mobilization of the economy was unnecessary. Accordingly, on September 2, 1939, OKW ordered that the previously planned mobilization should be only partially carried out. On this General Thomas writes:

> The Supreme Commander was of the opinion that a war with Poland did not necessitate a general mobilization, and any other form of mobilization was out of the question for political reasons. . . . This was especially applicable as far as the economy was concerned insofar as regulations for economy read that . . . only the most important war factories should be maintained at their former level and that only isolated war factories should be immediately speeded up to produce a large output.

> The preparations, covering many years of work, for the mobilization of the economy were consequently, for the most part, useless.[46]

Within a month or two the whole atmosphere had changed; the German war economy, it was discovered, had changed very little from peacetime. In a speech made in Vienna on October 14, Funk said:

> In war, however, most things usually come differently from what was expected, and that is particularly the case in this war, in a manner which is particularly advantageous for Germany. The plans which were previously laid must therefore in many cases be changed, economic life not having to be changed over the full extent the mobilization plans saw.[47]

45. Wagenfuehr, "Rise and Fall of the German War Economy," p. 8.
46. *Basic Facts for a History of the German War Economy.*
47. Wagenfuehr, "Rise and Fall of the German War Economy," p. 9.

An editorial, "A Peace-like Economy," in a leading German economic journal spoke of a "war economy as close as possible to that of peace." [48]

By October, however, it had become apparent that the Allies were not going to back down, and war production plans had to be revised upwards. These, however, fell far short of calling for the complete mobilization of the economy which was spoken of before the war. A substantial percentage rise in armaments production from the low level of the early months of the war was not a difficult task for the German economy to perform. The gains in armaments production are shown in Table 47, which discloses that from the fourth quarter of 1939 until the Battle of France began there was a substantial rise in armaments output, and that this continued until about August 1940. From the fourth quarter of 1939 until the third quarter of 1940, army weapons production increased by about 20 per cent, army ammunition production, 60 per cent, tank output, 150 per cent, and aircraft output increased by 100 per cent. In August total armaments production was some 50 or 60 per cent above the rate at the begin-

Table 47. Production of selected classes of armaments,
4th quarter 1939–1st quarter 1941
(1st quarter 1940 = 100)

Year and quarter	Army weapons	Army ammunition	Tanks[a] (total wgt. produced)	Aircraft (total wgt. produced)
1939				
4th	94	96	85	—[b]
1940				
1st	100	100	100	100
2nd	129	137	154	182
3rd	113	154	216	182
4th	109	95	250	157
1941				
1st	147	91	280	166

Source: *Indexziffern der deutschen Rüstungsendfertigung*, Planungsamt, June, 1944.
a. Includes assault guns mounted on tank chassis.
b. Not available.

48. Wagenfuehr, "Rise and Fall of the German War Economy," p. 9.

ning of the war.[49] Despite the impressive percentage rise, however, the level of munitions production was still very small in August 1940. During that month the value of total armaments production amounted to just over one billion marks,[50] 10 per cent of the monthly value of total industrial production.[51] Monthly tank and aircraft production amounted to only one fifth of the number produced during a later period of the war.[52]

In July 1940, in preparation for the invasion of Britain, aircraft production and ship construction were given top priority. Before these new production programs could be put into effect, however, the whole venture was called off. Seeing no necessity for keeping the economy under such a "strain," Hitler ordered a general cutback in munitions production and a resumption of some types of civilian luxury goods production. This was at a time, it may be noted, when total munitions production was about one third of the rate reached in July 1944, and when civilian consumption still was within 5 per cent of the 1938 level.

As can be seen in Table 47, from September 1940 until around February 1941, there was a general decline in armaments production. Especially noteworthy is the fact that aircraft production itself (operational as well as nonoperational types) fell more than most other categories of armaments — about 40 per cent. The decision to reduce aircraft production to this extent seems almost incredible, considering that in September, the very month the decision was made, the number of aircraft lost in the Air Battle of Britain was substantially in excess of new production.[53] In the following months, although the number of sorties was greatly reduced, fighter output

49. Estimated from the data on weapons, ammunition, tank, and aircraft output appearing in Table 47, and from data on other types of armaments production contained in a report of the Speer Ministry, dated 27 January 1945.

50. The official data for total monthly armaments production do not go back before January, 1941. An estimate of the value of total armaments production in August was obtained by extrapolating the January 1941 figure (found in *Indexziffern der deutschen Rüstungsendfertigung,* June 1944) by the detailed data on armaments output.

51. Value of total industrial production taken from "Industrial Sales, Output and Productivity, Prewar Area of Germany, 1939–1944," United States Strategic Bombing Survey.

52. *Indexziffern der deutschen Rüstungsendfertigung,* June 1944.

53. From data on aircraft losses found in the files of the Air Ministry.

failed to keep pace with losses, and the production of bombers just about equalled the number shot down over Britain.[54]

The only types of armaments production which increased during the autumn of 1940 were tanks and shipbuilding. The rise in tank output, as Table 47 shows, was only moderate. The amount of shipping tonnage constructed during this period cannot be accurately gauged since monthly or quarterly figures are not available. Both of these, however, comprised only a minor part of total armaments production. During 1940, 1.6 per cent of total armaments expenditures went for tanks and 4.4 per cent for shipbuilding, compared to 41 per cent for ammunition and 38 per cent for aircraft. Production of both ammunition and aircraft was declining sharply.

According to Wagenfuehr, the production of civilian items, especially in those plants engaged in the output of both civilian and war goods, was substantially stepped up during this period.[55] The actual degree of conversion to civilian production cannot be ascertained since monthly or quarterly data for the output of civilian goods are not available.

The decline in armaments production was brought to a halt in January 1941, when Hitler ordered preparations undertaken for the war against Russia. The scale of these was quite modest and entirely consistent with the idea that the conquest of Russia required no more than a blitzkrieg. As Table 48 shows, the total value of armaments production increased from 760 million marks in January to 1,100 million in April, and after several months of decline reached a peak of 1,150 million marks in August. Even then, however, total armaments output was hardly greater than in the peak month of the previous year.[56] The largest production gains occurred in aircraft, in tanks and antiaircraft weapons, and in ammunition. In July combat aircraft production was 120 per cent above the January figure, 10 per cent over the September 1940 total (measured in terms of weight). Even with this rise in production, Germany's output still fell far short of that of her enemies. In the middle of 1941, Britain alone was producing a total of 975 fighters and bombers per month,[57]

54. From data on aircraft losses found in the files of the Air Ministry.
55. "The Rise and Fall of the German War Economy," pp. 14–15.
56. *German Employment Statistics During the War,* FIAT, Office of Military Government for Germany (U. S.), 30 November 1945.
57. "Statistics Relating to the War Effort of the United Kingdom."

Table 48. Production of total and selected classes of armaments, 1941

Year 1941	Total armaments production	Production of combat aircraft		Tank[a] production		Army weapons	Army ammu- nition
Month	(millions of RM)	Weight (metric tons)	Num- bers	Weight (metric tons)	Num- bers	(1st quarter 1941 = 100)	
Jan.	760	2,780	391	4,840	231	} 100	100
Feb.	870	4,110	581	4,820	236		
Mar.	1,050	5,405	816	4,720	231		
Apr.	1,100	5,055	831	6,040	289	} 91	80
May	1,030	4,268	715	6,450	320		
June	1,040	4,373	701	6,240	310		
July	990	6,180	766	5,810	299		
Aug.	1,150	5,682	737	7,290	357	} 80	53
Sept.	1,060	5,242	674	7,220	367		
Oct.	1,070	4,830	643	7,590	378		
Nov.	1,000	4,276	563	8,000	394	} 62	48
Dec.	1,000	4,730	662	7,700	378		
Average 1941	1,010	4,700	670	6,393	316	93	70
Average 1940	1,000	–[b]	580	2,901	136	75	132
Highest Quarter 1940	1,200	–[b]	685	4,260	200	80	170

Source: *Indexziffern der deutschen Rüstungsenfertigung*, Planungsamt, June 1944.
a. Includes assault guns mounted on tank chassis.
b. Not available.

compared with Germany's 770. Tank output in midsummer reached 300 per month, about 30 per cent above the January rate. The production of antiaircraft weapons and ammunition (in value terms) increased by nearly 100 per cent from January to July.[58] The amount of resources that went into these armaments was surprisingly large; in mid-1941 expenditures on antiaircraft weapons and ammunition amounted to more than twice the amount spent on tanks.[59] The main impetus to the antiaircraft program was not, however, prepara-

58. *Indexziffern der deutschen Rüstungsendfertigung*, June 1944.
59. *Indexziffern der deutschen Rüstungsendfertigung*, June 1944.

tions for the Russian war but, rather, protection of the homeland from British bombers. Even though British bombing was on a small scale during 1940 and 1941, it was enough of a threat to make Germany take elaborate measures to protect her Western cities.

It was in infantry and artillery armaments that the preparations were smallest. No doubt, this was due to the feeling that the panzer divisions would spearhead the Russian offensive, with infantry divisions used only for mopping-up operations. As Table 48 shows, from January until June the output of army weapons fell around 15 per cent; army ammunition about 30 per cent. At that time ammunition production was only half as great as it was during the month preceding the French campaign.[60]

At the time the invasion of Russia began, Germany had approximately 2,000 bombers and 3,100 fighter planes, 5,100 combat planes in all.[61] This was only 1,000 more than she had for the French campaign,[62] and the tasks of the air force were far greater. For one thing, a considerable number of the fighters had to be used to protect German cities from British bombers. Moreover, unlike in France, the war in Russia required the supporting ground forces on a front extending for 2,000 miles. As of June 1, 1941, Germany had about 4,500 operational tanks, about half of which were the heavier Mark III and Mark IV types.[63] This was about 1,000 more than she had had for the French campaign.[64] Stocks of weapons and ammunition were also substantially above June 1940. But as future events were to show, Germany's supply of neither aircraft nor tanks, weapons nor ammunition, was adequate for the war against Russia.

However incredible it may seem for Germany to have undertaken a war with Russia without much greater economic preparations, even more incredible is the fact that she began to demobilize her war industries two months after the beginning of the Russian campaign. By the end of July, Field Marshal von Bock had covered 450 miles, two thirds of the distance to Moscow; von Runstedt was nearing Kiev in the South, whence he could proceed to the Russian oil fields. During these tremendous advances losses of tanks, aircraft, and

60. *Indexziffern der deutschen Rüstungsendfertigung,* June 1944.
61. From data on aircraft strength found in the files of OKL.
62. From data on aircraft strength found in the files of OKL.
63. *Effects of Strategic Bombing,* p. 165.
64. Effects of Strategic Bombing, p. 163.

weapons were less than new supplies from current production. Hitler ordered, in the latter part of July, a reduction of output for three major classes of armaments: army weapons, army ammunition, and aircraft. By August, as Table 49 shows, the production of all types

Table 49. Indices of aircraft, army weapons,
and army ammunition production, 1941

	Peak production month (= 100)	August	December
Aircraft			
Fighters	August	100	83
Bombers	April	59	53
Total	August	100	82
Army weapons			
Light infantry	February	80	63
Heavy infantry	March	84	31
Light artillery	January	79	12
Heavy artillery	February	69	40
Army ammunition			
Light infantry	April	69	53
Heavy infantry	February	65	54
Artillery	February	26	18

Source: *Indexziffern der deutschen Rüstungsendfertigung*, Planungsamt, June 1944.

of army weapons and ammunition had already fallen substantially. The light losses during the summer months, however, indicated to Hitler that additional cuts were in order. From August through December, total army ammunition and weapons output was cut 30 per cent. In December the Fuehrer well might have regretted this decision. For at that time, as we shall see, stocks of many types of ammunition were practically exhausted. The production of fighter aircraft fell from April onward. This, however, was due to a change over to bomber production during this period. Total aircraft production (measured in weight) reached its peak in August, and had fallen off some 20 per cent by the end of the year.

The decline in total armaments production — 13 per cent from August through December — was moderated by increases in explosives output, and in antiaircraft weapons and ammunition production.

During these months the first increased by 20 per cent, the second, by 30 per cent.[65]

Total armaments production in 1941 was hardly greater than in 1940; 12.1 billion marks compared with 12.0 billion marks.[66] Sizable increases in submarine, tank, and explosives output and a moderate increase in aircraft production were all practically canceled by the decline of ammunition output.

While Hitler was busy making postwar plans in Berlin, his Generals in Russia were finding a quick victory much less certain than was earlier assumed. Although von Bock took Smolensk at the beginning of August, his panzer divisions were then diverted to aid Runstedt's assault on Kiev, and it was not until the first week in October that he could begin his Moscow offensive. By mid-October, when von Bock's armies were some 100 miles from Moscow, the Russian winter set in. Then began Hitler's first defeat of the war. Offensive after offensive was mounted with no success. Finally, on December 6, the Russians undertook their counteroffensive, taking a heavy toll in German men and matériel.

At the same time that von Bock began his offensive, von Runstedt was ordered to proceed to Stalingrad and the Maikop oil fields (a mere 700 or 800 miles over snow and mud covered roads!). Part of his forces managed to get as far east as Rostov (about 250 miles from the oil fields), but at the end of November superior Russian forces drove his armies from the city and forced a very costly retreat.

The Generals blamed the defeats on Hitler's strategy. First, it was generally agreed that the full force of the attack should have been directed against the Russian armies massed in front of Moscow, rather than attempting this and the conquest of southern Russia simultaneously. Secondly, given the situation as it was, military leaders like von Brauchitsch, von Runstedt, and von Leeb, favored a withdrawal to safe winter lines as soon as the winter weather began. Von Bock, on the other hand, was convinced that a retreat during the winter months was folly; that his armies would meet the same fate as Napoleon's.

Hitler blamed the defeats on the Generals. Both von Brauchitsch,

65. *Indexziffern der deutschen Rüstungsendfertigung*, June 1944.
66. *Indexziffern der deutschen Rüstungsendfertigung*, June 144.

Commander-in-Chief of the Army, and von Runstedt, Commander of the German armies in southern Russia, were dismissed. So that the German armies never again would be embarrassed by "poor leadership," Hitler appointed himself Commander-in-Chief of the Army.

While a different military strategy might have enabled the German armies to take Moscow in the fall of 1941, or at least to have minimized their losses, there is no doubt that the lack of adequate economic preparations told heavily during these winter months. For the first time during the war, losses of practically all types of armaments exceeded current production. In October, November, and December, 1941, 2,500 tanks and self-propelled guns were destroyed or abandoned, more than twice the number produced during those months.[67] One reason why requirements were so seriously underestimated is that German Intelligence completely misjudged the effectiveness of the Russian tanks. According to Halder, when army units first encountered the heavy and well-armed Russian T-34 tanks, they were completely surprised, expecting to find the Russians using types of tanks discarded by the Germans at the end of World War I.[68] In the latter part of November, German technicians were ordered to design a tank which could match the T-34. Actual production of the Tiger tank, however, did not begin for nearly a year.

Aircraft losses during this period were not so large, primarily because the bad weather kept the air force grounded much of the time. Nevertheless the number of planes coming off the production lines was less than the number lost during the last three months of the year.[69] During the months of July, August, and September when the number of sorties flown was much greater, losses exceeded production by one third.[70]

Most serious, perhaps, was the shortage of ammunition. According to testimony of Speer, General Thomas, and Halder, the German armies were living on a hand to mouth basis in ammunition consumption during the fall of 1941.[71] The army planned to have a six

---

67. *Effects of Strategic Bombing*, p. 165.
68. Interrogation of General Halder, United States Strategic Bombing Survey.
69. Data found in the files of OKL.
70. Data found in the files of OKL.
71. Speer's Letters to Hitler, February and March, 1942; Thomas's *Basic Facts for a History of the German War Economy;* Interrogation of General Halder, United States Strategic Bombing Survey.

months' supply available and considered a three months' supply the irreducible minimum. It actually found itself during this period with total supplies generally sufficient for only one or two months' needs, and for particular army groups in the field the situation was even worse. Also, some types of ammunition were in much shorter supply than the general average. During November and December, 1941, the ratio between consumption and production of howitzer ammunition was 50 to 1.[72] The supply of artillery ammunition at the end of 1941 permitted only 35 per cent of the consumption as it had during the preceding summer.[73]

When Speer became Minister of Armaments and War Production in February 1942, he was asked by Hitler to investigate the causes of the ammunition shortage. According to Speer, it was due to nothing more than the army's setting its requirements too low, and not becoming aware of the shortage until after it was really serious.[74] Ammunition production, it will be recalled from the previous discussion, fell more than 50 per cent from the end of the French campaign until June, 1941, and another 30 per cent by the end of the year.

Besides underestimating requirements for all the above armaments, an equally serious defect of the planning for the Russian war was the lack of provision for special types of winter fighting equipment. During the winter months the troops were improperly clothed, tank operations were made difficult because winter lubricants were in many cases unobtainable, and some types of equipment were so designed that they could not be used at all during the extreme cold weather. Around October, special programs were inaugurated to produce several types of winter equipment (field heating stoves were given top priority), but at that time it was too late to rectify the situation.

By December, Hitler had come to the conclusion that the conquest of Russia would have to wait until the following summer. Discussion at his headquarters again changed from postwar economic planning to preparations for the final assault against Russia. However, the transcripts of the Fuehrer's conferences for the months of January, February, and March contain a number of entries such as the following:

72. Interrogation of General Halder, United States Strategic Bombing Survey.
73. Interrogation of General Halder, United States Strategic Bombing Survey.
74. Interrogation of General Halder, United States Strategic Bombing Survey.

The Fuehrer clearly stated that at the moment he had no interest in the 12 cylinder Daimler-Benz. After the war there would be no question of an export of luxury vehicles as it would be difficult to satisfy our own market.

The peacetime developments at the automobile works must be stopped and the experts thereby released switched into tank development work.[75]

On April 13, 1942, a decree issued by Reichsmarshall Goering suspended all economic peacetime planning until further notice. However, the actual decline of armaments production had been arrested several months earlier. In December, when the German armies were retreating with heavy matériel losses on both the northern and southern sectors of the front, there was a flood of orders for increased production of practically all types of armaments.

Beginning in January, there was a remarkable recovery of armaments output. As Table 50 shows, from January through March total armaments production rose 25 per cent, exceeding in that month the peak of August 1941. This substantial rise in total output was due to spectacular production recovery of just those three classes of arma-

Table 50. Indices of aircraft, army weapons, and army ammunition production, 1942 and peak month of 1941

(December = 100)

	March	April	Previous peak in 1941	
	1942			
Aircraft:				
Fighters	184	178	191	April
Bombers	152	131	122	August
Total	157	139	130	August
Army weapons:				
Light infantry	115	130	160	February
Heavy infantry	347	472	323	May
Light artillery	700	589	791	January
Heavy artillery	171	176	243	February
Army ammunition:				
Light infantry	138	165	189	April
Heavy infantry	233	312	184	February
Artillery	316	465	550	February

Source: *Indexziffern der deutschen Rüstungsendfertigung*, June 1944.

75. Transcript of Fuehrer's Conference, 23 March 1942.

ments which had been cut back during the preceding year: aircraft, army weapons, and army ammunition. As Table 50 shows, by March total aircraft production had increased 57 per cent over December, production increases for weapons ran from 15 per cent for light infantry types to 600 per cent for light artillery weapons; for ammunition, from 38 per cent for light infantry to 216 per cent for artillery. During March and April aircraft production surpassed the peak level of the previous year. Weapons and ammunition production had fallen so much during 1941 that not even these spectacular increases were enough to bring output back to the early 1941 levels.

After the large gain during the first three or four months of the year, however, the rise in armaments production slackened. From March until November total armaments production increased by about one fourth, no more than it had increased during the first three months of the year. As Table 51 shows, ammunition was the

Table 51. Increases in armaments production
from April until October–November, 1942
(April = 100)

	October–November average
Total armaments	122
Ammunition	173
Aircraft	99
Weapons	125
Tanks	112
Motor vehicles	92

Source: *Indexziffern der deutschen Rüstung-sendfertigung*, June 1944.

only type of armaments production which increased greatly throughout the year. The fact that ammunition output climbed faster than any other type of armaments during 1942, after having fallen more steeply than any other type of armaments during 1941, clearly confirms the fact that requirements for the Russian war had been grossly underestimated. During this period of about eight months, aircraft production remained about the same, motor vehicle output declined, and tank and weapons production increased moderately. Submarine construction (not shown in the table because of wide month-to-month fluctuations) fell off after the middle of the year. Excluding ammunition, the rate of total armaments production at the end of October was only 6 per cent above the March figure.

What is the explanation for this? To be sure, production of the Mark III tank was held up because of a temporary component shortage; submarine construction because steel sheets were not plentiful; powder production by a lack of skilled workers; gas generators by component difficulties. Inspection of all such cases, however, still does not satisfactorily explain why most types of armaments production remained nearly constant for a period of eight months. Much more convincing is the hypothesis that the principal limiting factor was the same one which had existed during the preceding year: a lack of demand. From about April until nearly the end of the year the Fuehrer's conferences are filled with statements like these: "The Fuehrer is completely satisfied with the production of the Mark III tank." "The Fuehrer expresses his satisfaction with the Flak program." "The Fuehrer expresses his satisfaction with – – –" etc. At the beginning of July 1942, Hitler declared that he was "quite prepared to put a ceiling limit to the munitions program." [76] At this time, it may be noted, Germany's total armaments production amounted to 1.4 billion marks per month, or about 65 per cent of Britain's (see Table 27). Whether or not a ceiling was actually placed on production we do not know, but at any rate such discussions suggest that the general atmosphere was not one which exerted pressure on the armaments industry for increased output.

This is again illustrated by discussions in the German Air Ministry during 1942. In March the following conversation took place between Goering (head of the German Air Force), Jeschonnek (Chief of the Air Force General Staff) and Milch (deputy Air Commander and head of Aircraft Procurement):

Milch:
> Herr Reichsmarshall, I have now studied the matter. Your total demand is 360 fighters per month [at the time Germany was producing 450 fighters per month]. I don't understand. If you were to say 3,600 fighters then I would have to say that America and England combined, 3,600 are too few, you must produce more. But to demand 360 fighters * * *!

76. Transcript of the Fuehrer's Conference, 10 July 1942.

Goering (to Jeschonnek):
    What do you think about it?
Jeschonnek:
    I do not know what I should do with more than 360 fighters.[77]

By the end of July, Hitler was willing to go much further than placing a ceiling limit on armaments production. At that time the German armies were nearing Stalingrad and the Caucasian oil fields, and it was thought, as in the summer of 1941, that the war was practically over. During a meeting with his economic advisers on July 29, Hitler proposed the cutting of armaments production in order to release capacity and workers for an increased output of civilian goods (it should be remembered that Germany was then at war with not only Russia, and Britain, but also the United States). If Speer had not interceded it is not at all unlikely that Germany would have witnessed a third period of economic demobilization. Speer argued "that such an action at this time would incite the discontent of all those, who have hitherto watched with displeasure the priority given to armaments production, to a renewed opposition against the present policy." [78] After considerable discussion Hitler finally agreed "that such an action should start only after a few months and then exclusively with foreign labor and within the limits permitted by the transport and coal position," adding "that the products produced in this drive could then be sold at exceptionally high prices." [79]

In the closing months of 1942, the period of economic lethargy was brought to an end by the impending disasters on the Eastern front.

This attitude of the German leaders explains not only the failure to more fully mobilize the economy, but also the reason the economic administration was allowed to remain so inefficient. With all of its defects, the economic administration was able to fill the limited demands for war material. What was the need, therefore, for instituting far-reaching reforms? Hitler's disinclination to give anybody full economic powers, the supervision of industry by incompetent military officers, the unwillingness to tighten raw material distribution con-

77. From a document found in the files of the Air Ministry.
78. Transcript of the Fuehrer's Conference, 29 July 1942.
79. Transcript of the Fuehrer's Conference, 29 July 1942.

trols — these were "luxuries" which the German leaders thought they could afford. Reforms are not sought in times of prosperity.

3. A CRISIS NEEDED

The preceding section may have left the reader with the impression that the failure to mobilize the German economy rested entirely with Hitler. In other words, the argument may have been taken to mean that if the Fuehrer had ordered the production of 30,000 planes a year instead of 10,000, or of 12,000 tanks instead of 3,000, the state of affairs would have been entirely different. While it cannot be denied such assertions contain a large element of truth, actually the aim of the inquiry was more modest, namely, to ascertain what Hitler actually did require of the economy for his military campaigns. What the level of armaments production would have been if Hitler had not undertaken a war with Russia in so cavalier a fashion is another question, and a more difficult question, since it is impossible to separate Hitler's own personality from the Nazi social setting, or his own aims from those of the Nazi movement. However, we want to suggest that besides Hitler's own reactions to Germany's military victories, the economic implications of Nazi ideology also played a role in setting the magnitude of the war effort.

It is not difficult to show that the Nazi economic and social aims were in conflict with the notion of "total war." We only have to recall the more important manifestations of this ideology. First, there was the idea that woman's place was in the home (and not in a munitions plant). By 1939, as a result of party propaganda and financial inducements by the State, this notion had become part of the accepted way of life. Second, Nazi policy aimed at providing the masses of the German people with a high standard of living. When the party came into power, this was one of its main objectives; until 1937, at least, it was the primary aim of economic policy. During the latter part of the 1930's, the party fought all proposals which would have required the people to surrender part of their high level of consumption. This was shown especially in the Nazi's reactions to Schacht's recommendations for higher income and consumption taxes, and for a reduction of food imports to save foreign exchange. The Labor Front, in addition to opposing all measures which would have cut the standard of living of the German worker, pressed for numerous

State-provided workers' benefits, as well as for shorter working hours. Third, extravagant expenditures on government and party buildings, municipal improvements, and especially the *Autobahnen,* were intended to provide lasting monuments to the founders of the Nazi state. However, a policy which removes women from the labor market, shortens working hours, and stresses a high level of public and private consumption, does not permit at the same time the construction of a huge war potential. To a nation with limited resources, spanning the countryside with superhighways and becoming self-sufficient in oil were conflicting aims.

Before the war, the Germans were not presented with a serious conflict of this sort because Hitler's blitzkrieg strategy did not require a large economic effort. As the war progressed, however, the conflict between social and military aims became increasingly evident. Hitler showed his unwillingness to ask for large civilian consumption sacrifices in a number of instances. At the beginning of the war, he decided against imposing the very high income and consumption taxes advocated by the Ministry of Finance. Both during the autumn of 1940 and the autumn of 1941, he ordered a reduction of war output and increases in the production of civilian goods. The fact that this was contemplated again in the summer of 1942 — after the lesson of the previous winter — shows that he must have placed a very high premium on an increased output of products for civilian use. The construction of public buildings continued into 1941, though not on the extravagant prewar scale. Speer persuaded Hitler to give up the construction of the *Autobahnen* only in 1942, the second winter of war with Russia. Throughout the whole war, there was no reversal of the policy against the employment of women; not even a disaster like Stalingrad could make Hitler reverse this policy. Writers like Gisevius claim that it would have been politically impossible for Hitler to draft women into war industries.[80] Whether or not this is true, it is certain that Hitler showed no inclination to make the attempt. Beginning in 1943, the conscription of women was frequently suggested, but always Hitler gave the same answer: "The sacrifice of our most cherished ideals is too great a price. . . ."[81]

How much of the failure to mobilize the German economy was due

80. *To the Bitter End,* pp. 276ff.
81. Records of the Fuehrer's Conferences, 13 March 1943.

to the inflexibility of an ideology which had developed during peacetime and how much to the belief that Europe could be conquered without giving up the social and economic aims of Nazism is something which cannot be determined. On a higher level of sophistication it might even be asked whether the belief in a cheap victory over Russia itself stemmed from the unwillingness to fight a long and expensive war.

The same sort of question, of course, could be asked about the attitude of the United States towards rearmament in the years 1936 through 1940. What prevented this country from spending 50 billion dollars a year on armaments as soon as it became apparent that Hitler's actions might sooner or later lead the world into war? One part of the answer is that Congress was unwilling to ask for such a sacrifice; another that at the time the threat was not regarded as very serious. Whatever weight one might attach to each of these factors, one thing is certain: the United States needed a real crisis, a Pearl Harbor, before large-scale preparations could be undertaken. Germany, on the other hand, was less fortunate; her "Pearl Harbor" did not come until the beginning of 1943.

Until Stalingrad, the German war production effort was restricted by the lack of a real sense of crisis. As we have seen, the defeat before Moscow did not shock Germany into making a tremendous war effort. Hitler viewed the failure to take Moscow as a temporary setback and fully expected that his armies would be victorious the following summer. The level of war production was substantially increased during the first few months of 1942, but after that it was permitted to level off until the closing months of the year. Nor was the United States' entry into the war viewed as a calamity. Hitler thought, first of all, that the American war production figures were grossly exaggerated.[82] General Thomas reports that when Hitler was informed that the United States could produce 50,000 planes and 25,000 tanks a year, he flew into a rage. He had no doubt that the United States could produce safety razors and refrigerators, but

---

82. Goebbels shared the Fuehrer's opinion: "Donald Nelson has issued a report about American armament production. It exceeds all previous American exaggerations. We simply must do something to offset this American munitions propaganda." *Goebbels' Diary,* Entry of 19 December 1942.

50,000 planes and 25,000 tanks! This was nothing but Jewish propaganda.[83] Moreover, Hitler was confident that the United States would be fully occupied fighting Japan. This is shown by testimony of German officials as well as by the transcripts of the conversations between Hitler and Matsouka.[84] If a war with the United States was greatly feared, Germany surely would not have declared war first. Even though it may have been felt that the United States would soon enter the war against Germany, there was no need to anticipate this decision.

Germany's awakening did not come until her defeat at Stalingrad in February 1943. From mid-November until February, when von Paulus was forced to surrender his armies, German casualties numbered at least 500,000[85] and the losses in material were 5,000 aircraft,[86] 3,600 tanks, and 15,000 guns.[87] Such losses had a very direct effect on increasing tremendously the level of war production, and in tightening the economy generally. The need to replace all the equipment lost at Stalingrad and to make Germany's matériel position much stronger than it had been before this catastrophe gave Speer sufficient reason to take the far-reaching measures discussed in the following chapter.

Hitler's own reaction was to view the defeat at Stalingrad as something less than a terrible catastrophe. In a historic meeting with his advisers on January 25, 1943 (by which time the fate of the German armies had been sealed), Hitler first ordered production increases for such armaments as tanks, flame-throwers, E-boats, ammunition, etc. Then he turned to a discussion of the construction of a tunnel through the Leibl Pass, expressing the opinion that a two-year construction period seemed too long and that the reported figure of 3,000 workmen seemed too high. Finally, Hitler took up a most important matter, the construction of a stadium at Nürnberg, suitable

83. From a report written by General Thomas shortly after the end of the war.

84. *Nazi-Soviet Relations, 1939–1941,* United States State Department; United States Strategic Bombing Survey Interrogations of General Thomas, General Halder and Albert Speer.

85. In a report written for Allied military personnel, General Thomas stated that Germany lost the equivalent of 45 full strength divisions during this period.

86. From the OKL's records of aircraft strength and losses.

87. General Thomas's Report.

for celebrating the conquest of Russia! The following is an extract from the discussion:

> Hitler points out that to enable the Party Congress to hold its victory celebration the construction of a new building to replace the Congress Hall must at all costs be prepared now. It has to be planned as a single hall of iron construction with accommodations for 20,000 people. The tower which is still standing in the old Congress Hall can be incorporated. The construction of this hall is particularly urgent as Nürnberg, the city of the Party Congress, possesses no large halls suitable for mass meetings.[88]

Nor was the defeat at Stalingrad a great crisis for the masses of the German people. The Propaganda Ministry invariably saw to it that major defeats were reported as minor setbacks. Reading Goebbels' Diary, one is impressed by the number of times the Propaganda Minister noted that "this defeat must be minimized."

What also helped bring war home to the German people and to Hitler, too, was the large-scale Royal Air Force attacks on German cities beginning with the thousand-plane raid on Cologne in the summer of 1942. Unlike the defeats in far away Russia, it was impossible for the Propaganda Ministry to minimize the spectacle of the bombings. Although R.A.F. Commander Sir Arthur Harris was of the opinion that these raids would weaken the will of the Germans to resist, they had the opposite effect until at least the very last part of the war. This is shown in the letters of Speer to Hitler, in Goebbels' diaries, in the writings of Gisevius, in the interrogation reports of a number of other German officials. Speer reports that nothing during the war moved Hitler more than the inspection of the ruins of Hamburg in the summer of 1943.[89] It is difficult to imagine a more effective way of converting the German leaders and the German people to a program of austerity than by bombing their cities.

The defeat at Stalingrad and the destruction of her cities were just the crises that Germany needed to make her mobilize her economy — the first, through its direct effect of calling for tremendous increases in the production of war matériel; the second, through weakening the resistance of the Nazi leaders to far-reaching mobilization measures. Had the large-scale attacks on German cities com-

88. Records of the Fuehrer's Conferences, 25 January 1943.

89. Memoranda written by Speer after the war for the Allied Control Commission.

menced in the summer of 1940, and had Stalingrad come a year earlier, there is no doubt that by 1942 the German economy would have been fully mobilized and the production of armaments substantially greater. And perhaps if these crises had come earlier, the course of the war would have been very different.

I X   *A Summary of Germany's Economic War Effort, 1942–1944*

This chapter summarizes the course of Germany's military production during the last two and one-half years of the war, it describes the principal factors responsible for the acceleration of production, and it states the author's views on the effects of strategic bombing. The reasons for omitting a more detailed treatment of this period of the war are, first, that on the whole it appears a much less interesting period than the period from the beginning of the war through the Battle of Stalingrad; and second, that the topic of main interest in this period — strategic bombing — is in my opinion adequately covered in the Bombing Survey studies, especially *The Effects of Strategic Bombing*.

I. MILITARY SUPPLIES, LATE 1942 TO MID-1944

As we saw in the previous chapter, in 1942 efforts were begun to speed up war production. During the first half of 1942, there were large increases in tank ammunition and weapons output. From the first to the third quarter of the year, as Table 52 shows, total munitions output increased about 40 per cent. The rise, however, was from a very low level of output, and it was contemplated that 1943 would be the year of final victory.

The real acceleration in munitions output was begun late in 1942, when the progress of the war made it apparent to Hitler that his strategic calculations were in serious error. In two major advances — the first of which tapered off in the late spring of 1943, the second

Table 52. Index of German munitions
output 1942–1944
(first quarter 1942 = 100)

1942:	First quarter	100
	Second quarter	125
	Third quarter	140
	Fourth quarter	152
1943:	First quarter	184
	Second quarter	205
	Third quarter	209
	Fourth quarter	211
1944:	First quarter	226
	Second quarter	260
	Third quarter	279
	Fourth quarter	244

Source: *Indexziffern der deutschen Rüstungsendfertigung*, Planning Board, Ministry for Armaments and War Production.

of which lasted from the end of 1943 to mid-1944 — total munitions output increased to more than twice the 1942 volume. By the third quarter of 1944, it had reached an annual rate of 34 billion RM, compared with about 12 billions at the time the war with Russia began and 16 billions in 1942. Both of these advances featured tank and aircraft output. During the first, when the total munitions index increased by about 40 per cent, aircraft output rose by 130 per cent, and total "panzer" (tanks and assault and self-propelled guns mounted on tank chassis) output by 125 per cent.[1] It was brought to a close by model changes in aircraft and submarines, component shortages, and by some relatively destructive bombing attacks on the aircraft industry. During the second period of increase, which brought the munitions index about 33 per cent above the level of the fourth quarter of 1943, the gain in aircraft was again 130 per cent and in panzer output about 70 per cent. It is remarkable that this increase in aircraft output was achieved during a period when 75 per cent of the factory space devoted to fighter production was either damaged or destroyed.[2]

1. *Indexziffern der deutschen Rüstungsendfertigung*, July, 1944.
2. *Effects of Strategic Bombing*, p. 156.

In numbers, aircraft production rose from about 15 thousand in 1942, to 25 thousand in 1943, and 40 thousand in 1944. Indicative of the effort that was put into increasing Germany's defensive capabilities, fighter output rose from just over 5 thousand in 1942 to nearly 29,000 in 1944 (which was nearly 40 per cent more than the number credited to Germany by Allied Intelligence).[3] Panzer output increased from a total of 6,000 in 1942 to 12,000 in 1943, and 19,000 in 1944.[4]

The increase in the output of other types of military equipment was more modest. As compared with an increase of 115 per cent in total munitions production from the fourth quarter of 1942 to the third quarter of 1944, weapons output increased 110 per cent; ammunition output 50 per cent; and production of motor vehicles declined about 10 per cent.[5]

In sharp contrast with their relative production achievements during the first three years of the war, in 1943 and 1944 Germany's military output increased a good deal faster than Britain's, and at the peak was considerably larger than Britain's. Thus, whereas Germany's munitions output more than doubled from the 1942 level to the peak rate, Britain was able to increase hers by only about a quarter.[6] The peak level of total munitions output in Germany probably exceeded Britain's by some 15–20 per cent.[7] In aircraft production Britain maintained a comfortable lead over Germany throughout the whole war period: though the margin narrowed in 1943 and 1944, and though in numbers Germany's output rose far above Britain's (approximately 40 thousand as against 26,500 for the U. K. in 1944) measured in structural weight, Britain's 1944 output was still nearly one-fifth greater than Germany's.[8] But in most other types of armaments, Germany's output rose far above Britain's. Whereas in 1942, Britain produced about 8600 tanks, and Germany, 6200, by 1944 Britain's output had declined to 4600, and Germany's

---

3. *An Appraisal of Pre- and Post-Raid Intelligence,* United States Strategic Bombing Survey, Table 3.

4. *Effects of Strategic Bombing,* appendix table 104, p. 278.

5. *Effects of Strategic Bombing,* appendix table 100, p. 275.

6. *World Munitions Production, 1938–1944.*

7. *World Munitions Production;* and Wagenfuehr, "Rise and Fall of the German War Economy," p. 14.

8. *Statistics Relating to the War Effort of the United Kingdom,* 1944 and *Statistische Schnellberichte zur Kriegsproduktion,* 1945.

had increased to 19,000.[9] In Germany, artillery output increased from 23,000 pieces to 71,000 between 1942 and 1944; while in Britain, output declined from 43,000 to 16,000.[10] In small arms ammunition, Britain outproduced Germany by 60 per cent in 1942; in 1944 Germany outproduced Britain by more than 100 per cent.[11]

In June 1944, Germany was much better stocked with most types of military equipment than she had been at any time during the war. From June 1941 to June 1943, the total number of operational fighters varied between about 1850 and 1950 planes.[12] At the time of the invasion, Germany had almost 2700 fighters.[13] When the war with Russia began, Germany had only 420 operational ground attack planes, and by December 1942, the number had shrunk to 280.[14] (These statistics may help to explain why the diaries of the German Generals hardly mention tactical air support during the Russian campaign). But as of June 1944, 1430 ground attack planes were reported in operational units.[15] Reflecting the wavering decision to discontinue the production of bombers, the bomber force fell from 1750 planes in June 1941, to 1410 in December 1943, to 1070 in June 1944.[16]

Although the losses of army equipment suffered in the Russian campaigns were enormous, Germany was able to make up these losses, and in addition provide the equipment for a large number of new divisions. General Thomas reports that up until the Battle of Stalingrad, total equipment losses roughly corresponded to the table of equipment for 45 full strength divisions; and that in the Battle of Stalingrad alone, equipment for fifty divisions was lost.[17] Subsequently, however, stocks of most types of army equipment rapidly

9. *Statistics Relating to the War Effort of the United Kingdom*, 1944; and *Statistische Schnellberichte zur Kriegsproduktion*, February, 1945.

10. *Statistics Relating to the War Effort of the United Kingdom*, 1944; and *Statistische Schnellberichte zur Kriegsproduktion*, 1945.

11. *Statistics Relating to the War Effort of the United Kingdom*, 1944; and *Statistische Schnellberichte zur Kriegsproduktion*, 1945.

12. *G. A. F. Strength and Losses*, Allied Expeditionary Forces, Control Party (OKL), July 7, 1945.

13. *G. A. F. Strength and Losses* (OKL), July 7, 1945.

14. *G. A. F. Strength and Losses* (OKL), July 7, 1945.

15. *G. A. F. Strength and Losses*, Allied Expeditionary Forces, Control Party (OKL), July 7, 1945.

16. *G. A. F. Strength and Losses* (OKL), July 7, 1945.

17. United States **Strategic Bombing** Survey Interrogation Report.

increased, reaching the high point of the war, both in terms of quantity and quality, at the time of the invasion of Normandy. Total stocks of tanks in army units increased from about 4500 in June 1941 to around 5 to 6 thousand at the end of 1942, and to 14,000 as of June 1944.[18] Moreover, an increasing proportion of the total was represented by the heavy Panther and Tiger tanks — tanks which had been designed to match the Russian T-34's. There was also a considerable increase in the stocks of army weapons, particularly army antitank weapons. Stocks of heavy infantry weapons as of June 1944 were reported at twice the post-Stalingrad amount.[19]

Curiously, while there was a major improvement in the supply position of nearly all other major types of army equipment, ammunitions remained in very short supply from the winter of 1942 until the end of the war. The large cutback in ammunition production that occurred early in 1941 resulted, by autumn, in a critical shortage at the fighting front. Although stocks were increased by a large acceleration of output in 1942, throughout the remainder of the war, ammunition stocks never reached the level of mid-1941.[20] Some of the German generals interrogated by the Bombing Survey did not appear particularly disturbed over the shortage, although they admitted that on ammunition supplies the German troops were at a considerable disadvantage at both the Eastern and Western fronts.[21] On the other hand, the diaries of Generals von Halder and Guderian are full of bitter complaints.[22] But despite the pleas of the Generals on the Eastern Front for more ammunition, only during a few months of 1942 was ammunition production a high priority program.

Despite the huge increases in military production during 1943 and 1944, it appears that throughout the war the Russian armies were not only numerically larger, but also better supplied with military equipment than the German armies. If the figures made public by Stalin in 1946 are correct, Russia outproduced Germany — by a very comfortable margin — in nearly all major items of military equipment during at least the last three years of the war. In terms of qual-

18. *Effects of Strategic Bombing*, pp. 167–169.
19. Wagenfuehr, "Rise and Fall of the German War Economy," p. 24.
20. *Effects of Strategic Bombing*, p. 188.
21. Interrogation of Field Marshal Kesselring. USSBS.
22. General Heinz Guderian, *Panzer Leader;* and diary of General von Halder (unpublished).

ity, the German aircraft were superior to the Russians', while in tanks the Russians had the edge, at least until Germany got the Panthers and Tigers into production. According to the diaries of Generals von Halder and Guderian, neither side made much use of air power throughout the war.

Although the differences are not as striking as those shown in Table 53, a German intelligence report, dated October 1944, gives

Table 53. German and Russian production of military equipment, annual average 1942–1944

	Germany	Russia
Aircraft	26,000	40,000
Tanks and self-propelled guns	12,000	30,000
Artillery	10,500	120,000
Machine guns	516,000	450,000
Rifles	2,060,000	3,000,000
Small arms ammunition (million rounds 1944 only)	5,370	7,400

Source: *Statistische Schnellberichte zur Rüstungsproduktion*, February 1945; and Stalin's speed February 9, 1946, *Pravda*, February 10, 1946.

the same general picture; namely, that in most types of military output — with the important exception of antiaircraft guns and ammunition — Russia's military output exceeded Germany's during the war period on a whole.[23] According to the estimates presented in this report, even in 1944, when Germany produced 19,000 tanks and other Panzer vehicles, which was more than 3 times the level of 1942, Russia's output of corresponding types of equipment was some 6,000 units larger. Russia's 1942 output was put at about 3 times Germany's. For most other types of military output, the intelligence estimates show a smaller difference between their respective outputs, and in the case of some items, Germany's 1944 output is reported above that of Russia. It is noteworthy that these estimates were prepared in 1944. Judging from earlier German appraisals of Russia's productive capabilities, such levels of military output never could have been approached.

23. *Rüstungsfertigung, deutsches Reich und Feindmächte*, OKW, October 1944.

It is possible — perhaps it is even likely — that both Stalin's figures and the German intelligence estimates late in the war exaggerated Russia's wartime military output. But even assuming some inflation, after allowing for the fact that the Germans had to keep a considerable amount of military equipment in the West to counter air attacks and the threat of invasion, it seems improbable that they supplied as much fighting equipment to the Eastern Front as the Russians did. The diaries of the German Generals insist that almost from the beginning of the war, the Russians were superior in both numbers of troops and quantity of equipment.[24] In their view, the 1941 and 1942 victories (not so easily won as the newspaper stories led us to believe) were exclusively attributable to the superior fighting qualities of the German soldiers, to their superior leadership, and to the unwillingness of the Russians to really oppose the Germans until they were deep inside Russia.

Although military supplies were probably far from adequate, a more severe limitation on Germany's fighting capabilities during the last two years of the war was imposed by the shortage of military manpower. Up until the beginning of the war with Russia, Germany had mobilized about 7.4 million men, and the active strength of the armed force was within several hundred thousand of this number. By May 1943, an additional 4 million had been called into the armed forces.[25] The total number mobilized, including casualties, was at that time equal to about 35 per cent of the entire German male population in the age groups 14–50.[26] After 1943, physical requirements were progressively lowered and occupational deferments were very carefully screened, but it was not possible to significantly increase the active strength of the armed forces. Between 1942 and 1943, armed forces strength was increased by about 1 million; between 1943 and 1944, only by 200,000.[27] Moreover, the quality of the newly conscripted troops progressively declined.

This is not to suggest that between 1943 and the end of the war

24. Diary of General von Halder (unpublished); and Guderian, *Panzer Leader.*

25. *German Employment Statistics During the War,* FIAT Office of Military Government for Germany (U. S.), 30 November 1945.

26. *German Employment Statistics During the War* (FIAT), 30 November 1945.

27. Summary Document of Armed Forces Strength Records, OKW.

it would have been impossible to increase further the size of the armed forces. A special survey prepared in the Ministry for Armaments and War Production, the results of which were reported to Hitler in July 1944, indicated that some 588,000 men who had been deferred for occupational reasons could be released for military duty.[28] In itself this is a considerable number, but it is a number which also suggests that military manpower reserves were at the time very slender.

2. MAJOR FACTORS ACCOUNTING FOR THE INCREASE IN MILITARY OUTPUT

A. *Changes in Total Available Output, Consumption, and Investment*

The tremendous increase in military output which occurred from late 1942 to mid-1944 was accomplished with a relatively small increase in the resources available for the German war effort. Between 1942 and 1943, Germany's gross national product rose about 10 per cent (in real terms).[29] Most of this increase, however, probably reflected the changing composition of output associated with the large shift towards munitions production. Though our estimates of total output do not cover 1944, it is likely that the gross national product did not rise significantly above the 1943 level.[30] Net acquisitions from foreign countries increased only nominally during 1943; and from the spring of 1944, as a result of territorial losses in both the East and the West and the disruption of the transportation system they shrank very rapidly.[31]

Until 1944, total consumption did not fall significantly from the 1942 level, which already had been reduced to the depression level. The quality of the German diet, however, continued to deteriorate, and an increasing proportion of civilian industrial goods had to be reserved for bombed-out civilians. Total employment in the civilian sector of the economy declined from about 13.2 millions in 1940 and

28. Speer's letter to Hitler, July 12, 1944, files of United States Strategic Bombing Survey.

29. See Appendix, Table 66.

30. *The Gross National Product of Germany, 1936–1944*, United States Strategic Bombing Survey.

31. See Appendix, section B.

1941 to 11.5 millions in 1942, 11.1 millions in 1943, and just over 10 million in 1944.[32] Although Speer attempted to carry out a wholesale closing-down of civilian goods establishments, he was bitterly and effectively opposed by the Nazi Party leaders. In fact, as the intensity of the bombings increased, all that he could do was to prevent an increased use of resources for civilian goods production.

The shortage of materials compelled a practical elimination of all types of public and private investment unessential to the war effort. Investment in basic industries, however, continued at a surprisingly large volume until nearly the end of the war. A special study of the Planning Board of the Ministry of Armaments and War Production showed that in 1943, the fourth year of the war, a considerable amount of resources was still being used for expanding the industrial potential.[33] Investment in manufacturing, power, and transportation amounted to around 8 billion RM, and in real terms was just as large as the 1939 level of corresponding types of investment. Investment in industry itself, after allowing for the change in prices, was about one-third larger than in 1938. In the heavy industries — iron, steel and coal — the 1943 volume of investment was almost twice the 1938 level. Expenditures on expansion of capacity in the chemical and synthetic oil industries were about a quarter greater. Steel quotas for plant expansion in oil and chemical industries rose from 2,900 tons in 1940 to 4,500 tons in 1942, and declined only slightly in 1943; in 1943 nearly one fifth of the total supply of finished steel went into chemical and synthetic oil expansion.[34] Power capacity increased at a substantial rate — about 6 per cent annually — during the whole war period.[35]

The large volume of resources which Germany used for such types of expansion — rather than for munitions output — represented the price she had to pay for prewar errors in planning. Despite the large acquisitions of petroleum from Rumania and other sources (which were not counted upon at the time the war broke out), oil remained critically short throughout most of the war period. A power shortage became a major problem because the prewar ex-

---

32. *Effects of Strategic Bombing*, appendix table 94, pp. 270–271.
33. *Die deutsche Industrie*, March 1944.
34. Steel Allocation data: first quarter 1939, second quarter 1944, Planning Board, Ministry for Armaments and War Production.
35. *Effects of Strategic Bombing*, appendix table 85, p. 265.

pansion plans did not take into account the enormous increase in requirements of the chemical, synthetic oil and rubber, and metallurgical industries.

B. *Availability of Specific Resources*

A more detailed examination of the supply position of major materials, power, machine tools, and labor also indicates that the doubling of munitions production which took place between 1942 and 1944 was accomplished with no major increases in resource availability. As Table 54 indicates, while total munitions output increased

Table 54. Indices of resource availability

(1942 = 100)

	1940–1941	1942	1943	1944
Metals:				
Steel[a]	87	100	111	89
Aluminum[b]	89	100	105	108
Copper[b]	94	100	91	66
Lead[b]	92	100	110	87
Tin[b]	83	100	57	86
Coal[c]	93	100	102	–[d]
Electric power[e]	–[d]	100	100	105
Petroleum[b]	89	100	120	102
Machine tool stock[g]	85	100	107	112
Labor force:[h]				
Total civilian	99	100	103	102
Industry	100	100	105	107
Addendum: munitions				
production	75	100	155	193

a. *Effects of Strategic Bombing*, Appendix Tables 71 and 72. 1940 partly estimated Includes production in occupied areas.

b. *Effects of Strategic Bombing*, Appendix Table 83. Estimates of supply include output in Greater Germany plus imports. Coal year beginning in March.

c. *Effects of Strategic Bombing*, Table 57, p. 94. Supply includes imports and brown coal converted to bituminous coal equivalent.

d. Not available.

e. *Effects of Strategic Bombing*, Table 70, p. 117. Annual data represent average total rated capacity for January, May, and September minus losses in capacity due to maintenance, repairs, water shortage, and enemy action.

f. *Effects of Strategic Bombing*, Table 57, p. 94; and *Statistische Schnellberichte zur Kriegsproduktion*. Total supply includes domestic crude, synthetic, booty, and production in occupied territories. The 1944 index based on January–April figures.

g. *Effects of Strategic Bombing*, Appendix Table 37. Inventory as of January 1.

h. *Effects of Strategic Bombing*, Appendix Table 5.

around 55 per cent between 1943 and 1944, total steel supplies increased by only 11 per cent, aluminum supplies by 5 per cent, and coal by only 2 per cent. There were sizable declines in copper and tin supplies. Despite the increase in capacity, the supply of power in 1943 was no larger than in 1942. The total civilian labor force, including foreign workers, increased 3 per cent, and the industrial labor force about 5 per cent. The only large gain was in petroleum output, a gain which had to be achieved through the building of new capacity. The increase in the machine tool supplies, which had been going on at a sizable rate since the beginning of the war, was not viewed by the Speer Ministry as altogether desirable. Although particular types of tools were in short supply, the main problem was to reduce output, thereby releasing capacity for military products. The enormous appetite of businessmen for general purpose tools as a hedge against inflation made this difficult.

In 1944, current supplies of all major metals except aluminum fell; the declines ranging from about 10 per cent for steel to 35 per cent for copper. Coal and electric supplies for the year as a whole were only slightly above 1943. The industrial labor force rose by less than 2 per cent. Although most of these declines began in the second half of the year, during the first half, when munitions output increased about 40 per cent, there was little increase in either the availability of materials or labor.

The increased labor, material, and machinery requirements for munitions output were partially met through a diversion of these resources from the civilian sector of the economy. In 1943, for example, production of consumer metal products — except household goods for the relief of the bombed-out — was practically eliminated. Similar action was taken with respect to those party-supported types of public investment, which previously had been spared.

But probably much more important in explaining the increase in munitions output was the tremendous increase in efficiency of resources devoted to war use. Prior to 1943, as we stated, procurement was characterized by insistence on the highest quality of workmanship, frequent changes in design, and improper scheduling of endproducts and components production — so that at particular times tanks could not be assembled for lack of turrets, while at others there were plenty of turrets but few chassis. Conducted in this manner, military production was extremely expensive in materials, manpower, and industrial facilities.[36]

Indicative of the saving of manpower, whereas total munitions output increased almost 200 per cent from mid-1941 to mid-1944, employment in the munitions industries during the same period increased from 2.7 million workers to only 3.9 million, or by 45 per cent.[37] Munitions output per worker rose by almost 60 per cent. Of course, the increase in labor productivity is hardly surprising. In both the United States and Britain, productivity in the munitions industries increased sharply as the scale of output was expanded. But more pertinent, inasmuch as metal supplies imposed a much more direct limitation on armaments output, a more efficient use of metals permitted the rise in munitions output to be accomplished without nearly a proportionate increase in armed forces' allotments. From mid-1941 to mid-1944, the quarterly allocations of steel to the munitions industries rose from only about 1.1 million tons to 1.5 millions, a 35 per cent increase, as compared with a 200 per cent increase in munitions output.[38] Although metals inventory figures for the munitions industries are not available, it appears that until late 1943, at least, accumulation was substantial. From 1940 through 1942, total current supplies of aluminum exceeded consumption by around 25 per cent annually.[39] Between 1941 and 1943, total copper stocks were estimated to have increased over 200 thousand metric tons, an amount nearly equal to the total rate of consumption in 1943.[40] As late as 1944, total stocks of steel were estimated at 15 million tons.[41] A very significnt portion of the metal stocks, it may be

36. Wagenfuehr summarized the direction of military production prior to 1942 as follows: "The well-known German thoroughness and the fact that during wartime decisions were handed down by leaders with exceptional powers led to constant changes in the equipment which was already in mass production, resulting in huge quantities of high-class scrap and a waste of scarce materials and scarce labor. Nearly every alteration was presented by the domineering heads of the respective committees as a demand originating from Hitler. . . ." "Rise and Fall of the German War Economy," p. 17.

37. *German Employment Statistics During the War,* Office of Military Government for Germany.

38. Steel allocation data, Planning Board, Ministry of Armaments and War Production.

39. *Monatliche Rohstoffübersichten, Statistisches Reichsamt,* Abtg. VIII.

40. *Monatliche Rohstoffübersichten, Statistisches Reichsamt,* Abtg. VIII.

41. Testimony of Hans Kehrl, director of material allocations, Ministry of Armaments and War Production, Interrogation Reports, USSBS.

assumed, was accumulated by munitions producers. As a conservative estimate, it appears that the allocations of steel, copper, and aluminum to munitions industries, in the period 1940–1942, would have supported at least twice the actual volume of output, though there may have been a problem with respect to some of the higher quality steels.

Finally, because capacity was generally ample, it was not necessary to divert a large volume of resources during the last two years of the war to expansion of capacity in the armaments industries. Throughout the war, most types of armaments capacity were used largely on a single shift basis. In the tank, motor transport, arms, and artillery plants only about 10 per cent of the workers were employed on a second shift.[42] In the aero-engine industry, where capacity was regarded as exceedingly tight, about 65 per cent of all workers were employed on the first shift.[43] In the ball-bearing industry (and in contrast to the experience of Britain and this country), about one fifth of the employees worked on a second shift, and none on a third.[44] In the industries using machine tools, the relationship between total employment and the stock of tools remained practically unchanged throughout the whole war period.[45] In spite of the resistance to such measures, during the latter part of the war quite a large proportion of the machinery capacity was converted to direct armaments production. By 1944, nearly half of the industry's sales was represented by munitions output.[46]

Although basic shortages did not significantly slow up the advance of military production during 1943 and the first half of 1944, it appears highly likely that even if bombing and territorial losses had not intervened, shortages of coal, power, and high-grade steels would have sharply limited further expansion.[47] Early in 1944, a serious

42. Testimony of Saur, head of the Technical Division, Ministry of Armaments and War Production, Interrogation Reports, USSBS.
43. Testimony of Saur, Interrogation Reports, USSBS.
44. Testimony of Saur, Interrogation Reports, USSBS.
45. *Effects of Strategic Bombing*, p. 44.
46. *Effects of Strategic Bombing*, appendix table 36, p. 230.
47. Early in 1944, Hitler ordered a drastic acceleration of military output. The "Victory Program" contemplated an increase of 57 per cent in total munitions output between March and December 1944. According to members of the Speer Ministry, however, an increase of this magnitude was entirely out of the question. (Wagenfuehr, "Rise and Fall of the German War Economy.")

coal shortage appeared imminent. Increasing output was made difficult both by a shortage of workers in the coal mines and by a lack of transport facilities. The power shortage, which had persisted throughout most of the war, had become so serious that by late 1943 it became necessary to sharply curtail aluminum and electric steel output, both of which were important power users. In 1944, practically the entire supply of high-grade steel was allocated for direct military use. Although electric steel capacity was still expanding, output actually was held back by the power shortage.

Besides these limitations on the output of munitions, there was the petroleum shortage which throughout most of the war had restricted the operational capabilities of the armed forces. Although during the course of the Russian campaigns a shortage of oil of the same character as the ammunition shortage of the winter of 1942 did not develop, the mobility of the armed forces had to be accommodated to very limited supplies of gasoline. According to General Guderian, most of the army supplies had to be moved by rail (often over rail lines constructed by the Germans) or by more primitive forms of transport.[48] The shortage of aviation gasoline was reported to have restricted the Luftwaffe's training program as early as 1942.[49] Even before the beginning of the large-scale air attacks on the petroleum industry early in 1944, it seriously limited the air force's operational capabilities.[50]

Curiously, the shortage of gasoline does not appear to have been given much consideration in the planning of military production. In his letters to Hitler, written in May and June of 1944, Speer was describing the aviation gasoline situation as desperate, and at the same time boasting of his accomplishments in increasing aircraft fighter production. Acceleration of production was continued after it had become apparent that the German air force could not get enough planes into the air to protect even the oil targets. It was not until the very last few months of 1944 that production of conventional fighter planes was given up and output was concentrated on the ME-262 jet. Despite the huge increase in production, the increase in opera-

---

48. *Panzer Leader.*
49. Testimony of General Koller, Chief of Staff for the Luftwaffe, Interrogation Reports, USSBS.
50. Testimony of General Koller, Interrogation Reports, USSBS.

tional strength was very small. Total fighter strength increased by only 3800 planes during 1944, compared with a total output of almost 29,000.[51] A substantial number of planes built during the accelerated program appear to have been destroyed on the ground.

It is true that shortages of petroleum, power, or steel do not impose an ultimate limitation on a nation's economic war effort in the same sense as man power or natural resources might; and it is also true that at the time Germany could have further expanded her civilian labor force. In 1944 there were still a substantial number of women who could have been taken into the labor force; in fact, the number of German women in the labor force in 1944 was only slightly larger than the 1939 total.[52] But even if the labor could have been made available, at that stage of the war Germany could not afford to divert other scarce resources — such as steel or power — to overcome basic shortages. Indeed, it is difficult to understand why some of the long-range expansion programs were not curtailed earlier.

C. *Speer's Program for Rationalizing German Industry*

In February 1942, when the Minister of Munitions Production, Todt, was killed in an airplane accident, he was succeeded by his assistant and Hitler's personal architect — Albert Speer. Unlike most of the civilian high officials, Speer did not rise to power through party affiliations but rather because he was able to win Hitler's confidence as an able administrator. Speer was disinterested in politics, and he participated in the general jockeying for power, in which most of the Nazi leaders were more or less completely absorbed, only to the extent that suited his sole interest — which was producing far more planes, tanks, and weapons than anyone else had ever contemplated. His interest in production problems was almost fanatical. (Since the war, Speer appears to have been mainly occupied in refighting the Battle for Production. The reports of his interrogations and the memoranda written by Speer since the war describing his production achievements number well over a hundred.)

When Speer succeeded Todt, he was made directly responsible for army supplies, and the procurement offices of the army were trans-

51. *G. A. F. Strength and Losses,* OKL Records, files of United States Strategic Bombing Survey.
52. *German Employment Statistics During the War,* 30 November 1945.

ferred to his Ministry (which until mid-1943 was called the Ministry of Weapons and Ammunition). It may be assumed from the transcripts of the Fuehrer's conferences that Speer was given such power, because Hitler, by late 1941, was finally persuaded that the army's logistic preparations for the Russian war were woefully inadequate. In addition, and on his own initiative, Speer was made chairman of *Zentrale Planung,* an agency set up in Goering's office of the Four-Year Plan, for the main purpose of allocating steel to all claimant groups. In 1943, the raw materials allocation function was officially transferred to Speer's Ministry (then the Ministry for Armaments and War Production), as was control over civilian production and naval armaments. Speer did not get control over aircraft production until after the beginning of the large-scale bombing attacks on the aircraft industry early in 1944. Despite his persistent efforts, he was never able to gain control over labor conscription; nor was he able to work out a satisfactory arrangement with Sauckel, the Plenipotentiary General for Labor Allocation, for allocating labor to armaments plants. Except as they had to do with armaments production, price control and tax policy remained outside of Speer's authority.

The principal accomplishments of the Speer Ministry were, first, the establishment of a more or less efficient system for scheduling and placing orders for military end-product and components output; second, the inauguration of a workable system for controlling the distribution of raw materials; and third, and by far the most important, the institution of a variety of effective measures for rationalizing the war and war-supporting industries.

We indicated that prior to 1943 contracts were placed with little regard to the availability of capacity in the munitions end-product industries or to the availability of components from the supplying industries. Speer succeeded in ending the chaos that resulted from this method of operation by collecting, as well as he could, requirements data from the armed forces; by distributing orders in such a manner that they could be speedily and efficiently processed; and by making arrangements for delivery of components at the appropriate dates.

As we have also seen, in 1942 the raw materials distribution system was on the verge of a complete breakdown, i.e., metal allotted to priority users substantially exceeded the total supply. Speer's first major achievement was the correction of this situation. Early in 1943, the steel priorities system was supplanted by an allocations system, and an attempt was made to tie the distribution of other metals to the distribution of steel.

This system of metals distribution, which was introduced at about the same time, did not appear to work very well by comparison with the Controlled Materials Plan used in this country. In the first place, not until late in 1944 was statistical data developed for obtaining accurate metals requirements for the component industries. Also, unlike the CMP, which embraced copper, steel and aluminum, the German system was only partly successful in relating the distribution of other metals to the distribution of steel.

The third accomplishment of the Speer Ministry, as described by Speer and his associates, was the rationalization of German industry. Shortly after Speer was made responsible for production of army equipment, he succeeded in relieving the army procurement officials from their supervisory powers over the munition plants; this in itself, according to his testimony, made possible an enormous increase in efficiency. The armed forces continued to be responsible for the formulation of requirements, for specifications for military equipment, and for the actual placing of contracts. Decisions on the distribution of military contracts, the building of new capacity, and the production processes that were to be employed became the responsibility of the Speer Ministry.

Speer was able to exert only a limited influence on requirements — in 1942 he was unable to persuade Hitler to further step up army production, and in 1943 such exhortations were not necessary — but his Ministry did have a considerable influence over the designs and specifications of military products. In numerous instances, the technical experts of the Ministry were able to persuade the armed forces that changes in design or in specifications of a particular type of military equipment, which had only a marginal influence on its operational value, would permit enormous increase in its producibility. Speer insists that this discovery was his principal secret weapon in the battle for production.

Control over military production was exercised through a system of Committees and Rings, the Committees being generally responsible for military end products, the Rings for the associated components. They were staffed by engineers, plant managers, and other types of technicians — men with backgrounds as members of boards of directors were seldom appointed. Speer ordered that all the key positions be filled by younger men. Only if it were absolutely necessary was someone over 45 selected; his assistant had to be under 45.

Overseeing the work of the Committees and Rings was the Technical Division of the Ministry for Armaments and War Production, which was headed by Speer's chief assistant. The Technical Division kept current records and judged the performance of individual plants mainly in terms of man hours of labor and volume of materials used per unit of output. Standards were prescribed, and those firms failing to meet the standards were singled out for special attention. Measures taken to increase efficiency included standardizing of components, increasing utilization of special-purpose tools, setting up machinery in a manner which would facilitate mass production, increasing the number of shifts in activities where capacity was a bottleneck, and disseminating information on efficient production techniques.

Besides promoting such measures, Speer and his associates were instrumental in introducing a tax and pricing incentive scheme for generally encouraging efficiency. Essentially, the effect of the scheme on incentives was just the opposite of the previously used combination of an excess profits tax and a cost-plus determination of prices of military goods. Under the new system a fixed-price contract replaced cost-plus contracts. The price paid for an individual type of equipment depended on the manufacturer's choice as to the efficiency group he would come under. Each type of production was divided into four efficiency classes, and the price set for each of them was determined on the basis of the costs of representative firms. However, if an individual manufacturer elected the lowest efficiency class, he paid the full excess profits tax; on the other hand, if he selected the efficiency group in which the permitted price was lowest, he was fully exempt from the wartime profits tax. Prices and tax rates were set in a manner that tended to make profitability of the most efficient producers highest.

Although Speer's accomplishments during the last two and one-half years of the war were very creditable, especially in contrast to the previous management of the war economy, the foregoing discussion does not imply that in any fundamental sense Speer was responsible for the acceleration of military production. The factors basically responsible, were the Allied air attacks and the losses suffered on the Eastern front. In this connection it should be noted that despite the high degree of inefficiency which, according to Speer and his associates, characterized aircraft procurement prior to their taking over responsibility for the program, in 1943 the increase in aircraft production was larger than the gain in any other major type of armaments, except for tanks.

The increased efficiency in production planning did not characterize the planning of military requirements. Though the course of the war after Stalingrad made such planning difficult, a much better integration of strategic considerations and planning of supplies would have been possible. The basic reason why the planning was not more intelligent is that Hitler made himself responsible for the ultimate determination of military requirements, and, as has been emphasized earlier, he was not an able planner, nor even interested in broad planning considerations. During the latter part of the war there were at least two major planning errors. The first was the failure to set the production objectives for ammunition sufficiently high (prior to 1944, at least, supply factors did not limit ammunition production). Although there were frequent complaints from the military commanders, the transcripts of the "Fuehrer's Conferences" indicate that Hitler was not interested in ammunition.[53] His principal interest (and the discussions of it run well over a hundred pages) was in all the details of tank design and tank production. A second major blunder was the failure to give up producing bombers, once it had become apparent that the air attack against Britain was a failure. Although General Milch, Director General of Aircraft Procurement, wanted to convert to fighters as early as 1942, he was overruled by Hitler and Goering, who could never quite give up the idea of destroying Britain through bombing. For a period of 18 months, the argument continued. Several times Milch almost won his point; plans were made for sharply expanding fighter output, industry was given orders — and then they were subsequently cancelled. For the period as a whole, however, bomber production accounted for over two thirds of total aircraft output (measured in terms of air frame

53. "Transcripts of the Fuehrer's Conferences, 1942–1944."

weight).[54] It was not until the autumn of 1943 that Hitler finally agreed to concentrate on fighter output.

3. THE COLLAPSE OF MILITARY PRODUCTION

Beginning in the summer of 1944, the then tremendous weight of aerial attack, territorial losses, and military conscription made it impossible to increase military output, and these factors eventually brought about Germany's economic collapse.

By the end of 1944, areas which had accounted for about 10 per cent of Germany's total industrial output, and a like amount of her munitions output, had been lost.[55] The loss of upper Silesia in January cut off nearly half of her hard coal supplies; by February, areas responsible for 40 per cent of Germany's total steel supplies had been conquered.[56] Numerous difficulties arose in adapting production to the loss of component supplies which had been produced in conquered areas.

The conscription of more than 1.5 million men into the armed forces during 1944, although not fully compensated for by recruitment of foreigners and German women, resulted not so much in a general manpower shortage as in a very serious shortage of skilled workers.[57] By autumn the rate of conscription had become so high (more than 200,000 a month) that it was no longer possible to give occupational status serious consideration.[58] Though in the metalworking industries the draftees were replaced (until January industrial employment rose), it was impossible to replace them with skilled workers. This loss was keenly felt because of Germany's major reliance on general purpose tools.

After the beginning of the year, military conscription was handled directly by the local military authorities, and as might be assumed under the circumstances, except for a relatively few key plants, the maintenance of production was given no consideration.

54. *Indexziffern der deutschen Rüstungsendfertigung*, Planning Board, Ministry for Armaments and War Production, 1944.

55. *Kriegseilbericht* (War Express Report) Special Paper, United States Strategic Bombing Survey.

56. Wagenfuehr, "Rise and Fall of the German War Economy," p. 24.

57. Labor Balance for 1944, Planning Board, Ministry of Armaments and War Production.

58. Labor Balance for 1944, Planning Board, Ministry of Armaments and War Production.

The third major factor was the enormous step-up in the weight of attack on German industry, cities, and the transportation system. In the third quarter of 1944 alone, the tonnage of bombs dropped by the Allied air forces almost equalled the total for the entire history of the European air war up to July 1, 1944.[59] The average monthly weight of attack during the second half of 1944 was more than seven times the average for 1943.[60]

The two highest priority target systems during the remainder of the war were oil and transportation. In the course of the systematic attacks on the oil industry, which got underway in June, production of aviation gasoline was reduced from a preraid average of 175,000 tons to 52,000 in June, and 10,000 in September.[61] After a minor recovery in the autumn months, production was stopped altogether in February. Soon after the attacks, both the air force and army were forced to curtail their gasoline consumption drastically. A major by-product of the oil attacks was a sharp reduction in nitrogen and methanol output, which in turn resulted in a substantial curtailment of ammunition production.

The attack on the transportation system, which began on a large scale in September, had as a principal objective the isolation of the Ruhr producing area. The tonnage of bombs dropped on the transportation targets from September through May was equal to about a fifth of the total tonnage dropped on tactical and strategic targets in Axis Europe throughout the war.[62] From the latter part of August to the week of December 23, freight car loadings fell from about 900,000 cars to about 550,000, and by the first part of March had declined to 214,000 cars.[63] Total coal shipments, which normally accounted for 40 per cent of total rail freight, fell from 7.4 million tons in August to 3.0 million in October and 2.7 million tons in December.[64] By March the tonnage hauled was barely adequate for the needs of the railroads.

Besides these two main campaigns, a comparatively large weight of attack was delivered against munitions plants; in particular against

59. Tabulating Branch, Secretariat, United States Strategic Bombing Survey.
60. Tabulating Branch, Secretariat, USSBS.
61. Oil Division, United States Strategic Bombing Survey.
62. Tabulating Branch, Secretariat, United States Strategic Bombing Survey.
63. Speer's letters to Hitler, January 1945.
64. Speer's letters to Hitler, January 1945.

tank, ordnance, motor vehicle and aero-engine plants. The attacks against the aero-engine plants, where equipment was much more of a limiting factor than in aircraft assembly, were particularly successful. Partly because of these attacks, partly because of the decisions taken as a result of the shortage of aviation gasoline, total aircraft output fell by more than 40 per cent between July and December.[65] The tank production loss on account of strategic bombing was put at 20 per cent for the second half of 1944.[66] Motor vehicle production fell considerably, though this had little effect on the total stock of vehicles, and less effect on the use of motor transport for the movement of supplies.

The attacks on the Ruhr transportation network, in addition to their effect on shipments of coal and other supplies out of the Ruhr, resulted in a considerable reduction of steel and power output. Besides denying them coal, the attacks resulted in considerable damage to auxiliary facilities in these industries. From May through January, total power losses attributable to these factors nearly doubled, and reduced available capacity throughout Germany by about one quarter.[67] Steel output in the Ruhr area fell from about a rate of over 1 million tons a month to 300,000 in December.[68]

In December, total raw materials output was about half of what it had been in July; and by February was further reduced to about 35 per cent of the July average. By the end of the year, or even earlier, however, the decline in raw materials output had ceased to be a limitation on the output of military or civilian goods. By then the problem was generally one of transporting sufficient coal to fabricate the semifinished inventories manufacturers had on hand.

The intensified scale of the air attack also caused a considerable diversion of labor to the clearing of debris, to reconstruction, and to dispersal, etc. The program for reconstruction of the oil industry alone involved some 120,000 workers.[69] It has been estimated that in the third quarter of the year, workers directly or indirectly engaged in repair work totaled in the neighborhood of 2 to 3 million.[70]

65. *Effects of Strategic Bombing*, appendix table 101, p. 276.
66. *Effects of Strategic Bombing*, p. 171.
67. *Effects of Strategic Bombing*, table 70, p. 117.
68. *Effects of Strategic Bombing*, p. 108.
69. *Effects of Strategic Bombing*, p. 80.
70. *Effects of Strategic Bombing*, p. 40.

But the attacks also had the effect of releasing labor from plants not restored to operating order, or from plants which could not operate because of a lack of coal or other materials. By autumn considerable unemployment was reported in some localities.[71]

Though there is no way to assess its importance, there is little doubt that by the end of 1944, if not sooner, military and other production was affected by another major factor, that is, by the increasing recognition that production no longer mattered. By February or March, even Hitler appears to have concluded that the war was lost. His last order to Speer was for the destruction of all types of vital plants to prevent their use by the Allied powers.[72] Part of Speer's defense at the Nuremberg trials was his refusal to carry out these orders.

All of these major factors — territorial losses, the manpower problem, the bombings, the willingness of the people to engage in a maximum production effort — affected production more slowly than might be supposed. In December, total industrial production, as estimated from a monthly sample survey, was within 15 per cent of the second quarter average.[73] Total industrial production in the area held by the Germans as of December was estimated at 99 per cent of the second quarter average; and output in the metal-working industries at about 95 per cent the second quarter average.[74]

Between July (the production high point of the war) and December, munitions production fell about 18 per cent.[75] Evidently it was more seriously affected by lack of components and skilled labor than industrial production as a whole. As late as December, however, total panzer output and the output of weapons was higher than in any previous month.[76] Though considerably reduced from the peak rate, production of fighter aircraft was at a higher rate than had been achieved prior to July.[77]

After the end of the year, military production rapidly collapsed.

71. Wagenfuehr, "Rise and Fall of the German War Economy," p. 26.
72. Speer's letters to Hitler, March 1945.
73. *Kriegseilbericht* (War Express Report).
74. *Kriegseilbericht* (War Express Report).
75. *Indexziffern der deutschen Rüstungsendfertigung,* Planning Board, Ministry of Armaments and War Production.
76. *Indexziffern der deutschen Rüstungsendfertigung.*
77. *Indexziffern der deutschen Rüstungsendfertigung.*

By March, which was the last month production data were collected, munitions production had been reduced 45 per cent below the December total.[78] Insofar as was possible, available capacity and material supplies were concentrated on a few high priority programs. For example, between December and March, it was somehow managed to achieve fairly sizable increases in output of the "people's rifle," assault rifles, flame throwers, and bazookas. Output of jet planes reached 286 in March, as compared with 124 in December and 19 in September.[79]

Paradoxically, even in March 1945, Germany's total military output was at a substantially higher rate than when she began her attack on Russia — an attack which was to have brought complete victory by the autumn of 1941.

4. SOME OBSERVATIONS ON STRATEGIC BOMBING

At the risk of oversimplification, I shall now turn to some brief observations on strategic bombing. These observations supply my own interpretation of some of the conclusions of the United States Strategic Bombing Survey, and needless to say, other participants in the work of the Survey may not agree with what follows.

The general objective of the preinvasion bombing campaigns was, as stated in the Casablanca directive, "the progressive destruction and dislocation of the German military, industrial, and economic system, and the undermining of the morale of the German people to a point where their capacity for armed resistance is fatally weakened." It is not unlikely that the author of this sweeping directive was British; United States objectives were considerably more modest. Because of operational limitations they had to be: prior to the spring of 1944, the capabilities of the air forces were limited not only by the relatively modest weight of attack they could deliver, but also by the availability of long-range escorts for deep penetrations, and by the necessity of frequent diversions of the air forces for tactical missions. The most important of these was the preinvasion attack on the French railway system, which for several months used almost the entire capacity of all the air forces based in the European theatre.

The U. S. Strategic Air Force, capable of daylight "precision"

78. *Indexziffern der deutschen Rüstungsendfertigung.*
79. Wagenfuehr, "Rise and Fall of the German War Economy," p. 12.

bombing, generally sought targets whose destruction would quickly affect the enemy's flow of military supplies. Because of operational limitations, only the most "economical" targets were selected; that is, targets whose destruction promised to maximize the enemy's short-term loss of military production. Prior to the time of the invasion, these considerations ruled out target systems like transportation and power and resulted in the choice of such systems as ball-bearing and air-frame and aero-engine plants.

The British, on the other hand, found early in the war that their bombers were unsuited for daylight precision attacks. First used as an expedient, later a general theory in support of area bombing was developed. This theory emphasized mainly the morale effects of bombing. As for economic considerations, the German economy was pictured as being so fully and efficiently mobilized that resources would have to be diverted for the restoration of civilian, as well as for military production. (The argument that such attacks could not maximize the immediate loss of military production was discounted by emphasizing the enemy's powers of recuperation.) On the assumption that the Germans were fighting a "total war," which meant that any transfer of resources would subtract from the war effort, general attacks on cities appeared to be as good a way as any to make the enemy divert his resources to recuperation.

After the invasion, when their operational capabilities were enormously greater than even a few months before, the U. S. air forces shifted their emphasis from an immediate reduction of the enemy's military production to bringing about a general attrition of his economy. Though the attacks on the oil targets, designed to have a maximum military effect, were continued throughout 1944, plans for attacking other types of military production targets were generally given up in favor of the transportation attack, the general objective of which was Germany's economic collapse. The tonnage of bombs delivered on transportation targets was far greater than on any other target system, and the scale of the attacks increased from September until almost the end of the war. As late as the end of February, the operation Clarion set out some 8 to 9 thousand planes against Germany's entire railway system.

It is apparent from the data presented in Section I of this chapter that the *preinvasion* attacks of the U. S. and British Forces could not prevent an enormous increase in German military production. From the beginning of 1943 to mid-1944 the rise in munitions production was nearly 50 per cent. Though the attacks, notably those against aircraft plants, prevented a somewhat larger increase, in general the production losses attributable to bombing were very modest. Based on a detailed examination of losses in the damaged industries, it was the conclusion of the United States Strategic Bombing Survey that prior to mid-1943, neither the British nor the U. S. attacks had a significant effect on military output as a whole; that in the second half of 1943 and the first half of 1944 they caused losses of some 5 and 10 per cent respectively.[80]

The expected effects of the attacks were, of course, much greater. The ball-bearing attacks alone were to reduce German armaments production by 30 per cent.[81] It was believed that in Germany, as had been the case in the United States and in Britain, bearings were in such short supply (the inventory cushion was estimated to be only one month's supply) that any reduction in current supplies would be almost immediately reflected in a curtailment of aircraft, tanks, and other fighting equipment using ball bearings. Moreover, it was believed that the main part of the German output was concentrated in a half-dozen cities, highly vulnerable to air attack.

But as it actually turned out, the Germans had time to disperse part of their production between the initial attacks in the autumn of 1943 and their resumption in February 1944. And though production initially fell substantially, the Germans were able to restore output much more quickly than was believed possible. Stocks of bearings turned out to be relatively generous, sufficient to tide the Germans over during the period when output was being restored.

In short, whereas Intelligence had estimated the ball-bearing production loss at 9 months, the actual loss was more like 3 months of the preraid rate of output.[82] And while it was estimated that the raids would cut armaments production by 30 per cent, after the war

80. *Effects of Strategic Bombing*, pp. 11–13.
81. *The German Anti-Friction Bearings Industry,* Equipment Division, United States Strategic Bombing Survey.
82. *The German Anti-Friction Bearings Industry,* Equipment Division, USSBS.

it was found out that no type of military production had been appreciably curtailed for a lack of bearings.[83]

The ball-bearing attack illustrates the difficulties of a plan of attack aimed at the Achilles' heels of the enemy economy. The soft spots must be correctly identified, which frequently they are not. To be successful they must result in a reasonably prolonged loss of output, which almost always they did not. Losses in output were restored much more quickly and easily than was believed possible, just as in this country production bottlenecks were eliminated much more easily than it was believed they would.

To have had nearly the effect on preinvasion armaments output that it was believed the bombing attacks actually did have, a very substantially larger amount of capital destruction would have been necessary. As it was, output was not limited nearly so much by plant capacity and machine tools as it was by steel and power. And since the attacks had little effect on the latter, they little affected the course of armaments production.

Much less successful were the British area raids on German cities. Though they did result in considerable physical destruction and cause some production losses, notably in steel, their effect on output as a whole was not very significant. As for their effect on "the will of the Germans to resist," it was to bring the war home to the Germans, and thereby to induce them to divert a much larger volume of resources for the war effort. According to Speer's account, reported earlier, more than anything else the bombing raids on Cologne and Hamburg won for him his long campaign for thoroughgoing economic mobilization measures. Though repair work in the bombed cities did require a substantial number of workers (in the main, foreign labor was conscripted for this work), the bombing also helped Speer in his efforts to close down civilian plants and thereby release materials and labor for the war effort.

The preinvasion air raids, however, did affect the German war effort — and in a manner which has been little commented on even since the war. This was in causing the Germans to devote a very significant part of their war production effort and also a large number of highly trained military personnel to air defense. From 1942 to the

83. *The German Anti-Friction Bearing Industry*, Equipment Division, USSBS.

first half of 1944 expenditures on air defense armaments — defensive fighter planes and their armament, antiaircraft weapons, and ammunition — nearly tripled, and at the time of the invasion amounted to about one third of Germany's entire munitions output.[84] Indeed, in mid-1944 production of air defense armaments was at a higher level than was munitions output as a whole at the time Germany went to war with Russia.[85] It can be seen, therefore, that where the preinvasion attacks really paid off was not nearly so much in the damage they did, but rather in the effect they had on causing the Germans to put a very significant part of their total war effort into air defense.

Beginning shortly before the invasion, the scale of attack was substantially stepped up. Indeed, the total tonnage of bombs dropped on Germany in the second half of 1944 was about equal to that which occurred during the entire preceding period of the war, and the attacks were maintained at about this level through April of 1945.[86]

As the level of attack mounted so did its effect on output as a whole. One of the attacks, that against the German synthetic oil industry, undoubtedly had a very significant effect on the progress of the war. This attack succeeded, by September 1945, in reducing output to practically nothing.[87] Because the Germans previously had not been able to accumulate sizable reserves of aviation gasoline and other fuels, the impact of the attacks on fighting units was almost immediate. By midsummer the Germans were able to use only a small fraction of the air strength available to them. Paradoxically, the drive to accelerate aircraft fighter output — conventional as well as jet — was continued for a matter of months after the harsh facts of the fuel situation had become plainly obvious.

The success of the raids on the oil plants was due in part simply to the scale of the attacks — every known major facility was attacked a number of times — and in part to the fact that because the oil industry was one of the most capital intensive in Germany, the amount of capital destruction per raid was very high. Despite an

84. *Indexziffern der deutschen Rüstungsendfertigung,* Ministry for Armaments and War Production.
85. *Indexziffern der deutschen Rüstungsendfertigung.*
86. *Effects of Strategic Bombing,* pp. 2–4.
87. *Effects of Strategic Bombing,* p. 13.

enormous effort to restore output by late summer, the Germans were unable to keep output above a bare trickle.[88]

As we have already recounted, by the end of 1944 the air attacks had begun to have a major impact on German industrial output as a whole, and between December and March output fell precipitously. However, by this time the course of production was of little matter to the German war effort. If anything mattered to the German leaders at this time, it was to press as many men as they could into Germany's sagging lines of resistance.

With the possible exception of the oil attack, by far the most effective attacks of the British and U. S. air forces were the attacks directed at purely military objectives. We speak primarily of the attacks on the French railway network, which in the period immediately preceding the invasion occupied a major part of both the British and U. S. air forces; and the attacks on air bases, which began early in the air war and were continued throughout.

The effect of the first was to make it enormously difficult for the Germans, after the invasion had begun, to move troops and supplies into the area opposite the invasion. The effect of the second was to play a substantial role in minimizing Germany's air strength. From mid-1943 to mid-1944 Germany's fighter air strength failed to show any increase despite the fact that during that period about 14,000 such planes were produced.[89] Although there is no reliable information on the number of planes actually destroyed on the ground, it may be assumed that the attacks on air bases were a major factor in preventing a large rise in German air strength.

Though we recognize that there is room for difference of judgment, in our view the principal contributions to the allied war effort of the bombings are mainly represented by the results of these attacks on military objectives, the results of the attack against the German oil industry, and in the effect which the bombings in general had in causing the Germans to devote a very substantial effort to air defense. These, of course, are considerable accomplishments, but they fall short of the expectations held by the experts at the time. Particularly in Britain it was believed that the air attacks would have

88. *Effects of Strategic Bombing*, p. 13.
89. *G. A. F. Strength and Losses* (OKL Records); and Speer's letter to Hitler, January 27, 1945.

a more decisive effect on the German economy and on the German will to resist. Indicative of the expectations the British held, they were willing to devote over one third of their war production effort to aircraft and allied armaments.[90]

The mistake of Sir Arthur Harris and his followers is simply that they anticipated history in imputing to their blockbusters the destructive power of atomic bombs.

SUMMARY AND CONCLUSIONS OF PART TWO

The general picture of the German war economy emerging from this study is not that of a nation geared to total war. It is rather that of an economy initially mobilized for fighting relatively small and localized wars, and subsequently responding to the pressure of military events only after they had become harsh facts. Thus, in the autumn of 1939 Germany's preparations in steel, oil, and other important materials were far from adequate for a sustained effort against the major powers. Her levels of civilian output were still very comfortable. Her total output of munitions was not impressively larger than Britain's.

The weakness of Germany's position in terms of a long war was fully understood by the German war leaders. The decision to undertake a lightning attack through the Lowlands was not made on the basis of a high confidence in its success; it was undertaken as the only possible way that Germany might avoid a major military defeat.

For the war against Russia, fuller preparations were made, but preparations which hardly strained the capacity of the economy. Indeed, one of the reasons for temporarily giving up the idea of an invasion of Britain in favor of a blitzkrieg attack on Russia was that the latter would not require a massive economic effort. Soon after the attack began some important types of munitions output were allowed to decline on the premise that the war would soon be over. And even the first winter's defeats did not result in a major revision of Germany's military or economic strategy; in Berlin they were regarded as only a temporary setback.

It was only after the Battle of Stalingrad and the initiation of

90. *World Munitions Production, 1938–1944.*

large-scale air raids on her cities that Germany began to mobilize in earnest. The peak of her war effort was not reached until mid-1944, and was reached only after her defeat was a foregone conclusion.

Contrary to the impression that most of us have had, the Germans did a far from distinguished job in managing their wartime economy. Both Britain and the United States moved much faster in developing efficient techniques for determining military production objectives and for assuring that the objectives were reasonably met. It was not until the third year of the war that the Germans finally managed to work out a realistic picture of materials requirements, and not until then that a partially effective materials rationing system was substituted for an unworkable priorities scheme.

The improvements in the economy brought about by Speer and his associates during the last two years of the war were very impressive (the gain in military output far outweighed the loss through the use of additional resources) but mainly by comparison with the previous state of affairs. Many of Speer's "revolutionary" measures were revolutionary only to Germany. For example, his great drive to rationalize fighter aircraft production in 1944 consisted essentially of adopting practices that were common in the United States and Britain.

Like the democracies, Germany relied almost exclusively on direct controls. Fiscal policy played an insignificant role in restraining inflationary pressures and in facilitating a transfer of resources to war purposes. But what is particularly paradoxical about German fiscal policy is that, whereas during the depression years any deficit financing was regarded as a dangerous threat to the future stability of the country, in wartime, when the inflationary pressures became acute, there was very considerable resistance to increases in tax rates and little apparent concern over the incurrence of huge deficits.

What the Germans really excelled in was in improvising. The measures taken to get around the shortage of ferroalloys were truly ingenious. The kinds of measures taken to restore production after bombing attacks and the speed with which production was restored were remarkable.

Behind the inability of those responsible for war production to increase the total effort as rapidly as they would have wanted, or to introduce various kinds of effective controls much earlier than they were able to, was the reluctance of the Nazi party and of the German industrialists to give up various peacetime objectives until events made it plainly clear they had to. There was a good deal of opposition to restrictions on the production of civilian goods. Speer's efforts to get more people into war production were seriously impeded by that part of Nazi ideology that claimed that women's place was in the home. The industrialists, remembering the inflation after World War I, were able to put up a very stout resistance to measures designed to prevent them from hoarding hard goods.

Thus it can be seen that the classic image of the ruthless efficiency of dictatorships — of their ability to subordinate a variety of competing objectives to such a central purpose, as winning the war — is not borne out in the case of Germany.

How then was Germany able to do so well militarily? Her conquest of France was certainly one of the greatest military victories of all times. And considering especially that she elected to attack on a front stretching from the Baltic to the Black Sea, it seems remarkable that Germany was able to come as close as she did to conquering all of western Russia.

Not being a military expert, I am not hesitant about giving my opinions. The French were completely defeated, it now seems, because they staked everything on a single strategy — the Maginot Line. When the attack did not come as expected, the French and British armies were unable to do anything except to attempt to retreat with a minimum of losses.

Though it is easy to blame the French for their single-mindedness and the British for their acquiescence, even now it may be wondered if the main lesson of this terrible defeat has really been learned. For example, when one hears of the apparent willingness of the British to put everything into building a powerful H-bomb capability, one cannot help wondering if they aren't simply building for themselves a new kind of Maginot Line.

As for Russia, doesn't the fact of the huge German victories — despite Hitler's decision to attack on a front running thousands of miles and despite Germany's limited preparations for the war — suggest simply that the Russians were not as formidable a military power as they were generally pictured to be? If we overestimated Germany — and we certainly did — by the same token we overestimated Russia. Russia did not withstand a maximum German effort. There is little doubt, to be sure, that on the basis of Russia's poor showing against Finland, Hitler underestimated the Russians. But considering how close Germany actually came to conquering all of Russia west of the Urals, it hardly can be said that he grossly underestimated them. And apparently the Russians have drawn the same conclusion, for what appears to concern them even more than the H-bomb is the rearmament of Western Germany. However, if Russia was a second-rate military power in World War II, we can take little comfort in that fact now. Today, unfortunately, her military strength appears to be enormously greater than it was then.

The main lesson that comes out of Germany's experience is simply that a nation's economic war potential may be a very poor measure of her actual military strength. It is hardly surprising that Germany eventually lost the war to a combination of powers whose economic war potential vastly exceeded hers. What is much more surprising is how well she did, despite the economic odds against her.

Conversely, from our own point of view we can take little comfort in the fact that it was America's resources that ultimately resulted in Germany's defeat. On the contrary, we ought to be telling ourselves that it was a matter of good luck that events turned out as they did. Suppose that Hitler had decided that conquering the whole of western Russia was too much of a gamble. Suppose he had taken Goering's advice and contented himself with Western Europe, North Africa, and the Middle East. Suppose that the Germans had managed to get jet fighters into production two years earlier than they did — something they could have easily done. In brief, if a few things had happened differently, Germany's ultimate defeat would have demanded an enormously greater sacrifice on our part — perhaps ten times the casualties we actually incurred.

The lesson that we ought to draw from this experience is that whether future wars be nuclear wars or conventional wars, we should count much less on our potential military strength than on our actual military strength.

Appendix, Bibliography, and Index

Statistical Appendix

A. GERMANY'S GROSS NATIONAL PRODUCT, 1928–1938

Prior to the war, the German Statistical Office published a national income series extending back to 1913, but did not prepare gross national product estimates. During the war, several German economists became interested in social accounting concepts as a means of broadly portraying the impact of the war on the economy. Although estimates of total output and its distribution among major uses were prepared, these estimates were very crude, and unfortunately were not carried back to cover the prewar years.[1]

Under the auspices of the Federal Reserve Board, Howard Ellis and Paul Hermberg have prepared estimates of Germany's prewar national income and national product.[2] Ellis' work, as indicated below, suffers from serious defects in the interpretation of the German national income concepts. The estimates presented here closely follow Hermberg's methodology. In a few cases (as, for example, valuation of inventory changes) it did not appear worth while to attempt the degree of refinement used by Hermberg. My estimates differ somewhat from Hermberg's insofar as they were based on official German data, some of which were not available to him at the time he prepared his study. The differences between the two sets of estimates turned out to be surprisingly small.

1. "National Income, Public Gross and Net Expenditures, and Private Expenditures," Wagemann Institute, 1945 (unpublished monograph).

2. "German Gross National Product Estimates," Paul Hermberg, 1945 (unpublished monograph). *Germany: National Income and its Uses, 1925–1938.* Federal Reserve Board Report, February 1944.

There are several good descriptive accounts of German national income methodology. The most complete and authoritative consulted was Dr. Paul Jostock's booklet "The Computation of National Income and its Meaning." [3] Ernest Doblin's National Income Conference paper, "Problems of Measuring German National Income in Wartime," [4] provides an adequate treatment and is one of the few works available in English. The clearest and most concise statement consulted was a monograph prepared during the war at the Wagemann Institute, "National Income, Public Gross and Net Expenditures and Private Expenditures." [5]

The gross national product concepts underlying my estimates are roughly similar to the U. S. concepts. The gross national product is defined as the market value of all privately produced goods, plus government services, valued at their cost. The national product totals have been built up from the official national income estimates, after adjustment for several of the major conceptual differences. Gross national product is the total of adjusted national income, indirect taxes, and depreciation. Like the U. S. estimates, total government expenditures for goods and services are valued net of depreciation. [6]

The German national income concepts differ from those employed in this country principally in the treatment of taxes and government services. The German Statistical Office computed national income as a sum of wages and salaries (including public payrolls except for the armed forces), agricultural income, and undistributed corporate profits, other business income, and income of public service enterprises — all gross of direct taxes and social insurance contributions. From this sum there was deducted an item called "taxes not included in private income," an adjustment which has given rise to much confusion. This adjustment is equal to government services to con-

3. *Die Berechnung des Volksinkommens und ihr Erkenntniswert,* Dr. Paul Jostock, Deutschen Wirtschaftswissenschaftlichen Gesellschaft, Berlin, 1941.
4. Conference on Research in Income and Wealth, April 1944.
5. Conference on Research in Income and Wealth.
6. Ellis is incorrect in his argument that a deduction for depreciation should be made from the government figures to put them on a "net" basis. Both in this country and in Germany, the GNP data on government expenditures are measured net of depreciation. To put them on a gross basis it would be necessary to set up separate capital and current accounts for the government, and to impute a depreciation item in the current account.

sumers plus public investment minus direct taxes and the government deficit. The nature of the adjustment has led Ellis and some other analysts to conclude that this treatment excluded military expenditures, along with other government "intermediate" services from the national income, and in their own estimates they have adjusted the German official estimates to include total public outlays (excluding transfer payments).

Although seemingly plausible, such an adjustment will not result in a national income total, as conventionally defined. The error involved in such reasoning is essentially that of failing to understand that the German "national income" estimates are in fact net national product estimates, net of depreciation and government "intermediate" services. The tax adjustment referred to above also can be defined — and in a way less subject to misinterpretation — as indirect taxes minus government "intermediate" services. Adding this item to the national income shares, as computed by the Germans, will result in a total somewhat greater than national income as conventionally defined. In the limiting case, with "intermediate" services valued at zero, the total would equal net national product. The adjustment, therefore, represents a deduction of government intermediate services from net national product, as we customarily define it.

The meaningfulness of the German treatment need not concern us. National income may be defined as simply "national income" (German concept) minus "taxes not included in private incomes," plus pay of the armed forces. The last item is treated in the German national income computations as a transfer item; that is, it is simply not included in wages and salaries.

The other principal difference between U. S. and German concepts is omission from the German accounts of imputed items, such as imputed interest and imputed rents. In the author's judgment, the analytical usefulness of national product estimates is not particularly enhanced by such imputations, and accordingly no adjustments of this character were made.

The national product totals were broken down into four principal components: government goods and services, gross private domestic investment, net foreign investment, and consumer expenditures. It was possible to obtain nearly all the data needed for the first three of these from official German sources. Consumer expenditures were obtained as a residual. The sources are indicated in the footnotes to the tables.

Available German data permitted satisfactory estimates of private capital formation and of net foreign investment. On the other hand, the derivation of government expenditures for goods and services from German budget data must be regarded as fairly crude. With the available data it was not possible to derive satisfactory separate expenditure and income accounts for the Reich, for states and municipalities, and for public service enterprises. On the receipts side, the difficulty arises from the complicated system of tax collections whereby, with respect to some taxes, the Central Government acted as a fiscal agent on behalf of the subordinate governmental units, and with respect to others, the states and municipalities collected taxes for the Reich. Another source of difficulty is that of separating out public service enterprises from other public expenditures and receipts. Finally, the expenditure data are not available for all years in sufficient detail to make satisfactory estimates of transfer payments.

The expenditure and receipts "Totals" for the Reich, states and municipalities, and for public service enterprises shown in Table 60 appear to be reasonably accurate, although the division between Reich and subordinate authority accounts does not exactly correspond with published German budget data. Thus, the Reich deficits are somewhat smaller and those of states and municipalities correspondingly larger than indicated by conventional sources. Public service enterprises are not shown separately in the expenditure and income accounts. In Table 63, however, investment of public service enterprises and of the government proper are shown separately. For any analysis of investment, public investment, including investment of publicly owned corporations, as well as private investment should be examined. It was not possible to check in detail Hermberg's estimates of transfer payments against the official data. Such crude checks as were made indicated that a detailed recomputation, if possible, would yield estimates of the same approximate magnitude and trend as Hermberg's.

For the purpose of obtaining a GNP series in constant prices, the major components were deflated by what appeared to be appropriate deflators. Thus, in constructing a constant price series for government expenditures for goods and services, total public investment was deflated by a construction cost series; other government expenditures by a wage cost series. It was not possible to separate out non-investment purchases from business, but the bulk of the "Other public expenditures" for the period covered were undoubtedly representel by wage and salary payments. Private investment in construction and equipment was deflated by a weighted index of construction and equipment costs, and inventories by the wholesale price index. The Germans published a constant price series on exports and imports, which were used to estimate net foreign investment in constant prices. Finally, consumer expenditures were deflated by the consumer price index. The biases implicit in price indices may have resulted in some overstatement of the rise in real output from the early to the late 1930's. On the other hand, there is reason to believe that relative to the 1928 and 1929 figures, real output in 1938 and 1939 was understated.

Comparison of the consumer expenditures series — estimated as residuals — with independent estimates provides a rough check on the reliability of the GNP estimates. Table 55 shows the consumer expenditure estimates and other related series. Unfortunately, however, the independent estimates of total consumer expenditures shown do not cover the period as a whole. Marschak has estimated consumer expenditures as national income (German definition) minus gross domestic and foreign investment, minus rents[7] (there was no apparent reason for excluding rents). For the overlapping years 1928 and 1929, his estimates average some 10 billion RM larger than mine. However, after deducting Government services to consumers and adding rents, the difference appears to be of the order of 3 billion RM. Dr. Jacobs, of the German Chamber of Commerce, built up consumer expenditure totals from detailed estimates of the output of consumer goods and services. For the years 1936, 1938, and 1939, his estimates were within 2 billion RM of mine.[8]

The annual changes in the consumer expenditure estimates appear

7. *Archiv fur Sozial wissenschaftund Sozialpolitik,* Bd. 67, Heft 2, April 1932. The method is described in Ellis' national income monograph referred to above.
8. Monograph on consumer expenditure prepared by Dr. Alfred Jacobs of the German Central Statistical Office.

Table 55. Indices of consumption, selected years, 1928–1938

GNP estimates	1928	1929	1932	1936	1937	1938
Consumer expenditures						
(billions of RM)[a]	68	72	46	56	61	62
Index (1928 = 100)	100	106	67	82	90	91
Consumer expenditures, 1928 prices						
(billions of RM)[b]	68	71	58	68	74	74
Index (1928 = 100)	100	104	85	100	109	109
Independent series						
Consumer expenditures (Marschak)						
(billions of RM)[c]	80	81				
Consumer expenditures (Jacobs)						
(billions of RM)[d]				55	59	63
Index of retail sales, 1928 prices						
(1928 = 100)[e]	100	100	81	92	107	119
Index of production for consumer						
goods[f]	100	99	78	98	117	127

a. See Table 58.
b. See Table 59.
c. *Archiv für Sozialwissenschaft und Sozialpolitik*, Bd. 67, Heft 2, April 1932.
d. Monograph on consumer expenditures prepared by Dr. Alfred Jacobs of the German Central Statistical Office.
e. *Standard of Living and Rationing*, Section S, German Economic Survey, Ministry of Economic Warfare.
f. *Monatzahlen über die industrielle Produktion*, Statistisches Reichsamt.

to be reasonably consistent with changes in retail sales and the output of industrially produced consumer goods. Because purchases of goods and services (in which rent is a major item) are more stable than clothing and other consumer purchases, the retail sales and industrially produced consumer goods declined somewhat more in the early 1930's and recovered somewhat faster than total consumer expenditures. The very large increases in the former series for 1938 and 1939 also reflect territorial additions, whereas the GNP estimates measure output in "old" Germany, excluding Austria and the Sudetenland.

As a result of his misinterpretation of the German treatment of indirect taxes and government "intermediate" services, Ellis was able to come out with reasonable estimates of consumption (estimated as a residual) despite the fact that his public expenditures were grossly overestimated.[9] In obtaining net national product as official national income plus government intermediate services and military outlays, instead of national income plus total indirect taxes minus "taxes not included in private incomes," he overstated net national product by an amount which was of the same magnitude as his overstatement of public expenditures. For 1938, for example, Ellis' estimate of net national output was about 15.5 billion RM larger than mine, government expenditures for goods and services about 12 billion RM larger, while his consumer expenditures exceeded mine by some 5 billion RM.[10] On the other hand, other analysts, like Mrs. Sweezey, whose work was not as painstaking as Dr. Ellis', crudely estimated changes in consumption as the difference between changes in national income (German definition) and changes in *their* estimates of government expenditures, and obtained estimates of consumption which were much lower than could be supported by independent information.

B. GERMANY'S GROSS NATIONAL PRODUCT, 1939–1943

Estimation of Germany's wartime national output involves a number of difficult problems. In the first place, the German Statistical Office suspended its detailed computation of national income estimates, substituting crude estimates of the totals. Second, most of the basic data, including national income estimates, refer to an expanding geographic area; output for the prewar area of Germany can be only roughly approximated. Third, only partial data exist for assessing the economic contribution of the occupied areas. Fourth, and this difficulty is not peculiar to Germany, deflating with the available price data will result in a fairly unpredictable overstatement of the growth in real output. This is because it is almost impossible to take into account statistically, quality deterioration and the increasing restricted availability of civilian products. Finally, most of the 1944 basic data are crude preliminary estimates, and between the various sources there are major inconsistencies which it was not possible to resolve. For these reasons the national product estimates were not carried beyond 1943.

Besides all of these difficulties, there are more basic analytic prob-

9. *Germany: National Income and Its Uses.*
10. *Germany: National Income and Its Uses.*

lems concerning the meaning of total national output in a period of pronounced change in both the consumption of final output, and in the composition of major inputs. To explain changes in real output and the proportion of total output, or resources, used for war purposes, it is necessary to look behind the aggregates into the requirements placed on and the availability of particular types of resources. For example, one of the major technological differences between military and civilian goods is their considerably larger requirements for labor per unit of metals fabricated. An important part of the explanation of the enormous increase in national output in the United States during the war includes this technological fact — plus the fact that during the war the supply of labor was considerably more elastic than the supply of metals.

Because of the difficulties of constructing reliable GNP estimates for Germany during the war, and their analytic limitations, the national product estimates have been relied upon only incidentally in the analysis of Germany's wartime economic achievements. Although the available data were carefully examined in the preparation of the estimates presented below, the estimates should not be construed to represent anything more than very crude approximations.

The economics division of the United States Strategic Bombing Survey prepared a special report on Germany's wartime gross national product.[11] The main source for the estimates was the monograph on Germany's national product by Dr. Grunig of the German Chamber of Commerce.[12] Grunig's data included independent estimates of consumer expenditures, the foreign balance, domestic investment, and government expenditures. Another set of wartime national product estimates is available in the Wagemann Institute monograph referred to above.[13] There are several major differences between the Bombing Survey–Grunig estimates and those of the Wagemann Institute. The former series was built up from independent estimates of all the major components of the national output, and adjusted to measure output in a single geographic area. On the other hand, the estimates prepared by the Wagemann Institute were built up from

11. *The Gross National Product of Germany, 1936–1944.*
12. Unpublished National Product monographs.
13. "National Income, Public Gross and Net Expenditures and Private Expenditures," 1945.

national income totals, which refer to the expanding German boundaries, and estimates of private consumption were obtained as a residual.

For several reasons it appeared necessary to rework the Bombing Survey estimates. An independent set of consumer expenditure estimates, prepared by Dr. Jacobs of the German Central Statistical office, were more easily reconciled with independent prewar and wartime data.[14] Dr. Grunig's estimates of public outlays, on which the Bombing Survey's Estimates were based, differ substantially from those contained in the Wagemann Institute monograph and from official budget data. Finally, since the preparation of the estimates, somewhat more reliable information has become available on the economic contribution of the occupied areas.

Insofar as was feasible, the estimates have been adjusted to measure output in the prewar area of Germany, including Austria and the Sudetenland. Estimates for gross private domestic investment were available on this basis. Dr. Jacob's consumption estimates which referred to "old Germany" were adjusted by means of national income data to relate to prewar boundaries. Conceptually, the measurement of government expenditures should have excluded public civil expenditures, such as were included in the total German budget, of the areas annexed after the outbreak of the war. The error involved in not considering such a refinement was, however, probably very small. To obtain output produced in Germany, there was deducted from total available output — Government expenditures, plus consumer expenditures, plus gross private domestic investment — an approximation of the net economic contribution of all the areas outside of Germany's prewar boundaries.

The estimates for government expenditures for goods and services during the war were derived in about the same way as the prewar estimates, described in section A, above, with one principal exception. Government interest payments, which became very large during the war, were treated as a transfer item. Estimates of transfer payments were contained in the Wagemann Institute monograph for the fiscal years beginning in 1939 and ending in March, 1943. For the remaining period, transfer payments were crudely estimated on the basis of budget data and other information. A final adjustment was

14. Unpublished monograph on Consumer Expenditures, 1936–1944.

necessary to convert the fiscal year goods and services estimates to a calendar year basis.

The estimates of gross private domestic investment and consumer expenditures are reasonably consistent with independent sources. A comparison of the consumer expenditure series, expressed as index numbers, with other indices of consumer output is shown in Table 56. Total industrial production of consumer goods declined somewhat

Table 56. Indices of consumption, 1939–1944

	1939	1940	1941	1942	1943	1944
Consumer expenditures, 1939 prices[a]	100	93	87	80	80	75
Industrial production of consumer goods[b]	100	94	96	86	91	85
Sales of consumer goods industries to civilians, 1939 prices[b]	100	90	88	74	74	72

a. See Table 66.

b. *Industrial Sales, Output, and Productivity Prewar Area of Germany, 1939–44*, United States Strategic Bombing Survey.

less than consumer expenditures, measured in real terms, because of the increasing volume of consumer goods which went to the armed forces. Sales of consumer goods industries to civilians, also measured in constant prices, showed a slightly larger decline than total consumer expenditures for goods and services.

The crudest part of the estimates is the measurement of the economic contribution from other areas. The total estimates of foreign contributions (external investment) is made up of German purchases financed through occupation levies, invasion currency, and the clearing debt, and the surplus of imports over exports in the foreign trade balance. The principal sources for the data were a monograph on foreign contributions prepared by the Research Office for Military Economy, which contained annual estimates of the contributions of France, Holland, Norway, Poland, Denmark, the Protectorate, and occupied Eastern Areas; the estimates contained in the Bombing Survey's National Product monograph; and the German budget and foreign balance data.

The estimates leave out of account captured stocks of military goods, materials and agricultural products, the contribution of foreign laborers and foreign troops, and part of the contribution of the areas formally annexed subsequent to 1939. Captured stocks may have represented a very sizable omission, but there is no way to obtain even a rough order-of-magnitude estimate for this item. From

Table 57. Gross national product, 1928–1938
(billions RM — current prices)

	1928	1929	1930	1931	1932	1933	1934	1935	1936	1937	1938
National income:[a] (official estimates)	75.4	75.9	70.2	57.5	45.2	46.5	52.8	59.1	65.8	73.8	82.1
Minus: taxes not included in private incomes[a]	3.0	3.7	4.0	3.7	2.6	2.5	2.3	2.3	2.3	2.3	2.3
Plus: armed forces pay and allowances[b]	0.2	0.2	0.2	0.2	0.2	0.2	0.4	1.0	1.6	2.4	3.4
National income at factor cost	72.6	72.4	66.4	54.0	42.8	44.2	50.9	57.8	65.1	73.9	83.2
Plus: depreciation allowances[c]	6.7	6.9	6.9	6.4	5.8	5.8	5.8	6.0	6.2	6.5	6.8
Plus: indirect taxes[d]	10.2	10.4	10.6	10.0	9.0	9.1	9.8	10.6	11.3	12.8	14.5
Gross national product	89.5	89.7	83.9	70.4	57.6	59.1	66.5	74.4	82.6	93.2	104.5

a. *Statistisches Jahrbuch* (1937), p. 534; *Statistisches Jahrbuch* (1941–1942), p. 604.
b. Grunig, "Monograph on Germany's Gross National Product," German Chamber of Commerce.
c. *Statistisches Jahrbuch* (1941–1942), p. 605; *Wochenbericht*, 1938, p. 356.
d. Hermberg, Paul, *Germany: National Income and Its Uses, 1925–1938*, Federal Reserve Board; and *Statistisches Jahrbuch* (1941–1942), p. 546–547.

the occupation levies, some reimbursement was made to the contributing governments for labor services, but in the main the contribution of foreign laborers is left out of account. The contribution of foreign laborers is roughly indicated by the fact that in the period 1941 through 1944, about 15 per cent of Germany's total civilian labor force was made up of foreign laborers.[15] On the other hand,

15. *Effects of Strategic Bombing*, p. 206.

that part of the contribution of the annexed areas not included is relatively small, probably not more than 2 to 3 billion marks annually.

The estimates shown in Table 65 on total foreign contributions are substantially smaller than those contained in the Bombing Survey

Table 58. Gross national product by major components, 1928–1938
(billions of RM)

	1928	1929	1930	1931	1932	1933	1934	1935	1936	1937	1938
Gross national product[a]	89.5	89.7	83.9	70.4	57.6	59.1	66.5	74.4	82.6	93.2	104.5
Government purchases of goods and services[b]	13.0	13.0	12.5	11.0	9.5	9.0	11.5	13.5	16.5	20.5	30.0
Gross capital formation[c]	9.7	5.0	1.5	−1.8	0.3	3.2	4.7	7.2	9.2	10.5	12.2
Construction and equipment	7.1	6.3	5.3	3.3	2.2	2.6	3.7	4.8	6.2	7.1	8.5
Inventories	2·6	−1.3	−3.8	−5.1	−1.9	0.6	1.0	2.4	3.0	3.4	3.7
Net foreign investment[d]	−1.3	−0.4	2.0	3.2	1.4	1.0	0.1	0.5	1.1	1.0	0.6
Consumer expenditures[e]	68.1	72.1	67.9	58.0	46.4	45.9	50.2	53.2	55.8	61.2	61.7

a. See Table 57.
b. See Table 61.
c. See Table 64.
d. *Statistisches Jahrbuch* (1933), p. 498; *Statistisches Jahrbuch* (1938), p. 562; *Statistisches Jahrbuch* (1941–1942), p. 282. Net foreign investment includes net export balance on goods and services plus net changes in monetary stocks of gold and silver.
e. Residual.

report. The estimates prepared by the Research Office for Military Economy measure the value of goods received from foreign areas in terms of their current prices in Germany; and it appears that the same method of valuation was used in the German budget expenditure data. On the other hand, the *current price* estimates contained in the Bombing Survey report were not adjusted to take into account the very large rise in the prices paid for foreign goods relative to

German prices. Though it was attempted to take this into account in deflating the figures, the deflated figures are still somewhat larger than mine. For the years 1940 through 1943, my estimates of total foreign contributions, measured in 1939 prices, total about 85 billion RM, as compared with the Bombing Survey's estimate of 104 billion RM. The foregoing also appears to be the principal reason for the much larger estimates of public expenditures contained in the Bombing Survey's national product study.

Table 59. Gross national product by major component,
measured in 1928 prices, 1928–1938
(billions of RM)

	1928	1929	1930	1931	1932	1933	1934	1935	1936	1937	1938
Gross national product	90.8	88.5	83.8	76.1	71.9	73.7	83.7	92.3	101.2	114.2	126.2
Government purchases of goods and services[a]	13.0	12.6	12.4	11.9	12.1	11.9	14.8	17.4	21.1	26.5	36.1
Gross capital formation	9.7	4.9	2.0	−0.3	1.5	4.4	6.2	9.6	12.1	13.6	15.7
Construction and equipment[b]	7.1	6.2	5.4	3.7	2.8	3.5	4.8	6.3	8.1	9.1	10.8
Inventories[c]	2.6	−1.3	−3.4	−4.0	−1.3	0.9	1.4	3.3	4.0	4.5	4.9
Net foreign investment[d]	−0.9	0.6	1.4	2.0	−1.1	−1.4	−2.6	−1.3	–	–	−2.7
Consumer expenditures[e]	68.1	71.0	69.4	64.5	58.3	58.8	62.7	65.3	68.0	74.1	74.4

Note: Details will not necessarily add to total because of rounding.

a. Government investment (see Table 63) deflated by index of building costs (*Statistisches Jahrbuch*, 1941–1942, p. 360); remainder by index of average hourly wage rates (*Statistisches Jahrbuch*, 1941–1942, p. 384).

b. Construction and equipment deflated by weighted index of building costs and machinery costs (*Statistisches Jahrbuch*, 1941–1942, p. 360; and *Weekly Report*, Institute for Business Cycle Research, January 27, 1937).

c. Inventories deflated by index of wholesale prices (*Statistisches Jahrbuch*, 1941–1942, p. 350).

d. Imports and exports of goods, *Statistisches Jahrbuch* (1941–1942), p. 284. For services the current price balance was used.

e. Deflated by cost of living index (*Statistisches Jahrbuch*, 1941–1942, p. 376).

Table 60. Budget expenditures of the Reich, states and municipalities, 1933–1938[a]
(billions of RM)

	1933	1934	1935	1936	1937	1938
Total expenditures	15.3	17.4	18.9	23.0	27.3	39.4
Reich expenditures[b]	6.3	8.2	10.2	13.2	17.3	29.2
Rearmaments	1.9	1.9	4.0	5.8	8.2	18.4
Other	4.4	6.3	6.2	7.4	9.1	10.8
State and municipality expenditures[c]	9.0	9.2	8.7	9.8	10.0	10.2
Total receipts	14.9	17.2	18.2	21.7	26.4	31.6
Reich[b]	7.7	10.0	10.7	13.8	17.0	21.3
Taxes and customs	6.9	8.3	9.7	11.6	14.0	18.2
Other	0.8	1.7	1.0	2.2	3.0	3.1
State and local[c]	7.2	7.2	7.5	7.9	9.4	10.3
Taxes	3.7	3.6	3.7	4.0	4.6	5.0
Other[d]	3.5	3.6	3.8	3.9	4.8	5.3
Excess of expenditures over receipts	0.4	0.2	0.7	1.3	0.9	7.8

Note: Details will not necessarily add to total because of rounding.
a. Fiscal year beginning April 1.
b. *Geld-und Finanzprobleme der deutschen Nachkriegswirtschaft, deutschen Institut für Wirtschaftsforschung.* Excludes tax transfers to states and municipalities.
c. Hermberg, *German Government Finance,* Division of Research and Statistics, Federal Reserve Board; and *Statistisches Jahrbuch* (1941–1942), p. 543.
d. Includes income from public service enterprises.

Table 61. Government expenditures for goods and services, 1928–1938
(billions of RM)

	1928	1929	1930	1931	1932	1933	1934	1935	1936	1937	1938
Total budget expenditures[a]	20.8	20.9	20.4	17.0	14.5	15.3	17.4	18.9	23.0	27.3	39.4
Less transfer payments[b]	7.8	7.8	8.1	6.4	5.3	6.4	4.8	4.8	5.7	5.9	6.5
Loans and transfers	1.8	1.9	1.2	0.6	0.3	1.7	0.3	0.4	1.0	1.3	1.8
Relief and subsidies	2.1	2.3	3.4	3.9	3.6	3.5	3.3	3.2	3.5	3.5	3.6
Pensions	1.7	1.6	1.6	1.3	1.2	1.1	1.1	1.1	1.1	1.0	1.0
Reparations	2.2	2.0	1.9	0.6	0.2	0.1	0.1	0.1	0.1	0.1	0.1
Expenditures for goods and services	13.0	13.1	12.3	10.6	9.2	8.9	12.6	14.1	17.3	21.4	32.9
Adjusted to calendar year basis	13.0	13.0	12.5	11.0	9.5	9.0	11.5	13.5	16.5	20.5	30.0

Note: Details will not necessarily add to total because of rounding.
a. For the period 1928–1932, *German Government Finance;* 1933–1938, Table 60.
b. *German Government Finance.*

Table 62. Public and private investment, 1928–1938
(billions of RM)

	1928	1929	1930	1931	1932	1933	1934	1935	1936	1937	1938
Total	16.3	11.5	6.6	1.3	2.5	5.7	9.3	13.6	17.3	18.9	22.5
Public investment in construction and equipment	6.6	6.5	5.1	3.1	2.2	2.5	4.6	6.4	8.1	8.4	10.3
Government proper	4.0	3.9	3.1	1.9	1.4	1.6	3.2	4.7	6.1	6.2	7.4
Public service enterprises	2.6	2.6	2.0	1.2	0.8	0.9	1.4	1.7	2.0	2.2	2.9
Private investment	9.7	5.0	1.5	−1.8	0.3	3.2	4.7	7.2	9.2	10.5	12.2
Construction and equipment	7.1	6.3	5.3	3.3	2.2	2.6	3.7	4.8	6.2	7.1	8.5
Inventories	2.6	−1.3	−3.8	−5.1	−1.9	0.6	1.0	2.4	3.0	3.4	3.7
Addendum: Total investment in construction and equipment	13.7	12.8	10.4	6.4	4.4	5.1	8.3	11.2	14.3	15.5	18.8

For sources see Tables 63 and 64.

Table 63. Public investment, 1928–1938
(billions of RM)

	1928	1929	1930	1931	1932	1933	1934	1935	1936	1937	1938
Total	6.6	6.5	5.1	3.1	2.2	2.5	4.6	6.4	8.1	8.4	10.3
Public investment	4.0	3.9	3.1	1.9	1.4	1.6	3.2	4.7	6.1	6.2	7.4
Roads[a]	0.5	0.5	0.4	0.2	0.2	0.4	0.4	0.4	0.5	0.6	0.9
Waterways and harbors[b]	0.2	0.2	0.1	0.1	0.1	0.2	0.2	0.2	0.2	0.2	0.2
Housing[c]	1.3	1.2	1.0	0.4	0.2	0.2	0.3	0.2	0.2	0.2	0.3
Other[d]	1.9	2.0	1.6	1.1	0.9	0.9	2.3	3.9	5.2	5.2	6.0
Public service enterprises	2.6	2.6	2.0	1.2	0.8	0.9	1.4	1.7	2.0	2.2	2.9
Public utility[e]	1.0	1.1	0.7	0.4	0.2	0.2	0.3	0.4	0.5	0.6	0.7
Railroad[f]	0.9	0.8	0.8	0.5	0.4	0.6	0.7	0.6	0.6	0.7	1.0
Trams and subways[f]	0.3	0.3	0.2	0.1	−g	−g	−g	−g	−g	−g	−g
Post office	0.3	0.4	0.3	0.2	0.1	0.1	0.1	0.2	0.2	0.2	0.3
Superhighways[f]						−g	0.2	0.5	0.7	0.7	0.9

Note: Details will not necessarily add to totals because of rounding.
a. *Statistisches Jahrbuch* (1938), p. 564; *Statistisches Jahrbuch* (1941–42), p. 609. Does not include superhighways.
b. *Statistisches Jahrbuch* (1941–42), p. 609; Wirtschaft und Statistik (1939), p. 2; Wochenbericht (1939), no. 10, p. 54.
c. *Statistisches Jahrbuch* (1941–42), p. 565. Period after 1934 estimated from fragmentary data.
d. Residual Estimates, 1935–1938. Totals from *Statistisches Jahrbuch* (1941–1942), p. 609, and *Reichkreditgesellschaft* (1937–1938), p. 6. Includes military construction.
e. *Statistisches Jahrbuch* (1941–1942), p. 610.
f. *Statistisches Jahrbuch* (1941–1942), p. 609.
g. Less than 50 million RM.

Table 64. Private investment, 1928–1938
(billions of RM)

	1928	1929	1930	1931	1932	1933	1934	1935	1936	1937	1938
Total	9.7	5.0	1.5	−1.8	0.3	3.2	4.7	7.2	9.2	10.5	12.2
Construction and equipment[a]	7.1	6.3	5.3	3.3	2.2	2.6	3.7	4.8	6.2	7.1	8.5
Industry	2.6	2.0	1.6	0.9	0.4	0.6	1.1	1.7	2.2	2.8	3.7
Transport	0.4	0.3	0.3	0.1	−[b]	0.1	0.1	0.2	0.3	0.4	0.5
Agriculture	0.9	0.9	0.9	0.7	0.6	0.6	0.7	0.8	0.9	1.0	1.1
Housing	1.5	1.6	1.4	0.7	0.6	0.7	1.1	1.3	2.0	1.9	2.2
Other	1.7	1.4	1.1	0.9	0.5	0.7	0.7	0.8	0.9	1.0	1.0
Inventories[c]	2.6	−1.3	−3.8	−5.1	−1.9	0.6	1.0	2.4	3.0	3.4	3.7
Industry and trade	1.9	−1.2	−3.5	−4.8	−2.4	0.5	1.4	2.1	2.4	2.7	3.2
Agriculture	0.7	−0.1	−0.3	−0.3	0.5	0.1	−0.4	0.3	0.6	0.7	0.5

Note: Details will not necessarily add to totals because of rounding.

a. For the period 1928–1934, *Statistisches Jahrbuch* (1938), pp. 564–565; for 1934–1938, *Wirtschaft and Statistik*, 1938, p. 30; *Wochenbericht*, 1938, Vol. 51–52, p. 365; *Statistisches Jahrbuch* (1941–1942), pp. 610–611.

b. Less than 50 million RM.

c. For the period 1928–1934, *Statistisches Jahrbuch* (1941–42), p. 610; *Wochenbericht*, No. 21, 1938, p. 113.

Table 65. Gross national product, 1938–1944
(billions of RM — current prices)

	1938	1939	1940	1941	1942	1943	1944
Government expenditures[a]	32	45	63	80	98	117	
War	17	30	53	71	91	112	
Other	15	15	10	9	7	5	
Consumer expenditures[b]	69	71	68	65	61	61	58
Food and clothing	44	45	40	38	36	37	36
Other	25	26	28	27	25	24	22
Gross capital formation	14	13	1	−8	−16	−18	
Internal[c]	13	14	10	7	6	6	
External	1	−1	−9	−15	−22	−24	
Total gross national product	115	129	132	137	143	160	
Total available output	114	130	141	152	165	184	

a. See Table 68.

b. Based on a monograph on Consumer Expenditures, 1936–1944, Dr. Alfred Jacobs, German Central Statistical Office.

c. USSBS Report, "Gross National Product of Germany, 1936–1944."

d. Rough estimates based on memorandum of Research Office for Military Economy data 10 October 1944 (a portion of this document is contained in *Nazi Conspiracy and Aggression*, VII, 264); estimates of Government receipts from other countries contained in *Geld-und Finanzprobleme;* and a report of the German Statistical Office Deutschland, *Der Aussenhandel nach Ländern 1936–Juli 1944.*

Table 66. Gross national product, 1938–1944
(billions of RM — 1939 prices)

	1938	1939	1940	1941	1942	1943	1944
Government expenditures[a]	33	45	62	77	93	109	
Consumer expenditures[a]	70	71	66	62	57	57	53
Gross capital formation	14	13	1	−8	−14	−16	
Internal[a]	13	14	10	7	6	5	
External[b]	1	−1	−9	−15	−20	−21	
Total gross national product	117	129	129	131	136	150	
Total available output	116	126	138	146	156	171	

a. Implicit price indices from USSBS Report "The Gross National Product of Germany, 1936–1944."
b. Implicit price index from "Wehrmacht purchases from German Industry," USSBS Report, "Industrial Sales, Output and Productivity, Prewar Area of Germany, 1939–1944."

Table 67. National income, 1938–1944[a]
(billions of RM)

	1938	1939	1940	1941	1942	1943	1944
Total, Germany proper[b]	82	90	92	98			
Total, Greater Germany[c]	87	98	110	120	125	135	130

a. Source: USSBS Report, "The Gross National Product of Germany, 1936 to 1944."
b. German area prior to annexations of Austria and Sudetenland.
c. Current boundaries, including annexed areas.

Table 68. Government expenditures, 1938–1943
(billions of RM)

	1938	1939	1940	1941	1942	1943
Total budget expenditures[a]	39.4	59.5	84.0	107.9	132.9	51.6
Reich[b]	29.2	49.5	75.4	98.9	124.9	145.1
War	18.4	32.3	58.1	75.6	96.9	117.9
Other	10.8	17.2	17.3	23.3	28.0	26.2
States and municipalities[c]	10.2	10.0	8.6	8.5	8.0	6.5
Transfer payments	7.8	10.9	16.8	25.2	30.9	30.6
Interest on the national debt[d]	1.3	1.9	2.8	4.2	5.9	6.6
All other[e]	6.5	9.0	14.0	21.0	25.0	24.0
Total government expenditures for goods and services	31.6	48.6	67.2	82.2	102.0	121.0
Adjusted to calendar year basis	32.0[f]	45.0	63.0	80.0	98.0	117.0
War expenditures	16.5	30.0	53.0	71.0	91.0	112.0

a. Fiscal year beginning April 1.

b. *Geld-und Finanzprobleme der deutschen Nachkriegswirtschaft.* Excludes tax transfers to state and municipal authorities.

c. Estimates based on "National Income, Public Gross and Net Expenditures," Wagemann Institute, 1944. Includes tax transfers from Reich.

d. *Geld-und Finanzprobleme.*

e. Estimates for the period 1938–1943 based on "National Income, Public Gross and Net Expenditures"; for 1938 estimate see Table 61.

f. Adjusted to include Austria and Sudetenland.

Bibliography

UNPUBLISHED SOURCES

CONFERENCE IN RESEARCH IN INCOME AND WEALTH, APRIL, 1944

Doblin, Ernest, "Problems of Measuring German National Income in Wartime."

FEDERAL RESERVE BOARD RESEARCH REPORT

Ellis, Howard, "Germany: National Income and its Uses, 1925–1938," 1944.

Hermberg, Paul, "German Gross National Product Estimates," 1946.

FIELD INFORMATION AGENCY, TECHNICAL

"German Employment Statistics During the War," Office of Military Government for Germany (U. S.), November, 1945.

Hahl, Hans, "The Achievements and Difficulties of the Reichsvereinigung Eisen and the Iron Industry," Economic and Financial Branch, Control Commission for Europe, 1946.

Hettlage, "German War Finance," 1946.

Interrogation Reports, Office Military Government (U. S.): Interrogations of Albert Speer and Members of the former Reich Ministry for Armament and War Production, 1945–1946 (reports 1–95 inclusive).

"Rationalization of the German Armaments Industry," a symposium of essays prepared by a number of German technical experts, 1943.

Rohland, Walther, "The German Coal Problem," 1946.

——— "New Processes in the Steel Industry Introduced During the Second World War," 1946.

——— "Rationalization of the German Steel Industry," 1946.

——— "The Role of Foreign Ores in the German Iron Industry," 1946.

Schmelter, "Manpower Utilization," 1946.

Speer, Albert, "The Industrial Mobilization of Germany for War," 1946.

Wagenfuehr, Rolf, "The Set-up and Method for the Over-all Plan of Industrial Requirements," 1946.

GERMAN RECORDS DIVISION

The Halder Diary (seven volumes), manuscript, War Department.
Heerespersonalamt Records, Department of Defense.
Summary Data of Armed Forces Strength, Department of Defense.

HARVARD UNIVERSITY LIBRARY

Minutes of the Meetings of the Central Planning Board, 1942–1944.
Minutes of the Meetings of the Four-Year Planning Office, 1939–1942.
Statistisches Jahrbuch für das deutsche Reich, Statistisches Reichsamt (1939/1940 "Secret edition").
Transcripts of the Fuehrer's Conferences, 1941–1944.

HIS MAJESTY'S STATIONERY OFFICE, 1944

"Statistics Relating to the War Effort of the United Kingdom," Cmd. 6564.

NÜRNBERG TRIAL DOCUMENTS

Memorandum on the Contributions of Foreign Areas, Research Office for Military Economy, 1944.
Gen. Thomas, "Basic Facts for a History of the German War Economy."

THE RAND CORPORATION LIBRARY

"Der Aussenhandel nach Ländern, 1936–Juli–1944," Statistisches Reichsamt.
Die deutsche Industrie, 1943, Planungsamt, Ministry of Armaments and War Production.
"The Economic Situation, 1943–1944," Ministry of Armaments and War Production.
Die Entwicklung der Rationssätze in den Kriegen, 1914/1918 und 1939/1943, Study prepared by the German Food Ministry.
"G.A.F. Strength and Losses," Allied Expeditionary Forces, Control Party (OKL), July 7, 1945.
"German Iron and Steel Industry, Ruhr and Salzgitter Areas," Combined Intelligence Objectives Sub-committee, June, 1945.
Hitler's Directive to Goering, 1938.
"Investment in 1943," Planning Board, Ministry for Armaments and War Production.
Jacobs, Alfred, "Monograph on Consumer Expenditures, 1936–1944."
"Labor Utilization, 1943," Statistisches Reichsamt, 1943.
Monatliche Rohstoffübersichten, Statistisches Reichsamt.
"National Income, Public Gross and Net Expenditures and Private Expenditures," Wagemann Institute, 1945 (manuscript).
"The Raw Materials Situation as of July 1, 1941," Economic and Armament Office, Supreme Command of the Armed Forces.

Rüstungsendfertigung, deutsches Reich und Feindmächte, OKW, October, 1944.

"Statistical Survey of Quantity of Steel Rights Issued," Planungsamt, Ministry for Armaments and War Production.

"Statistische Schnellberichte zur Kriegsproduktion," Planungsamt, Ministry for Armaments and War Production.

"Statistische Schnellberichte zur Rüstungsproduktion," Planungsamt, Ministry for Armaments and War Production.

Wagenfuehr, Rolf, "The Rise and Fall of the German War Economy," manuscript, 1945.

Woermann, "Die Ernaehrungslage der Welt."

UNITED STATES DEPARTMENT OF COMMERCE

National Income Supplement, Survey of Current Business, July, 1951.

UNITED STATES STRATEGIC BOMBING SURVEY, FILES

"Ergebnisse der amtlichen Lohnerhebungen," Statistisches Reichsamt.

"The Gross National Product of Germany, 1936–1944," Washington, 1945.

Grunig, "Monographs on investment, government expenditures, and contributions from foreign areas."

Interrogation Reports

Officials of the Ministry of Armaments and War Production: Karl Hettlage, economic and financial advisor to Speer; Hans Kehrl, Chief, Planungsamt; Dr. Otto Saur, Chief, Technisches Amt; Walter Schieber, Chief Rüstungslieferungsamt; George Seebauer, Chief, Produktionsamt; Albert Speer, Reichsminister for Armaments and War Production; Rolf Wagenfuehr, Chief economist, Planungsamt.

Other civilian officials: Karl Lange, head of the Wirtschaftsgruppe Machinenbau; Fritz Sauckel, Plenipotentiary for Labor Mobilization; Hjalmer Schacht.

Military officials: Admiral Karl Donitz; General Alfred Jodl; Field Marshal Albert Kesselring; General Wilhelm Keitel; Field Marshal Karl von Runstedt; General Thomas.

Kriegswirtschaftliche Kraftebilanz, 1939–1944.

"The Labor Situation in 1943," Statistisches Reichsamt.

"Report on Aircraft Production, July, 1944," Planning Board, Ministry of Armaments and War Production.

Report of Referate for Metals, July, 1944.

Speer's Letters to Hitler, 1942–1945.

Tonnage of Bombs Dropped by British and U. S. Air Forces on Axis Europe, Secretariat.

Transcripts of Air Ministry Meetings, 1942–1943.

"Übersichten über die eisenschaffende Industrie, 1939," a report prepared for the Hermann Goering Works.

Weekly Reports of the Planning Board, Ministry for Armaments and War Production.

Zusammenstellung über die personnelle und materielle Rüstungslage der Wehrmacht, OKW.

UNITED STATES STRATEGIC BOMBING SURVEY, REPORTS

Report of the Aircraft Division
  The German Aircraft Industry, Washington, 1945.
Report of the Equipment Division
  The German Anti-Friction Bearings Industry (mimeographed).
Report of the Oil Division
  German Oil, Chemical, Rubber, Explosives and Propellants Industries, Washington, 1945.
Reports of the Over-all Economic Effects Division
  An Appraisal of Pre- and Post-Raid Intelligence (mimeographed).
  The Effects of Strategic Bombing on the German War Economy, Washington, 1945.
  The Effects of Strategic Bombing upon the Operations of the Hermann Goering Works During World War II (mimeographed).
  The German Bomb Damage Statistics (mimeographed).
  The Gross National Product of Germany, 1936–1944 (mimeographed).
  Industrial Sales, Output and Productivity, Prewar Area of Germany (mimeographed).
  War Express Reports (mimeographed).

WAR PRODUCTION BOARD

"Wartime Production Achievements," October 9, 1945.
"World Munitions Production," July 15, 1944.

PUBLISHED SOURCES

Ciano, Galleazzo, conte. *Ciano Diaries, 1939–1943,* New York: Doubleday, 1945.
Clark, Colin. *The Conditions of Economic Progress,* London: Macmillan & Co., 1951.
Ellis, Howard. *Exchange Control in Central Europe,* Cambridge: Harvard University Press, 1941.
——— "Exchange Control in Germany," *Quarterly Journal of Economics,* Supplement, Vol. LIV (1940).
Ford, Franklin. "Twentieth of July," *American Historical Review,* July 1946.
Foreign Logistical Organizations and Methods. A report for the Secretary of the Army, 15 October 1947.
German Army Mobilization, Intelligence Division, War Department, 1946.
Germanicus, pseud. *Germany, The Last Four Years,* Boston: Houghton, 1937.
Gisevius, Hans B. *To the Bitter End,* Boston: Houghton, 1947.

Goebbels, Joseph. *Diaries, 1942–1943,* New York: Doubleday, 1948.

Goldsmith, R. W., "The Power of Victory — Munitions Output in World War II," *Military Affairs,* Vol. X, No. 1, Spring 1946.

Guderian, General Heinz. *Panzer Leader,* London: Joseph, 1952.

Guillebaud, Claude W. *The Economic Recovery of Germany from 1933 to . . . March 1938,* Toronto: Macmillan & Co., 1939.

International Military Trials, *Nazi Conspiracy and Aggression* (ten volumes), Washington, 1946.

Jostock, Paul. *Die Berechnung des Volkseinkommens und ihr Erkenntniswert,* Statistisches Reichsamt, Stuttgart, 1941.

Kuczynski, Jürgen. *Germany: Economic and Labor Conditions under Fascism,* New York: International Publishers, 1945.

Laurie, Samuel. *Private Investment in a Controlled Economy, Germany, 1933–1939,* New York: Columbia University Press, 1947.

Lichtenberger, Henri. *The Third Reich,* New York: Greystone, 1937.

Marschak, Jacob. *"Substanzerluste," Archiv fur Sozialwissenschaft und Sozialpolitik,* Bd. 67, Heft 2, April, 1932.

Nathan, Otto, and Milton Fried. *The Nazi Economic System,* Durham: Duke University Press, 1944.

—— *Nazi War Finance and Banking,* New York: National Bureau of Economic Research, 1944.

Neuman, Franz L. *Behemoth,* New York: Oxford, 1944.

Noll von der Nahmer, Robert. "Die Dekung des oeffenlichten Bedarfs-durch nichtinflatorische Papierausgabe," *Finanzarchiv,* 1934.

Poole, Kenyon E. *German Financial Policies, 1932–1939,* Cambridge: Harvard University Press, 1939.

Reynaud, Paul. *Le Problème Militaire Française,* Paris, 1937.

Rostas, L. "Industrial Production, Productivity and Labor Distribution in Britain, Germany and the United States, 1935–1937," *Economic Journal,* Vol. LIII, April 1943.

Shulman, Milton. *Defeat in the West,* New York: Dutton, 1948.

Stocking, George W., and Myron W. Watkins. *Cartels in Action: Case Studies in International Business Diplomacy,* New York: Twentieth Century Fund, 1946.

Stolper, Gustav. *German Economy, 1870–1940,* New York: Reynal, 1940.

Sweezy, Maxine. *The Structure of the Nazi Economy,* Cambridge: Harvard Univ. Press, 1941.

Tissier, Pierre. *The Riom Trial,* London: Harrap, 1943.

United States State Department, *Nazi-Soviet Relations, 1939–1941,* Washington, 1947.

Wolf, E. *Geld-und Finanzprobleme der deutschen Nachkriegswirtschaft,* Institute for Business Cycle Research, Berlin, 1946.

PERIODICALS

Annual Economic Review, Council of Economic Advisors

The Banker Magazine

Der deutsche Volkswirt
Finanzarchiv
Institut fur Konjunkturforschung, *Konjunkturstatistisches Handbuch*
——— *Statistik des In-und Ausland*
——— *Vierteljahrshefte*
——— *Weekly Report*
——— *Wochenbericht*
International Labor Review
London and Cambridge Economic Series
Reichsarbeitsblatt
Reichsgesetzblatt
Der Vierjahresplan
Weltwirtschaftliches Archiv
Wirtschaft und Statistik
Wirtschaftskurve

Index

Agriculture, production program, 48–50

Air Force, 169; "court-martial" system of procurement, 160; Quartermaster General, 158

Air Ministry, 159, 161; files, 189, 199

Allied Control Commission, 204

Aluminum: potential in 1933, 31; production program, 46, 50; stockpiling of, 57; supply, 111–2

Annual Economic Review, 12, 89, 90

Archiv für Sozialwissenschaft und Sozialpolitik, 245–6

Armed Forces, 128; Armament Inspection Offices, 157–8, 166; Supreme Command, 128; War Economy and Armament Office, 150–1, 156–7

Army Equipment, Chief of, and Commander of Replacement Army, 156

Baran, P., 22

Bauxit-Trust A.G., 46

Beck, General: Chief of Staff, 20; Commander of Army Group, 176

Bergius process, 32

Bericht vom Westwall, 14

Blomberg, Minister of War, 150–1

von Bock, Field Marshal, 191, 193

von Brauchitsch, Commander-in-Chief of the Army, 176, 178, 193–4; meeting with Hitler, November 6, 1939, 176

Britain, Invasion of (Operation Sea Lion), 180–1

British Air Force, attack on, 180

British Ministry of Economic Warfare, 114, 118; report, 120

Brüning administration, 5, 8; and imports, 59

Calcium chloride, potential in 1933, 34

Canaris, Admiral, head of OKW Intelligence, 176

Capital formation, for war potential, 13–6; classification of investments, 14

Cartels, 29–30, 81, 167

Cejke, of the Air Ministry, 129

Central Planning Board, minutes of meetings, 54–5, 123

Central Statistical Office, report, 93–4

Chemicals: potential in 1933, 33–4; supply, 110

Chrome, potential in 1933, 31

Churchill, W., 16, 20, 123, 180

Ciano, G., 64

Civilian production, control of, 161–2

Clark, C., 87–8

Coal, 121–5; potential in 1933, 33

Comb-out commissions, 165

Conference on Research in Income and Wealth, April, 1944, 242

Construction, curtailment of nonwar, 105–6

Copper: potential in 1933, 31; production program, 46–7; stockpiling of, 58–9; supply, 112–4

Coordination, top-level, 168–172

Council of Economic Advisers, 12, 89, 90

Council of Ministers, 9, 22–3
Crisis and Stalingrad, 200–205

DAF, Rohstoffe-Dienst, 41–2
Defense Law, May, 1935, 148
Die deutsche Industrie, 15, 214
Deutschland: der Aussenhandel nach Ländern, 1936—Juli 1944, 93–4, 256
Doblin, E., 242

Economic controls, system of, 152–172; civilian production, 161–2; coordination, top-level, 168–172; government finance and price control, 153–5; procurement, 155–161; resources, 162–8
Economic General Council, 169
Economic Group for Machine Construction, 109, 167
Economic mobilization, limiting factors of, 20–7
Economic objectives, 1939–1942, 185–200
Economic policy and fear of inflation, 4–9, 22
Economic rearmament of Germany, conclusions on, 76–82
Economic recovery, nature of, 9–16
Effects of Strategic Bombing, 40, 62, 85, 88, 118, 125, 177, 191, 194, 206–218, 231–4, 251
Ellis, H., 7, 60, 241–7
Employment of women, 136, *passim*

Farben, I. G., 33; and "Buna-S," 33
Federal Reserve Board, report, 241, 251, 254
Ferroalloys, 118–122; potential in 1933, 28–31; stockpiling of, 57
Fey, W., interrogation, 92
FIAT (U.S. Office of Military Government for Germany), 37, 53, 155, 189, 212
Finanzarchiv, 8
Fischer-Tropsch process, 32, 39–40
Food consumption, 89
Ford, F., 20
Foreign trade policy and raw material position, 59–63
Four-Year Plan, Second, 18, 39–42, 44–7, 53–5, 60, 133

Four-Year Planning Office, 37–8, 47, 62, 126, 149, 151–2, 164; minutes of meetings, 37, 47, 62; reports, 54; Iron and Steel Section, 128
France, conquest of, 179–180
von Fritsch, Commander-in-Chief of the Army, 150
Fromm, Colonel General, Chief of Army Equipment and Commander of the Replacement Army, 157
Fuehrer's Conferences: minutes, 132; record of, 162, 201, 204; transcript of, 105, 196, 198–9, 224
Funk, W.: Commissioner-General for the Economy, 161, 164; head of Ministry of Economics, 129, 150, 161; head of Ministry of Food and Agriculture, 161; speech in Vienna, 186

G.A.F. Strength and Losses, 209, 220, 234
Geld- und Finanzprobleme der deutschen Nachkriegswirtschaft, 254, 256, 258
The German Anti-Friction Bearings Industry, 231–2
German Armaments Industry, 43
German Army Mobilization, 17–8
German Central Statistical Office, 241–2, 245–6, 249, 256
German Chamber of Commerce, 245, 248, 251
German economic policy, pre-Hitler, 6
German Employment Statistics during the War, 212, 217, 220
German Food Ministry, 89
German General Staff, 64
German Government Finance, 1933–1938, 254
German Institute for Business Cycle Research, *Weekly Reports*, 5, 35, 68, 71, 122, 253
German Institute for Business Research, 48–9, 61–2
German Intelligence, 177, 180, 194
"German Iron and Steel Industry, Ruhr and Salzgitter Areas," 119
German Labor Front, 66, 80
German Munitions Production com-

pared with Intelligence estimates, 101–3

German-Romanian Treaty of March, 1939, 62

German Statistical Office Deutschland, 256

German Statistical Yearbook, 1929–1942, 115

German War Economy Office, 86

"Germanicus," 3

Germany's Economic War Effort, 1942–1944, summary of, 206–238

Germany's Gross National Product, 1928–1939, 241–7; 1939–1943, 247–258; prewar composition of, 11–12; *Gross National Product of Germany, 1936–1944*, 92, 248

Gisevius, H. B., 176, 178, 201, 204

Goebbels, J., Diary, 202, 204

Goerderler, Lord Mayor of Leipzig, 20

Goering Corporation, 44; acquisition of Alpine Montangesellschaft, 44. *See also* Hermann Goering Ore and Foundry Company

Goering, H.: Chairman of Economic General Council, 152, 169; Chairman of Four-Year Planning Office, 128, 148, 169, 221; Commander of Air Force, 150, 198–9; Plenipotentiary of Second Four-Year Plan, 18, 35, 42, 150; Plenipotentiary for War Economy, 152, 169; temporary Minister of Economics, 1938, 149–150; decree suspending peacetime planning, 1942, 196; and inflation, 23; interrogation, 37; speech before Air Ministry, 25

Goldsmith, R. W., 102

Government finance and price control, 153–5

Gross capital formation, private, 89

Grunig, 248–9, 251

Guderian, H., 95, 210–2, 219

Guillebaud, C. W., 5, 7

Hahl, H., 118

von Halder: Chief of Army General Staff, 37, 176, 178; diary, 210–2; interrogation, 20, 37, 180, 183, 194–5, 203

Harris, A., 235

Henschel Aircraft Company, 159–160

Hermann Goering Ore and Foundry Company, 43

Hermann Goering Works, 43–4, 53–4

Hermberg, P., 241, 244, 251, 254

Hettlage, K., 153–5; Financial Advisor to Speer Ministry, 94, 109, 153; interrogation, 53

Hitler A.: Commander-in-Chief of the Armed Forces, 151; Commander-in-Chief of the Army, 194; director of economic planning, 169–171; conversations with Matsouka, 203; directive for "Case Barbarossa," 181–3; directive to Goering, 1936, 35–7, 43, 1938, 37, 57; directive on Second Four-Year Plan, 53; first defeat of war, 193; meeting with von Brauchitsch, 1939, 176; memorandum to Goering, October 1936, 18; plot against, 1939, 20; and raw material situation, 1936, 35–6; and Sauckel, 166; speech to Commanders-in-Chief, August 1939, 63–4, November 1939, 174–5; "Victory Program," 218; war plans, 25–7, 78, 173–185

Hyming, C., 22

Indexziffern der duetschen Rüstungsendfortigung, 133, 171, 187–193, 196–7, 207, 225, 228–9, 233

Industrial Sales, Output and Productivity, Prewar Area of Germany, 1939–1944, 250

Industrial capacity, shortages in, 104–110; machine tool situation, 107–9

Die Industriewirtschaft: Entwicklungstendenzen der deutschen und internationalen Industrieproduktion (1860–1932), 86

Inflation, fear of, 4–9, 22, 52, 78, 104

Investment, control of, 167–8

Investment outlays, memorandum on, 105–6

Iron ore, 117–8, 121–2; imports, 1940, 116; potential in 1933, 28, 30; production program, 50–1; stockpiling of, 58–9

Iron and Steel Production, Main Committee for, 125, 134

Iron and Steel Trade Association, reports, 55

Jacobs, A., 89, 155, 245–6, 249, 256
Jeschonnek, Chief of Air Force General Staff, 198–9
Jostock, P., 242

Karin Hall Plan, 39–40, 50
Kehrl, H., 53, 161; head of Raw Materials Division of Armaments Ministry, 128; interrogations, 37, 53; testimony, 217
Keitel, W., Generaloberst, 24, 64; Hitler's Chief of Staff, 150
Kesselring, A., Fieldmarshal, interrogation, 210
Koller, General, Chief of Staff for the Luftwaffe, testimony, 219
Konjunktur-Statistisches Handbuch, 1936, 30–3; 1938, 32
Kordt, T., German chargé in London, 20
Kriegseilbericht (War Express Report), 225, 228
Kriegswirtschaftliche Kraftebilanz, 105, 124, 137, 142–4
von Krosigk, S., Minister of Finance, 16, 22
Kuczynski, J., 3, 12, 65

Labor, balance of, 1944, 225; government control over, 66–7, 164–7; distribution of manpower, 65, 72; employment of women, 136–7, 140; expansion of supply, 65; workweek, 136–8;
    mobilization, 136–7; and German Labor Front, 66; from legal point of view, 65–7; statistical appraisal of, 67–70
Labor Ministry, 164–5
Labor offices, 165–6
"The Labor Situation in 1943," 165
"Labor Utilization," 140, 142
Lange, K., 109, 168
Laurie, S., 54, 167
Lead: potential in 1933, 32; production program, 46–7; stockpiling of, 58; supply, 112, 114
Leibl Pass, tunnel, 203

Ley, Dr., 66
Lichtenberger, H., 3
London Economist, 97

Maginot Line, 237
Manganese, potential in 1933, 31
Manpower: mobilization of, 65–7, 77–8; Germany and Great Britain compared, 69–70; occupational distribution of labor force, 72; requirements, military and industrial, 166; shortages in, 104, 136
von Manstein, Runstedt's Chief of Staff, 178–9
Marschak, J., 245
Matsouka, conversations with Hitler, 203
Methanol, potential in 1933, 34
Milch, Deputy Air Force Commander, 157, 198–9; Director General of Aircraft Procurement, 224; Fieldmarshal, 129
"Military and economic aid" from occupied areas, 93–5
Military objectives, attacks on, 234
Military output: collapse of production, 225–9; German and Russian compared, 210–1; low level of, 103; major factors for increase in, 213–225; Speer's program, 221–5
Military supplies, late 1942 to mid-1944, 205–213
Ministry of Armaments and Munitions, 148–9, 152
Ministry of Armaments and War Production, 105, 107; "Index of German War Production," 100; Machine Report Unit, 94; Planning Board, 98, 214, 225, 228; Report, 120, 122; Survey, 213; "Survey of Armaments Production," 99; Steel allocation data, 1939–1944, 214, 217; Technical Division, 218; "World Munitions Production," 100
Ministry of Economic Warfare, 101; German Economic Survey, 246
Ministry of Economics, 38, 126, 148–150, 162–5, 167–9
Ministry of Food and Agriculture, 149
Ministry of Labor, 149
Ministry of Weapons, ammunition, 221

Molybdenum, potential in 1933, 31
Monatliche Rohstoffübersichten, 58, 111, 217
Munitions production, comparison of Germany and United Kingdom, 96–101, 206–9
Mussolini, opposition to Hitler's strategy, 63–4

Nathan, O., 7, 16, 21, 65
National Income and Expenditure of the United Kingdom, 1938–1946, 89; *1939–1940,* 96; *1946–1947,* 90
"National Income, Public Gross and Net Expenditures and Private Expenditures," 241–2, 248, 258
National Labor Law, January, 1934, regulation of, 66
National Product, monograph, 250
Naval Armaments Board, 158
Nazi Conspiracy and Aggression, 23–7, 35, 45, 52, 60, 63–4, 87–8, 141, 173–7, 180–3, 185, 256
Nazi ideology: conflict between military and social aims, 201; influence on war effort, 200
Nazi-Soviet Relations, 1939–1941, 183, 203
Nelson, D., 202
Neuman, F. L., 148
Nickel: potential in 1933, 31; stockpiling of, 57
Nitrogen, potential in 1933, 33–4
Noll von der Nahmer, R., 8, 154
Nonferrous metals, potential in 1933, 31–2
Norway, conquest of, 178
Nuremberg trials: documents, 64; testimony, 181
Nürnberg stadium, 203
Nonmilitary expenditures, 90; contribution of occupied areas, 93; government administration, 92; public works projects, 91

Office of the Reich Forest Master, 149
Office of the Price Controller, 149
Oil: potential in 1933, 32–3; production program, 39–41, 50–51; stockpiling of, 58

OKL records, 177, 191, 194, 209, 220, 234
OKW (Intelligence), 131, 137, 151, 156–8, 176, 185–6, 211–2
Operation Barbarossa, 181–3, 185
Operation Clarion, 230
Operation Gruen, 26
Operation Sea Lion, 180–1
Ordnance Inspections, 158
Organization Todt, 93
Output: of exploited countries, 87–8; of Germany, 85–9

von Papen government, 5; and imports, 59
von Paulus, surrender at Stalingrad, 203
Phosphorus, potential in 1933, 34
Pig iron production, 1939, 115–6
Pleiger, P., 43; interrogations, 54, 122; manager, Hermann Goering Works, 53
Poole, K. E., 5, 7, 12
Procurement, 155–161; agencies and industry, 158–161; coordination of armed forces procurement, 156–8; determination of requirements, 155–6
Prussian Geological Institute, 42
Public works projects, 91

"Rationalization of the German Armaments Industry," 159–161
Raw materials: controls, 54–6, 162–4; distribution, 77; and foreign trade policy, 59–63; potential in 1933, 28–34; production program, 34–54; shortages, 104, 110–135; supply, 110–4; and war strategy, 63–4
"The Raw Materials Situation as of July 1, 1941," 126, 128; as of July 1, 1944, 131
Raw Material Situation in Case of Mobilization, 57–8
Rearmament expenditures, 16–9, 22, 76; reasons for small scale, 78–81
Referate or Metals, Report, July 1944, 113
Reichkreditgesellschaft (1937–1938), 255
Reichsgesetzblatt, 66–7, 140, 165

Reichskanzlei, Conference of, 27
Reichstellen, 149, 162–4
Reichsvereinigung Eisen, 117–8, 133
Reichsvereinigung Kohle, report, 124
Research Office for Military Economy, 250, 252, 256; memorandum on foreign contributions, 93–4
Resources: control of, 162–8; limitation of, 104–106
Reynaud, P., 17
Rohland, W., 116–9, 122, 124–6, 133–4
Rostas, L., 96–7
Royal Air Force attacks on German cities, 204
Rubber: potential in 1933, 33; production program, 45–6, 50; stockpiling of, 58–9; supply, 111
von Runstedt, K.: Commander of German Armies in Southern Russia, 185, 191, 193–4; Field-Marshal, 178–9; interrogation, 180–1, 183–4
Russia, conquest of, 181–3; pact with, 1939, 62–3
Rüstungsendfertigung deutsches Reich und Feindmächte (OKW), 211

Sauckel, F., 164–6; Commissioner for the Mobilization of Labor, 1942, 140; and conscription of workers, 141–2; foreign labor policy, 125; interrogation, 158; and supply of labor, 166; testimony, 218
Saur, K.-O.: Head, Technical Division, Speer Ministry, 161; interrogation, 113, 119, 122; testimony, 218
Schacht, H., 8–9, 16, 20; Minister of Economics, 6, 16, 18, 20, 22, 35, 42, 52; Plenipotentiary of War Economy, 35; President of Reichsbank, 22–3, 52; Reich Ministry of Finance, 23, 24, 52, 53, 148–9
Schieber, W.: interrogation, 158; procurement agent, 158; report, 161
von Schleicher government, 5
von Schlieffen, plan of attack, 178
Schmelter, head of Manpower Utilization Branch, Speer Ministry, 166
Shortages in industrial capacity, 104–110; in manpower, 104, 136; in raw materials, 104, 110–135

Shulman, M., 179–181
Siegfried Line, 175
Siemens-Martin (open-hearth) steel, 133–4
Speer, A., 129, 162, 165, 194, 203; defense at Nuremberg trials, 228; diary, 155–8, 161; Director of *Zentrale Planung*, 128, 221; and distribution of labor, 166; interrogations, 37, 53, 158; letters to Hitler, 152, 156–9, 161, 194, 204, 226, 228, 234; memoranda, 169; memoranda for Allied Control Commission, 204; Minister of Munitions Production (successor to Todt), 220–1;
    Minister of Armaments and War Production, 37, 52–3, 128, 148, 159, 169–170, 184, 195, 221–3; accomplishments of, 221–2; Committees and Rings, system of, 222–3; files, 175; Machine Report Unit, 91; Ministry report, 127–8, 159, 188; Technical Division, 222; Technical Office, 107
Stalin, speech of February 9, 1946, 211
Stalingrad, Battle of, 209; defeat at, 203–4
Standard of Living and Rationing, 246
"A Statistical Survey of the Quantity of Steel Rights Issued," 131
"Statistics Relating to the War Effort of the United Kingdom," 70, 96, 99–100, 115, 139, 143–4, 189, 208–9
Statistischer Bericht, 121, 123
Statistische Schnellberichte zur Kriegsproduktion, 47, 100, 110–3, 116, 118, 124, 208–9, 215
Statistische Schnellberichte zur Rüstungsproduktion, 99, 211
Statistisches Jahrbuch für das deutsche Reich, 1930, 32; 1931, 29, 33; 1933, 252; 1934, 68; 1936, 68; 1937, 13–4, 34, 251; 1938, 4, 252, 255–6; 1939/40, 51, 70, 75, 138; 1941/42, 10, 14–5, 32, 34–5, 41, 45–8, 51, 60, 62–3, 67, 68, 73, 121, 139, 251–6
Statistisches Reichsamt, 69, 145, 165
Steel, 114–130; allocation, 1939–1942,

126–130; Eisenschnellplan, 1943, 130; Emergency Plan, March 1943, 134; nonessential uses of, Hitler and Goebbels vs. Speer, debate, 132; potential in 1933, 28–31; priority allocation, 55–6; procurement areas, 41–5; production, 1939–1942, 115–126; production program, 41–5, 50–1; shortage, limitation to armaments production, 130–5; stockpiling of, 57; supply, 114–5

Steel cartel, German, 29–30, 81; opposition to expansion of capacity, 53; role in international, 29

Stocking, G. W., 30

Stockpiling program, 56–9, 77

Stolper, G., 3, 6

Strategic bombing, 229–235; aerial attack, 225–7; ball-bearing attacks, 231–2; raids on German cities, 232; raids on German oil industry, 233

Sulphur, potential in 1933, 34

Sweezy, M., 3, 12, 16, 247

Textiles, production program, 47–8

Thomas, General, 37–8, 64, 163–4, 186; comment of, 181, 184; head of War Economy and Armaments Office, 20, 38, 64, 129, 148, 150–1, 156–8, 165, 168–9, 176, 178, 184, 194, 203

Thomas (Bessemer) steel, 133–4

Tin, supply, 112, 114

Tissier, P., 177

Todt, F.: director, Ministry of Armaments and Munitions, 152, 165; General Plenipotentiary for Construction Industry, 109–110, 167; head, Organization Todt, 152; Inspector General for Roads, 152; Inspector General for Water and Power, 152; Minister of Munitions and Production, 220; Minister of Weapons and Ammunition, 168; succeeded by Speer, 220

Trade agreements, 1932, 59–61; with Balkans, 61

Tungsten, potential in 1933, 31

Ubersichten über die eisenschaffende Industrie Deutschlands, 1937, 45

United Kingdom, War Production Board, Planning Division, 97

United States: Controlled Materials Plan, 222; Department of Commerce, National Income Supplement, 92; Foreign Economics Administration, 118; Strategic Air Force, 229–231;

Strategic Bombing Survey: conclusions, 229; files, 117, 150, 152, 155, 159–160, 162, 171, 179, 220; interrogations, Fey, 92, Halder, 176, 194–5, 203, Hettlager, 53, 94, Kehrl, 53, Speer, 53, 203, Thomas, 176, 203; interrogation report, 22, 208–9, 217, 219; Oil Division, 226; special paper, 225; Tabulating Branch, Secretariat, 226;

War Department: Historical Division, 38; War Production Board, Planning Division, 102

Vanadium, stockpiling of, 57

Vierteljahreshefte zur Wirtschaftsforschung, 1938/39, 71–2

Wagemann Institute, 241–2, 248–9, 258

Wagenfuehr, R., 17, 81, 103, 161, 184–7, 189, 208, 210, 217–8, 225, 228–9; chief economist, Armaments Ministry, Planning Board, 37; interrogation, 37

War Economy and Armament Office, 148–151, 163–5

War Crimes Trial Commission, 37

War Economy Office, history of, 37–8, 64

War Express Reports, 225, 228

War Production and Armaments Board (OKW), 158

War Production Board, 19; reports, 171

Warlimon, General, SHAEF interrogation, 176

Watkins, M. W., 30

Wirtschaft und Statistik, 1938, 256; 1939, 13

Wirtschaftsgruppe Machinenbau, 105, 108–9

von Witzleben, General, 20; Commander of Army Group, 176

Wochenbericht des Planungsamtes, 105, 251, 255–6
Woermann, Dr., 49
Wolf, E., 153
World Munitions Production, 1938–1944, 100–102, 208, 236

Zentrale Planung, 129–130, 134, 166; evidence presented before, 124; Hitler's directive for, 128; meeting of, 125; minutes of meetings, 100, 122, 124
Zinc: potential in 1933, 32; production program, 46–7; stockpiling of, 58; supply, 111–2
Zusammenstellung über die personnele und materielle Rüstungslage der Wehrmacht (OKW), 137